D0759394

ED SHEERAN

Also by Sean Smith

George
Adele
Kim
Tom Jones: The Life
Kylie
Gary
Alesha
Tulisa
Kate
Robbie
Cheryl
Victoria
Justin: The Biography
Britney: The Biography
J.K. Rowling: A Biography
Jennifer: The Unauthorized Biography
Royal Racing
The Union Game
Sophie's Kiss (with Garth Gibbs)
Stone Me! (with Dale Lawrence)

BY SEAN SMITH

SUNDAY TIMES BESTSELLING AUTHOR

HarperCollins*Publishers*

HarperCollins*Publishers*
1 London Bridge Street
London SE1 9GF

www.harpercollins.co.uk

First published by HarperCollins*Publishers* 2018

1 3 5 7 9 10 8 6 4 2

A catalogue record of this book is
available from the British Library

HB ISBN 978-0-00-826751-3
TPB ISBN 978-0-00-826752-0
EB ISBN 978-0-00-826755-1

Printed and bound in Great Britain by
CPI Group (UK) Ltd, Croydon

For Hilaria

CONTENTS

PART TWO:
THE NEXT BIG THING

PART THREE:
THE SHAPE OF THINGS

INTRODUCTION

PRINCIPALITY STADIUM, CARDIFF, 24 JUNE 2018

He's on time. There's no messing about with Ed. He doesn't need to build up the excitement artificially by being late onstage. Instead, at 8.45 p.m. precisely, the lights go down and the video screens show him making his way casually down a corridor towards the stage as if he's strolling to the pub for a pint. The only giveaway that this is an extraordinary event is the deafening roar from 60,000 people.

And there's the man himself. The pedals of his famous loop station are at his feet and a small guitar bearing the logo of his latest album ÷ (*Divide*) is in his hands. He cuts a solitary figure. If you didn't know he was the biggest pop star in the world in 2018, you'd be forgiven for thinking this was the warm-up act who couldn't afford a proper band.

Standing a couple of rows in front of me, a young girl has the symbol ÷ etched in glitter on her cheek. I'm surrounded by people wearing official T-shirts with the logo on the front and the cities he's playing on the back. This will please Ed, who has always been switched on regarding the promotional and financial importance of official merchandise. As a schoolboy, he would try to flog a few of his self-financed CDs to his audience, even if it was just half a dozen people in a social club.

The first chords of 'Castle on the Hill' are all anybody needs to get up and dance. Ed Sheeran is only one man but he seems to create an enormous power and charisma. There's nobody else quite like him. Not everyone was brought up in a small town with a view of a magnificent castle, but we can all identify with thoughts and feelings about home. There's something reassuring about making your way back, perhaps at Christmas or just to see Mum and Dad or old friends who haven't moved on.

While he's getting his breath back, Ed announces, 'Good evening, Cardiff! Howya doing?', which is not especially original but meets with a very positive response. Ed's very relaxed between songs. The night before, he had left the stage twice to go for a pee.

He didn't need to do that tonight. Instead, he tells us this is the biggest tour that has ever come to Wales. More than 240,000 people have swarmed into the stadium to see him during the last four nights. Apparently, Friday night was the largest single audience, although, to loud cheers, Ed suggests that tonight's crowd is even bigger.

It's the last night of the UK leg of his 2018 world tour. I wonder idly if I'm the millionth person to see him since he played the Etihad Stadium in Manchester last month. It's not just a million teenage girls either. This is truly a family event with mums and dads, nans, grandads and children under ten all eager to enjoy themselves.

I'm next to a young couple from Barry Island who have brought their seven-year-old son Theo with them. 'Who's the fan?' I ask. They chorus that they all are, although Dad told me he usually preferred Iron Maiden and Def Leppard.

He would have enjoyed the start of 'Eraser', the opening track on the ÷ album that begins with a wall of sound, courtesy of the loop station. It's the first number of the night to feature some trademark rapping. In Ed's hands, rapping seems to be more poetic than aggressive. He has made the genre acceptable to millions who might not have appreciated it before.

He launches into 'The A Team', the song he wrote ten years ago that changed everything for him. 'If you know the words, then sing along,' he says. It seems as if 60,000 people do. 'There's no such thing as "Can't sing",' he tells us, 'only "Can't sing in tune".' That is certainly the case of practically everyone near me, but nobody cares.

Cleverly, he merges 'Don't' from his second album, × (*Multiply*), with 'New Man' from ÷, both harsh and slightly bitter break-up songs. Between numbers, Ed may not have the distinctive patter of Adele but he chats in a relaxed fashion that appears perfectly natural and friendly, not at all scripted.

Apparently, he last played in Cardiff in 2011 and vowed then that he wouldn't come back until he could fill this great stadium. That ambition didn't take long to achieve.

He asks for our biggest scream before changing pace to 'Dive' perhaps the most underrated song on ÷. It's a romantic ballad but not a soppy one. 'Don't call me baby/unless you mean it' is a chorus to sing at the top of your voice in the shower.

As each song passes, I'm more and more struck by how everyone knows the words. I suppose it's an indication of the sheer scale of his popularity. Ed's strategy is that it's a participation show and he wants everyone to sing and dance, although he reminds us that he can't dance – even if the famous video to 'Thinking Out Loud' gives the impression that he's a natural.

Ed wants us all to dance whether we can or not. Amusingly, he points out that there is always two per cent of an audience that refuses to sing or dance. They're either the grumpy reluctant boyfriend or the 'superdad' who's being a hero acting as chaperone for their son or daughter. Ed's own dad, John Sheeran, was exactly that, taking his boy along to countless gigs that gave him a vitally important musical education when he was young enough to absorb any influences.

Ed moves easily between different styles, often in the same song. They might build from a rap or a quiet verse into one of those anthemic choruses you can't get out of your head. He sings three songs in a row that reflect the agony of love. 'Bloodstream', from the × album, starts quietly before transforming into one of his most dramatic crescendos and a powerful wall of sound.

'Happier' is, for me, his most melancholy song, a story of love lost, a recurring theme with Ed. The poignant lyric touches anyone who has ever taken a wrong turn in love – and that would be everyone. 'I'm a Mess' is another song that reflects Ed's own intelligence and openness in his lyrics. I wish I had a fiver for every time someone's told me that they like the autobiographical touches he includes in his songs.

It's time to lighten the mood a little and 'Galway Girl' does exactly that. Some critics don't like this song and I've heard it described as Marmite – you either love it or you hate it – but we're all up, having a hooley in the aisles. Ed has always embraced his Irish heritage and my guess is that this will become a party classic in the years ahead.

Ed doesn't do many covers so it's a surprise when he slips 'Feeling Good' into the set list. Although many people know it as a Michael Bublé song from a decade ago, it's actually a much older stage-musical number that became an instant classic when it was recorded by the matchless Nina Simone in 1965. The late George Michael also featured it on his last studio album, *Symphonica*, in 2014. I wonder if there are any similarities between Ed and George – arguably the two greatest solo male pop stars the UK has produced. Ed cleverly mashes his version into the haunting 'I See Fire', the song he wrote for the 2013 film, *The Hobbit: The Desolation of Smaug*.

Ed changes guitars for practically every number. He is handed an electric guitar for the first time and mentions Amy Wadge, one of his original collaborators, who still lives locally in South Wales and is in the audience tonight. 'If you don't know the words to this one then you're probably at the wrong show,' he announces, then plays the opening chords of the sublime 'Thinking Out Loud', which he wrote with Amy.

Everyone goes into a huge romantic sigh. Instead of the thousand stars in the lyric, I can see a thousand and more torch lights from mobile phones shimmering in the darkened stands. Considering that he has only released three mainstream albums, Ed has already produced many classics – songs that will be first dances at weddings, reminders of first dates and kisses or just simply 'our songs'.

This is the beginning of four peerless ballads. He follows 'Thinking Out Loud' with 'One' and 'Photograph', also from the × album. During the latter, the big screens behind him flash up images of Ed as a child. Could it get any more poignant? And then he plays 'Perfect'.

Ed explains one of his secrets. This song is 'super-personal to me', he reveals. We know it's written for Cherry but it doesn't have the same emotion for everyone: 'It's my song before it comes out, but when it comes out, it becomes your song.' This is a universal truth about music.

As if to prove that point, the grey-haired couple behind me put their arms around each other. The young mum next to me picks up her son and cuddles him, while a few rows down I can see a small boy standing between his mum and dad and they all have their arms around each other. It's an 'I was there' moment that they will always remember. Perfect, indeed.

'Nancy Mulligan', the song he wrote about his Irish grandparents, wakes everyone from their romantic reverie and we all start dancing again – all except one superdad I spotted, who was determined to stay seated while his young daughter bopped away enthusiastically next to him. Even he got up for 'Sing', the closing number.

Ed pops offstage briefly to change his shirt. He's back wearing a number-eleven jersey with Gareth Bale on the back, which gets a cheer. The reception for the first number of the encore, his biggest hit to date – 'Shape of You' – is the loudest of the night. He finishes with a frantic wall-of-noise version of 'You Need Me, I Don't Need You', which is the song he traditionally performs as his last of the night.

Part of me thinks he should have ended with 'Thinking Out Loud' or 'Perfect', but that's clearly not what he's decided to do. He wants to leave with a dramatic climax, and that he achieves. This is the song that sums up his philosophy: be true to your own dreams and follow them. He wishes us a safe journey home and is gone – no fuss, no unnecessary milking of the applause, no insincere 'I love you, Cardiff' nonsense. He came, he played, he conquered.

On my way out with 60,000 other people, I thought about the end of the video for 'Photograph', perhaps my favourite. There's a shot of Ed at the top of a hill and a voice asks, 'Are you at the top of the mountain?' His phenomenal success – in terms of record sales, downloads, streaming, audience figures – doesn't lie. He is unarguably at the top of the mountain, looking down on the rest of the music business. My job, I thought, is to discover how on earth a scruffy, ginger-haired bloke climbed up there.

PART ONE

FAMILY IS ALL

1
PAINTING THE PICTURE

Undeniably, Edward Sheeran was a cute baby. The proof is in the many home movies his doting parents, John and Imogen, took of their second son as he crawled and gurgled, whooped and squealed around their first family home.

The footage was used charmingly in the nostalgia-packed video that accompanied his 2014 ballad 'Photograph'. While the sweet film had little to do with a melancholic lyric that declared how much 'loving can hurt', it provided a fascinating window on to his world.

We see Ed grow from baby to small boy, with ginger hair, large blue NHS specs and a small port-wine stain near his left eye, to a teenager busking in the street while learning his craft and, finally, to the man acknowledging the applause of thousands at a pop festival.

The large late-Victorian stone house that is the setting for many of the clips is not, however, in his beloved Suffolk, the county so closely associated with Ed, but in West Yorkshire where he was born, and where he spent his early years in the cosmopolitan market town of Hebden Bridge.

John and Imogen Sheeran lived halfway up Birchcliffe Road, one of the steepest hills in the town and a lung-bursting trek from the centre for a young mum with a baby and a toddler. Their first child, Matthew Patrick, was born eight miles away in Halifax General Hospital not long after the couple had relocated from London. Edward Christopher followed just under two years later, on 17 February 1991.

Calderdale, the valley in which Hebden Bridge sits, is ideal for bringing up a young family if you want to be sure of fresh air, spectacular countryside and wonderful walks. The road the Sheerans settled in winds its way to the crest of the hill where the views over the town and its distinctive streets of stone-built cottages are breathtaking.

Everything about Hebden Bridge shouts character. The town, which takes its name from the old packhorse bridge across the River Hebden, has bundles of it – from the quirky craft shops, the organic restaurants and boutique cafés to the tall, narrow terraced houses that seem to cling to the hillside as if stuck there with glue. Recently, the town has featured as a location for the hit television series *Last Tango in Halifax* and *Happy Valley*.

When Ed was born, the place was a work in progress – more basic and much less touristy than it is today. It had thrived as a bustling mill town specialising in corduroy and moleskin goods, but that prosperity ended in the 1970s when the textile industry went into decline. Hebden Bridge began to flourish again towards the end of that decade when it was transformed into a destination for creative minds and free spirits. It became well known for its strong sense of community and tolerance, in particular becoming a welcoming haven for lesbians and gay men.

Local author Paul Barker explained, 'It was a small mill town in steep decline. There were lots of squatters who had creative skills – writing, painting or music – so it started as an arts-based thing. It's a tolerant place, which allowed this scene to develop. People came to visit friends and realised the freedom to be able to live how they wanted.'

A strong literary connection already existed, although not a particularly happy one. The controversial poet laureate Ted Hughes was born in the village of Mytholmroyd, two miles down the road towards Halifax. His former home at Lumb Bank, two miles in the other direction, is now a residential writing centre.

Of more interest to literary pilgrims is the grave of Hughes's first wife, Sylvia Plath, in the village church in nearby Heptonstall, where his parents lived. She immortalised the location in her bleak poem 'November Graveyard' that spoke of 'skinflint trees'. The revered American poet had tragically committed suicide in London in 1963 but Hughes arranged for her to be buried in this most picturesque of locations. Many devotees of her work wishing to pay their respects stay in Hebden Bridge.

John and Imogen were drawn to the artistic nature of the town when they decided to settle there. Hebden Bridge was perfectly situated for a young and ambitious couple forging strong reputations in the world of art. They had begun promising careers in London where they were brought up in neighbouring districts south of the river – John in South Norwood and Imogen, a vivacious blonde, in Forest

Hill. They were married in May 1984 at the historic Christ's Chapel of Alleyn's College of God's Gift in the aptly named Gallery Road, Dulwich. He was twenty-six and she was twenty-four.

John was always a man who grasped an opportunity, impatient to make something of his life. Unsurprisingly, therefore, he had been appointed keeper of the Dulwich Picture Gallery in 1980 at the age of twenty-three. He had been taken under the wing of the gallery's charismatic first director, Giles Waterfield, and together they transformed its fortunes from a threadbare museum with a skeletal staff and no financial support into one respected throughout the world.

Giles took a chance on his protégé's youthful talent – as so many would with Ed in the future. When he died unexpectedly in November 2016, John wrote in appreciation of his old friend: 'You transformed a sleepy, forgotten capsule of late Georgian taste into a world-renowned art museum with its own dynamic exhibition and education programme.'

Giles and John were a formidable partnership. In 1983, they held a life-drawing class in the permanent collection to attract visits from schools and colleges, an initiative that proved to be the start of their acclaimed learning programme. Throughout the 1980s, John seized the chance to organise major new exhibitions, including a universally admired collection of Old Masters.

While the famous paintings of great artists would bring in the crowds, he also promoted a new generation of British artists – many of whom were based in the north of England – including the distinguished landscape painter David Blackburn, who was from Huddersfield. John curated an exhibition of his work in Dulwich in 1986 and wrote the catalogue that went with it.

John brought a refreshingly intelligent and critical eye to paintings. His goal, right from those early days at the Picture Gallery, was to encourage visitors to take the time to really look at a painting – not just to take a photograph and move swiftly on. He explained, 'When you read paintings, you start to look at people and places differently. Once you can read art, you have a gift for life.'

After seven years' working in the world of museums, John moved on from Dulwich. He had found other opportunities with galleries in Manchester and Bradford, and he and Imogen decided to base themselves in Yorkshire. They were ambitious to become independent and had an entrepreneurial spirit that rubbed off on their younger son at an early age.

In 1990, the year before Ed was born, they set up their own company, a fine-art consultancy called Sheeran Lock, with an office in Halifax. Their new direction meant lots of travelling, particularly the well-worn path down the motorway to London – long, tedious trips that provided Ed with some of his earliest memories as he listened over and over again to his dad's distinctly mainstream musical preferences. John Sheeran seemed to be stuck in a time warp, listening to music from the sixties and early seventies.

Even as a very young boy, Ed was displaying some of the characteristics that would serve him so well as a professional musician. He picked up words and melodies very quickly.

He would learn all the songs on classic Beatles and Bob Dylan albums and be able to sing along happily, if a little tunelessly.

One of his father's favourites was Elton John's 1971 album *Madman Across the Water*, which contained the track 'Tiny Dancer'. Ed would memorably reference it in his own classic song 'Castle on the Hill' when he reminisces about driving down the country lanes near home at ninety miles an hour. Many years later Elton would become an important figure in Ed's own story.

Despite his connection to 'Tiny Dancer', Ed chose another song from that album as a Desert Island Disc. He went for 'Indian Sunset', the elegiac orchestral number that opened side two and told the story of an Iroquois warrior contemplating defeat and death at the hands of the white man. The sensitive lyric revealed Elton's song-writing partner, Bernie Taupin, at his most poetic.

John and Imogen envisaged Sheeran Lock as a multi-faceted concern. They saw the company setting up exhibitions and educational projects not just in Yorkshire but also around the world. They acted as consultants to a growing band of artists, whom they felt deserved a wider audience.

One of their first steps was to set up a publishing arm to promote the work of their talented friends and clients, including northern painters Mary Lord, Marie Walker Last and Katharine Holmes, the Lancashire-based Anglo-Dutch sculptor Marjan Wouda and the printmaker Adrienne Craddock. A beautifully produced book would often accompany an exhibition of the artist's work. It was an approach that would serve their son Ed well in the future: make use of every aspect of your work.

As well as sorting out the day-to-day administration and editing the books, Imogen was a creative force not to be underestimated. These days, she is given a postscript in biographies of her famous son as a mum who dabbles in jewellery design. That sells her very short. She graduated with an MA in art history from the University of St Andrews, the same degree Kate Middleton would later obtain. After completing her studies, she worked in the press office at the National Portrait Gallery in London before moving north with John and becoming the gallery services officer at the Manchester City Galleries.

She used her artistic flair to transform the somewhat austere interior of the house in Birchcliffe Road into a magical pot-pourri of beautiful paintings and sculptures. She ditched wallpaper and emulsion in favour of a patterned fabric that she hung on the walls, like tapestry. Her little touches made the rather cold house, which used to be the local doctor's surgery, feel far warmer, especially in winter when a roaring fire was essential.

The boys shared the attic space as a bedroom and, looking out through the window, they could see across the valley to the spire of Heptonstall Church, where Sylvia Plath is buried. Imogen knocked through the wall into the next room to create an opening with a private play area they could crawl through. It was like a giant Wendy house for boys.

Lock is Imogen's maiden name and her family was well connected and high-achieving – particularly in the contrasting worlds of music and medicine. She was named after Imogen Holst, a family friend and the daughter of Gustav Holst, composer of the classical favourite *The Planets Suite*. Imogen Holst was a gifted composer in her own right. Significantly, she was the personal assistant of Benjamin

Britten, one of the most famous of all British composers, who co-founded the Aldeburgh Festival in Suffolk in 1948.

Ed's grandmother, Shirley Lock, sang for Britten and for many years she and her husband, Stephen, would spend their summers on the Suffolk coast to be part of the annual musical celebration. Britten and his partner, the tenor Peter Pears, were both godfathers to their eldest son, Adam. On one memorable occasion the little boy spotted one of the famous men walking along the seafront at Aldeburgh. 'Look!' he exclaimed. 'It's Uncle Ben-Peter!'

Shirley had an impressive musical CV as a founder second violinist with the National Youth Orchestra of Great Britain in 1948. She was also a member of the Cambridge University Musical Society (CUMS) orchestras, as well as a number of prestigious singing groups, including the Purcell, BBC and Ambrosian Singers.

In a family of high-achievers, Shirley's husband, Dr Stephen Lock, perhaps stands pre-eminent. He is a CBE, one rank below a knight, and has a long entry in *Who's Who*. For sixteen years, he was the much-respected editor of the *BMJ* (*British Medical Journal*) until he retired from the role the year Ed was born. His speciality, for which he won a worldwide reputation, was the future of the editing of scientific data and the responsibilities of 'journalogy' as he called it.

Stephen also supported the new venture of Sheeran Lock. He joined forces with his son-in-law John to write a book entitled *The Gift of Life*, which explored the paintings of Sir Roy Calne, the organ-transplant pioneer. Imogen continued the family's medical heritage by producing *A Picture of Health*. Her book accompanied a landmark exhibition of

Susan MacFarlane paintings at the Barbican Gallery, London, about the clinical treatment of breast cancer.

Stephen shared his wife's artistic passions, for opera in particular. In *Who's Who* he declares, amusingly, his recreations as 'reading reviews of operas I can't afford to see' and 'avoiding operas whose producers know better than the composer'. For many years he has been a popular volunteer at the Britten-Pears Foundation library in his beloved Aldeburgh.

Although Ed was close to his grandparents, he never knew his Uncle Adam. He had been fatally wounded at his home in Alleyn Crescent, Dulwich, two weeks after Matthew's birth in March 1989. The local newspaper, the *South London Press*, described the distressing circumstances under the stark headline 'Man Shoots Himself'.

Adam, an investment manager in the City, shot himself twice with a shotgun he used for clay-pigeon shooting. According to the paper, he left his girlfriend asleep upstairs at about 4 a.m. one Friday morning while he let himself into the garage. There, he sat in an old armchair and turned the gun on himself. The first bullet pierced his left shoulder. He then reloaded and shot himself a second time.

Adam died two hours later in King's College Hospital, Camberwell. He was thirty-one. The death certificate was issued by the Inner South District coroner Montagu Levine after an inquest in June. He listed the cause of death as 'Gunshot Wound to Head and Chest. He killed himself'.

On the first anniversary of his death, in 1990, a dignified notice appeared in the In Memoriam column of *The Times*, remembering Adam Timothy Southwick Lock and quoting Tennyson:

But trust that those we call the dead
Are breathers of an ampler day
For ever nobler ends.

The poet wrote his monumental elegy *In Memoriam*, also known as *In Memoriam A.H.H.*, as a tribute to his friend Arthur Henry Hallam, who had died tragically young from a brain haemorrhage. The most often quoted lines are: ''Tis better to have loved and lost than never to have loved at all.' Tennyson took seventeen years to write his masterpiece as he struggled to deal with the effects of sudden bereavement.

In March 1991, when Ed was six weeks old, the same notice appeared again in *The Times*. In 1995, without fuss, a painting was adopted in memory of Adam Lock at the Dulwich Picture Gallery. The peaceful work by the seventeenth-century Dutch artist Adriaen van Ostade is an oil on panel entitled simply 'Interior of a Cottage.' Adam would not be forgotten.

Ed's grandparents' love of music rubbed off on his mother, Imogen, who has a lovely voice and has been a mainstay of her church choir for many years. Ed, however, has never shared the family's enthusiasm for classical music, unlike his brother Matthew, who had an obvious talent for it from an early age.

Ed enjoyed musical instruments, though. In his first classroom there was a musical bar where the children could help themselves to drums, recorders and other instruments and make as much noise as they liked. Ed loved this – much more than sport, for which he never had much of a taste.

By the time Ed began school, his birthmark had been successfully treated by laser but he was painfully shy, with a pronounced stammer. He later revealed that it was a result of one of his laser treatments, when the technicians forgot to administer the anaesthetic cream. Although the two brothers started at Heathfield Junior School at the same time, they were in separate classes because of the difference in age. Matthew, who was much more confident, never fussed around his younger brother but he was always there if Ed needed him.

Ed began in Reception, the infants' class. The teaching assistant, Gillian Sunderland, remembers that the two brothers had very contrasting personalities, with Ed being by far the quieter: 'He was rather nervy. He wasn't needy in the sense of needing looking after but he was extremely shy. Extremely shy! He found mixing with other children rather challenging so he needed to be encouraged to mix really. He had a slight stutter but it was noticeable and I think he probably struggled with that.'

Looking back, Ed recalled that he had a 'really, really bad stammer'. His own memories confirm that, as a little boy, he found it difficult to join in. He told Kirsty Young on *Desert Island Discs* that he was a bit of a weird kid: 'I lacked an eardrum so I couldn't go swimming – which helps get friends.'

Heathfield is a private co-educational school in the small village of Rishworth, a ten-mile drive from Hebden Bridge down demanding country lanes, but it was worth it for the idyllic setting. Heathfield and its senior equivalent, Rishworth School, occupy 130 acres. The youngsters could spend much of the summer outdoors, playing and being taught in the open air. Gillian explains, 'There are other schools but if you want your child to enjoy the environment then you would choose here.'

While Ed would learn the basics of English, maths and phonics, much of the teaching at the school revolved around being creative. A small river ran through the grounds and the class would be taken down to look at the water and were encouraged to write a little story about it or perhaps draw a picture. Ed particularly liked to sit outside quietly and draw with his crayons.

The teachers liked Edward, as everyone called him at school, because he was such a gentle boy. While he was small for his age, he stood out with his bright ginger hair and big round glasses. 'He wasn't the type of boy who liked fuss, though,' recalls Gillian. 'He was very much a "Let's get on with it" type. He wasn't in need of stroking all the time.'

In the well-known photograph of young Ed in his burgundy-coloured school blazer and grey shorts he is wearing the Heathfield uniform. Throughout his childhood he was fortunate in that his parents were sociable, and popular with other parents and teachers. Gillian observes, 'They were the type of people that you don't forget because they were lovely – so genuine and very supportive and caring.'

When it came time for the Sheeran boys to move on because the family were relocating to Suffolk, Imogen presented Gillian Sunderland and form teacher Christine Taylor with a thank-you card – a pencil drawing of her two sons.

Growing up, Ed and Matthew were the subject of many works of art. One important creative decision that Ed's parents made was to commission paintings, sculpture and lihographs of their children so that there would be a lasting record of their early lives. As a result, there is a superb archive of them, not just sentimental camcorder shots. A further consequence of their foresight is that Ed has always been entirely comfortable posing for camera or paintbrush, and thousands of pictures of him are in circulation. Imogen's thoughtful gift ensured the boys would not be forgotten at Heathfield. One of the key reasons for their departure was the discovery that Matthew – not Ed – had considerable musical talent. He was showing potential as a treble soloist and there were greater opportunities for a boy soprano in Suffolk, near his grandparents in Aldeburgh and at St Edmundsbury Cathedral in Bury St Edmunds.

Imogen let slip why they were moving when she showed potential buyers around the house in Birchcliffe Road. Eventually it was bought by a local vet, Clare Wright, who was in awe of the art scattered throughout their home. She recalls, 'There was wonderful, beautiful artwork everywhere.' Every inch of wall seemed to have a painting hung on it, making the walls look bare when she moved in just before Christmas in 1995, when the family had left with their artworks. Ed was nearly five.

The Sheerans did, however, leave behind the piano, which also features in the 'Photograph' video, with Ed attempting to play it. Pianos are notoriously difficult to move and this was no Steinway, so it stayed put in the front room.

Eventually, Clare decided to give it away and, consequently, Ed Sheeran's first piano moved ten miles down the Burnley road to the Elland Working Men's Club. The family would need a new one when they moved into their next home in the Suffolk market town of Framlingham.

2

PUGILISM NOT VANDALISM

One item of furniture that was not on the removal firm's inventory was a television. The Sheerans didn't own one. Imogen and John were keen that their two boys should not become little couch potatoes. Theirs was an artistic household and they wanted the children to develop their creative nature in the important early years. It was a policy that would pay off handsomely.

Ed would later moan, tongue in cheek, that when they did eventually get a television, all they were allowed to watch was a box set of David Attenborough's *Life on Earth*. They didn't own a TV licence so it was videos or nothing. Nevertheless, Ed formed a lifelong appreciation of Attenborough and his standing as a true national treasure. 'I was a massive fan,' he admitted.

Imogen and John were very strict where TV was concerned. Edward and Matthew were allowed to watch one video each evening before they were directed to more meaningful play. Ed enjoyed *Pingu*, the long-running animated series about a family of penguins at the South Pole. When he was seven, he liked *The Land Before Time*, the classic animated feature film about the adventures of a family of dinosaurs.

After their viewing allowance, they were encouraged to draw or paint or, in Ed's case, build with Lego. He loved it, and those happy hours spent as a child would benefit him later when he needed to apply himself patiently to constructing a song. Even as an adult, Lego was comforting.

His mother and father finally weakened and bought a TV licence when Ed was nine. He wondered what all the fuss was about until he discovered *The Simpsons* – but it was shown at 6 p.m. and clashed with choir practice on a Friday evening. Ed's heart wasn't in that musical activity. One regular church-goer still smiles when she remembers the two Sheeran boys scampering out of the Sunday service at St Michael's almost before the organist had played the last notes of the final hymn. Their mother's continued support for the choir, on the other hand, was much appreciated locally: 'You can tell when she's singing,' observes one member of the congregation.

Ed nagged his parents to let him off singing in the church choir. Eventually, they agreed on the understanding that he joined his school choir instead. He was now a pupil at Brandeston Hall, which was in a beautiful location that could rival that of his first school in Yorkshire. The imposing stately hall is at the heart of the village of Brandeston, about four miles south of Framlingham. From its position next to the River Deben, the views across the water meadows would inspire any painter.

The hall was destroyed by fire in 1847 but was rebuilt as an almost exact replica of the Tudor original. It became the prep school for Framlingham College in 1949, and still has the stopped-in-time quality that J. K. Rowling might have imagined for her Harry Potter stories. At Brandeston Hall, Ed came out of his shell. He made a best friend called James Mee and the two boys would take it in turns to go to each other's houses after school.

James did not have the same television restrictions and it was at his house that Ed was introduced to *The Simpsons*. He also tasted meat for the first time. Imogen had been keen to start her sons on a healthy diet so the household was vegetarian for a few years. Ed was somewhat taken aback when he sat down for tea in James's kitchen and was presented with a hearty plate of bangers and mash. He told his friend's mum, 'These are the best sausages I've ever eaten', which was true, as he had never tried them before.

From then on, sausages would become a particular favourite. Imogen's full English fry-ups were a sought-after breakfast when they had friends or visiting musicians to stay. The Sheerans soon became popular hosts in Framlingham, or 'Fram', as it's known locally. Their sociability and ease in company contributed to their younger son's cautiously growing confidence.

Everything about the market town of Framlingham was cosy – a picture postcard of old England, steeped in history. It was compact, easy to get around and surrounded by delightful countryside. An added bonus was that it was only fourteen miles to the coast where Imogen's parents lived in Aldeburgh. The drive to Ipswich station to catch the train to London, a journey Ed would become very familiar with over the years, took forty minutes on a good day.

Just like Hebden Bridge, Framlingham has a strong sense of community, with traditional local pubs, independent shops and higgledy-piggledy streets full of the pink cottages so representative of the heart of Suffolk. On any day in the Market Square, the hub of the place, you are likely to see at least six people you know.

The cream-tea atmosphere of the present hardly matches the town's colourful and somewhat violent past. Framlingham Castle was the seat of the earls and dukes of Norfolk until it passed to Henry VIII's daughter Mary – 'Bloody Mary', as she was known. This was where she gathered her troops before she was proclaimed Queen of England and marched to London to take her throne in the summer of 1553.

The castle was a short walk from the new family home, a spacious detached house, which they bought for the relatively bargain price of £125,000. Today it would cost you £600,000. Ed had his own bedroom and a new piano was installed downstairs in one of the reception rooms at the back, which was perfect for entertaining.

In pride of place amid all the artwork the Sheerans continued to acquire, there were framed photographs of the two boys meeting the Prince of Wales. The family's association with Prince Charles represented the pinnacle to date of John Sheeran's career as a curator of prestigious exhibitions. He was appointed to organise and co-ordinate the prince's fiftieth-birthday exhibition, in 1998. Entitled 'Travels with the Prince', it celebrated his work as a watercolourist. It included paintings by contemporary artists such as Emma Sergeant, Derek Hill and Susannah Fiennes, cousin of the Oscar-winning actor Ralph Fiennes. The artists had been specially chosen to accompany Charles on his tours abroad.

The exhibition at the Cartoon Gallery in Hampton Court Palace, in Surrey, proved a big success. With little fuss, Prince Charles has become one of the UK's most successful artists, whose paintings have raised millions for the Prince of Wales Charitable Foundation. The deal for the travelling artists was that their trip was paid for, the prince had first choice of their paintings and, subsequently, they were free to sell their own work. It was a formula that worked exceptionally well.

Sheeran Lock produced a sumptuous book to accompany the exhibition, in which Imogen wrote the preface and John the text. It was part of a golden period for the couple as John's star continued to rise. In 2003, he was commissioned by the then President of Nigeria, Olusegun Obasanjo, to curate a special show of present-day Nigerian art in Abuja where the Commonwealth heads of government were meeting. The exhibition included a ground-breaking art-education project for young people from all regions of Nigeria. John and Imogen were inspired by that success to devise other programmes to help disadvantaged young people in the UK. Their philosophy was simple – nobody should be excluded from appreciating art and participating in it.

Ed was shielded from hardship in Framlingham and settled in well to life at a gentle Suffolk pace. The family had a more lively time on their frequent trips to Ireland to visit John's parents in County Wexford. John is one of eight children – five boys and three girls including his twin sister, Mary Anne – which meant Ed had cousins all over the country. The Sheerans are a large close-knit clan: Ed has always been aware of the importance of family, and has often sung about it.

Despite John being born in South London, the Sheerans were very much an Irish clan so Ireland and its music have had a profound influence on Ed's life.

Ed's grandfather, Bill Sheeran, was born in Magera, a small town in Londonderry, Northern Ireland. He grew up in the East End of London after his father, James, became a local doctor in Bow. James, who was Ed's great-grandfather, was reputedly a decent boxer and family legend has it that he once fought the great heavyweight champion Jack Johnson in an exhibition bout in 1913. After a spell of bullying at school when Bill was spotted carrying his violin case, his father had enrolled him in a boxing club and taken him to local tournaments, which had led to a lifelong love of the sport. In a similar way, Ed's love of music was enhanced by joining his own father for evenings out at pop concerts.

During the Second World War, Bill Sheeran boxed for his school, Epsom College, then trained as a dentist at Guy's Hospital in Southwark. He continued his love affair with the noble art and became captain of the hospital's boxing club, where he was trained by Matt Wells, a former world welterweight champion. One of Bill's favourite jokes was that the hospital's motto, *Dare Quam Accipere*, was perfect for boxers. More familiarly translated, this means, '[It is better] to give than to receive.'

While studying at Guy's, Bill took on his most infamous bout – against Charlie Kray, the elder brother of the notorious gangsters, Ronnie and Reggie. Expert opinion gave Bill no chance. Walter Bartleman, boxing correspondent of the old London evening paper the *Star*, and later the *Evening Standard*, told him before the fight, 'He'll eat you.' It didn't work out like that: Bill won the bout on a stoppage when Charlie was unable to continue.

Bill met his future wife Anne Mulligan at Guy's where she worked as a nurse. She had been raised on a farm near Gorey, a small town in County Wexford, about sixty miles south of Dublin. Ed romanticised their story on his ÷ album. The track 'Nancy Mulligan', a traditional Irish jig, describes how theirs was a *Romeo and Juliet* story. In Ed's tribute to his grandparents, he highlights the religious divide between a Protestant boy from Northern Ireland and a Catholic girl from the Republic. Her father, according to the song, did not approve of their marriage. He relates their love affair from Bill's point of view and would later explain, 'They got married and no one turned up to the wedding. He melted all his gold teeth in his dental surgery and turned them into a wedding ring.'

Exactly how much of the story is true and how much is artistic licence is a guessing game that fans can play with the majority of Ed's songs. He takes a genuine fact or feeling as a starting point and develops it into a song that resonates with every listener. Everyone has their own stories of love and can relate to the observation that Bill had never seen 'such beauty before' when he met his future wife. Fortunately the song met with a thumbs-up from his gran, although she was very modest about it: 'Oh, it's fine as long as I'm not there while he's playing it!'

In real life, Bill and Anne married in 1951 and settled in South Norwood, an area of London south of the River Thames, which seems slightly less glamorous than the 'Wexford border' Ed sings about.

Bill's second love – after his family – remained boxing while he built a thriving dental practice. When his own boxing days had passed, he became more involved in the administration of the sport as a respected steward. A popular figure, he was in charge of many of the biggest nights in British boxing and was on good terms with the sport's then best-known names, including Muhammad Ali, Henry Cooper and, Ireland's finest, Barry McGuigan.

While boxing might seem an unlikely bedfellow for the artistic world so enjoyed by his son John, Bill had a passion for collecting art connected to the sport. When the family moved to the quieter waters of Chislehurst in Kent, he filled the house with paintings, drawings, ceramics, sculpture and silver.

In his affectionate tribute to his father after his death at eighty-six in December 2013, John recalled how, in later years, Bill had given away most of his collection to friends. Touchingly, he gave the World Light Heavyweight Championship belt and trophy, won by Freddie Mills, back to the boxer's widow, Chrissie.

Two years before Ed was born, his Irish grandparents retired to the same farmhouse where Anne had been born in County Wexford. In 'Nancy Mulligan', they have twenty-two grandchildren. By the time of Bill's death that number had risen to twenty-three and there were also four great-grandchildren, a number that Ed has often said he is looking forward to increasing.

Bill loved to show the finer points of boxing to the younger members of the family. Ed's cousin Jethro Sheeran, better known as the recording artist Alonestar, became a huge fan of the sport, especially after Bill gave him a video one Christmas of Sugar Ray Leonard versus Marvin Hagler, one of the most celebrated fights of all time. From an early age he would be down at Bill's gym practising Sugar Ray's moves. Jethro, like many of the younger generation, idolised his grandfather: 'He always instilled into us to be humble and respect others.'

It's easy to imagine Bill teaching Ed, who was quite a small boy, self-defence. Anne proudly remembers that her grandson was 'lovely as a kid'. Ed revelled in his visits to the farm in the summer holidays when he would camp with his cousins in the big barn beside the house. He forged a lifetime love of Ireland, its people and its traditional music, and still visits his grandmother whenever he can.

Boxing proved to be the focus of the 2017 video for 'Shape of You', Ed's biggest-selling single to date. He displayed some promising moves as an aspiring boxer in love with a female fighter in his gym. By then his grandfather had died, after a battle with Alzheimer's disease but, in the poignant 'Afire Love', Ed recalls his dad telling him as a boy that it wasn't his grandfather's fault he no longer recognised his grandson's face.

Bill was president of the Gorey Boxing Club and members formed a guard of honour for his funeral, paying a personal tribute to him: 'In Bill Sheeran we have lost a mentor, inspiration and role model whose generosity and kindness has helped thousands of young men and women.' He was buried with a pair of boxing gloves in his coffin. In his obituary for Bill, published in the Guy's Hospital journal, the *GKT Gazette*, John Sheeran recalled his father's car-bumper sticker, which robustly declared, 'Pugilism not vandalism'.

Ed fell in love with the Irish music he heard on his childhood holidays. He adored the traditional Irish folk groups

Planxty and The Chieftains, but most of all he loved an artist who, ironically, he had first heard his dad play on one of the long drives south from Yorkshire. Van Morrison was the first of three major musical influences on Ed Sheeran. He listened to his classic albums *Moondance* and *Irish Heartbeat* and was hooked.

Moondance, which was released in 1970, is often hailed as a masterpiece of modern music and remains one of the best-loved albums of all time. Perhaps more interesting with regard to Ed's musical development was *Irish Heartbeat*, a collaboration between Van and The Chieftains.

Van, who was born in Belfast, had been an Irish icon for more than thirty years since he first came to prominence in the group Them, with whom he recorded classics such as 'Here Comes the Night' and, more significantly, 'Gloria'. His most famous song, 'Brown Eyed Girl' was his first solo single in 1967. He became a master of soulful blues, releasing a string of acclaimed albums.

While he had never deserted his Irish background in his songs, *Irish Heartbeat* was a return to more traditional music – albeit overlaid with Van's inimitable vocal style. Three tracks in particular resonated with young Ed, who was seven when the album was released in 1998. He loved the folk songs 'Carrickfergus', 'On Raglan Road' and, most of all, the elegiac title track. Ed has yet to release these songs himself but acknowledged, 'Van Morrison is a key influence in the music that I make.' He paid homage to Carrickfergus by including a reference to it in 'Galway Girl' as well as mentioning 'Van the Man' in his hit, 'Shape of You'.

And if you had been lucky enough to be drinking in the back room of the Cobden Arms in Mornington Crescent in

2010, you might have heard nineteen-year-old Ed enjoying a pint with musician friends and singing these favourites at the top of his voice. That, though, was many years in the future and the last thing on the mind of a quiet schoolboy still trying to conquer his stammer. It was time to do something about that.

3

THE EMINEM REMEDY

Ed was trying all sorts of things to help with his stutter. He had coaching sessions with a speech therapist and took a variety of different homeopathic remedies but nothing seemed to make much difference. He didn't have the worst stammer in the world but it did become more pronounced when he was excited and rushing to search for the right word. Interestingly, it didn't affect him when he was singing in the choir or in his dad's car. But conversation remained difficult.

When Ed was nine, Eminem was one of the biggest acts in the charts. Rap music was selling millions of records and Eminem was at the forefront of its popularity. When he released *The Marshall Mathers LP* – his real name – in May 2010, it became the fastest-selling album of all time in the US. More importantly, perhaps, his work was well received by the critics, who compared his autobiographical songs to those of Bob Dylan.

In Framlingham, this had passed John Sheeran by as he continued to play his old favourites. His brother, Ed's uncle Jim, was more enlightened about contemporary music and told him that Eminem was the next Dylan. John was always receptive to new ideas across the artistic spectrum so he went ahead and bought the album for his younger son even though he had never listened to it and had no idea that it contained controversial and sexually explicit lyrics. Ed would later describe rap music as storytelling.

Ed had a great capacity to absorb things – he had the musical equivalent of a photographic memory. He set about learning the songs on the album, including all the bad language: 'I learned every word of it, back to front, by the age of ten.' That would invariably be the case with music he liked. He had an enviable talent for working out how to play songs just by listening to them.

He discovered that rap was the best therapy for his speech. In 2015, while receiving an award at the New York benefit gala for the American Institute for Stuttering, Ed spoke about being indebted to Eminem: 'He raps very fast and very melodically, and very percussively, and it helped me get rid of the stutter.'

Ed's remedy was not unique: many young people used singing as the best form of therapy – although not all of them chose *The Marshall Mathers LP*. Ed's favourite track from it, and the one that had most influence on him, was the UK number one 'Stan'. The song combined two elements that are very important in Ed's music: a catchy melody line, which was sung by Dido, and a poetic, rhythmic rap by a master of the craft. Ed included the song in his *Desert Island Discs* and a separate list of his all-time favourites, which he gave to *Rolling Stone* magazine.

The song, which told of an obsessive fan's suicide, gradually builds into a rage, then takes it back a step for the Dido chorus, which was basically a sample from her hit 'Thank You'. Ed enjoyed its contrast of different emotions.

Even when so young, Ed seemed able to appreciate different musical genres. He still loved Van Morrison but now he was discovering new artists for himself. He noticed that Dr Dre, the producer of *The Marshall Mathers LP*, had a new album coming out entitled *2001*, much of which featured Eminem. Ed, who earned pocket money from odd jobs, including washing cars, made sure he bought it, then widened his collection to include Jay-Z, Snoop Dogg, Tupac, who had been killed in a drive-by shooting in 1996, and the Notorious B.I.G., who had been shot dead in a similar fashion a year later. Hip-hop music seemed wild and exciting to a boy soon to start high school in a small Suffolk town.

Ed was fortunate in that his older cousin Jethro had similar tastes, which meant there was someone to appreciate his new music on family holidays. Jethro, who was brought up in Bristol, had been inspired to become a rap artist when he heard Tupac's hit 'Dear Mama', a tribute to his mother whom he loved dearly despite her addiction to crack cocaine. Jethro was already fifteen when Ed first discovered hip hop but over the years the two worked closely together on each other's songs, particularly when Ed was still learning his craft in Framlingham.

Tupac's stories were grittier than those of Hollywood A-lister and rapper Will Smith, but Ed had become a big fan of the latter, too, when he discovered that *The Fresh Prince of Bel-Air* was on TV after *The Simpsons* on a Sunday night. He lost little time in learning Will's theme-tune rap. He loved it and is liable to drop a verse randomly into a song at one of his concerts.

Curing his stutter undoubtedly enhanced Ed's confidence but he still had his problem eardrum. That was finally operated on when he was eleven, which was obviously a relief, although he would continue to have problems with it in the coming years.

While Eminem undoubtedly influenced Ed's choice of more contemporary music, his love affair with the guitar was triggered by an old master on TV. He watched Eric Clapton performing 'Layla' at Party at the Palace, the June 2002 concert to celebrate the Queen's Golden Jubilee in the gardens of Buckingham Palace.

The concert became famous for Brian May playing 'God Save the Queen' on the palace roof, but Eric was the highlight for Ed. He had slipped unassumingly onstage after an unlikely collection of Emma Bunton, Atomic Kitten and Cliff Richard had joined Brian Wilson to perform 'Good Vibrations'. He commanded the space, dressed immaculately in an expensive dark suit and playing a guitar that was itself a work of art. The renowned New York graffiti artist John 'Crash' Matos had painted one of Eric's signature Stratocasters and presented it to him as a gift. Eric was delighted and commissioned others from the artist, who had made his name spray-painting trains across the city. The guitars became known as 'Crashocasters' and Eric played the original on a world tour. The big video screens to the side of the stage zoomed in on his hands as they moved nimbly around the musical work of art.

'Layla' is an iconic rock anthem that Eric has played thousands of times since 1970, when the track first featured on an album by his band Derek and the Dominos. An intensely passionate composition about love, the song changes halfway through into a much more melodic number that features a long, melancholic guitar solo.

Ed was spellbound by the whole magnificent performance – the majestic riff, the guitar and the sheer presence of Eric. 'I was like "Wow. That was so cool. I want to play that."' Even at eleven, once Ed had decided to do something, he did it. Fortunately his parents would invariably back him up.

Ed was in danger of always being half a step behind his elder brother, Matthew, who played the violin and continued to progress as a young classical musician. Ed had started taking cello lessons at school and his parents initially wanted him to tread a traditional musical progression of passing exams. Ed went along with it, but even at eleven he saw a different future for himself. He explained in the book *A Visual Journey* that classical music didn't inspire, excite or do anything for him whatsoever.

Instead, two days after watching Clapton, he walked into a pawnbroker's in Ipswich with £30 in his pocket and came out with a black Stratocaster copy. From that moment, Ed spent the majority of his leisure time shut away in his bedroom playing guitar. For the first few weeks, it was just 'Layla'. One can only imagine what the rest of the Sheeran household thought, hearing its famous riff played badly again and again … and again.

His parents decided he needed proper lessons and found a guitar teacher, Graham Littlejohn, who played with a local band and taught Ed to widen his repertoire. Under Graham's guidance, he learned to play rock classics, including 'A Million Miles Away', a thrilling piece by the celebrated Irish guitarist Rory Gallagher.

Just a month after seeing Eric Clapton on TV, Ed went to his first live concert. He persuaded his dad to take him to see the enduring American punk band Green Day when they brought their *Pop Disaster* tour to Wembley Arena in July 2002. He was eleven, and due to start high school in a couple of months. It was the first of many occasions when John Sheeran would accompany his son – in fact, he would be with him on every step of his musical journey. Many of Ed's friends were fans of the band, who were one of the biggest-selling acts in the world, and going along to see them in London earned him plenty of bragging rights.

Ed was pretty much a guitar geek by the time he started at Thomas Mills High School in September 2002, but not in an irritating way. He wasn't a loner and found it easier to make friends than he had in the past, especially if they were keen on music, too. Many of the mates he already had, including James Mee, moved to Framlingham College and inevitably they lost touch. James, who went on to become head boy, was more academically minded than Ed and achieved nine A*s at GCSE.

Thomas Mills was in the town, meaning Ed could walk to school – which was a bonus. His first form teacher was Georgie Ross, a charismatic young woman who was also in charge of drama. She noticed Ed among the new boys and girls right from the start, not just because of his striking ginger hair and glasses but also because he had brought his guitar with him on the first day. She recalls, 'It was his passion. That was the first thing I noticed about him. We had a getting-to-know-you exercise and he talked about his guitar. He was very funny and endearing, a jovial sort of cheeky chappie.'

Ed has never explained why, having been to fee-paying private schools, he moved on to attend a state secondary. He has intimated that he found Brandeston Hall sporty and competitive, adding, 'The other kids had a lot of money. I didn't enjoy it.' The huge fees at Framlingham College may also have had something to do with it. His parents' business was successful but was at the mercy of supply and demand, and there were no guarantees that they could afford the five-figure sum needed to keep two boys at public school for the next five years.

Ed has hinted that he was bullied during his school years but he has never been specific about when and where. He accepted that he was a 'weird-looking kid' and that everyone suffers 'a bit of bullying at school'. A particularly unpleasant boy threw a milkshake over him from a car while he waited at the bus stop. Such treatment motivated Ed to beat them at life.

Thomas Mills had a growing reputation as a school that encouraged children to make the most of their talents, particularly in the arts. The school dates back to the eighteenth century but was established as a comprehensive in 1979 by the merger of the old Mills Grammar and Framlingham Modern schools. Matthew was already being noticed by the time his younger brother joined him. He had been praised for his crystal-clear singing of 'Pie Jesu' at an end-of-term prizegiving. Both boys were fortunate that they arrived at the school when it was going through a golden period under the then headmaster David Floyd. He is one of the unsung heroes of the Ed Sheeran story in that he gave Ed and others the breathing space to develop their talents.

Georgie Ross observes, 'There was a sense of pride about being at the school. I think the majority of the children knew they were sort of lucky to be at this school. David had a real vision of what he wanted the school to be – an outstanding school. And he managed to convince us all to go on this journey with him.' Ofsted agreed, declaring, 'This is a good school where pupils make good progress and reach high standards in an atmosphere of civilised collaboration.'

Ed seemed equally at ease with boys and girls. His parents' close friends, Dan Woodside and Wendy Baker, had two daughters. Lauren and Martha were of similar ages to the Sheeran boys, and the families spent many sociable Sundays together. Dan was a decorative artist and Wendy an artist and art teacher, so they shared John and Imogen's creative tastes. Dan had worked on major restoration projects, including the ceiling at the entrance to the National Gallery, London, and the gilding of the Crimson Drawing Room at Windsor Castle.

Dan and Wendy had moved to the town a couple of years after their like-minded friends and turned their new home in Market Square into the Dancing Goat Café, which soon became a focal point for wiling away sunny afternoons. Ed and his new friends from Thomas Mills would gravitate there after school. He was always calling round on his own as well, to see if Lauren was coming out. In recognition of their families' long-standing friendship, Ed would give Dan and Wendy a gold record of his first album +, which now hangs proudly on the café wall.

Ed had a close circle of friends but was never constrained by Framlingham. The regular trips to Ireland and London, combined with his mum and dad's sociability, had broadened his horizons. John continued to extend his son's musical education by taking him to concerts and he managed to get tickets for a great night in April 2003, when Ed was twelve: they saw Paul McCartney in concert at Earl's Court. The most famous name in pop played a mammoth set of thirty-seven songs that spanned his entire career, from the heyday of The Beatles, to Wings and his solo material. David Lister, writing in the *Independent*, observed that Paul dished up a generous two-and-a-half-hour set of classics with 'such panache and emotion that it made the nerves tingle'. It was a tour de force and Ed decided that he preferred it to the Green Day gig.

Friends became used to Ed taking a guitar everywhere. By this time, he had a Faith, a decent-enough learning instrument. It was like a young child's teddy bear: he was rarely seen without it. He showed precocious bravery when he took to the stage and played 'Layla' at his school's spring charity concert. Inside, he wasn't feeling too confident but he blossomed in front of an audience of several hundred people in the school hall. By then he had mastered the song, so playing it was second nature and, to his relief, he was warmly applauded: 'It was fun. No one could have said a bad word, because I was so young and enthusiastic.'

At the end of his first summer term, Ed's year went to a resort in Holland, which was very exciting as they would all be away from home for a week. John and Imogen were keen for their sons to have adventures that would take them away from the narrow confines of Framlingham. Naturally, Ed took his acoustic guitar with him. On the coach he was determined to give everyone a song. His art teacher, Nicky Sholl, recalls that they asked for volunteers to go up and do a turn: 'Of course Ed went up and sang a song and then went back to his seat. And then he came back and sang one again. And everyone was like "Get him off the microphone!" It was very funny.'

He was also one of 140 pupils who sat around on the beach and chilled out at the end of a sightseeing day as the sun went down. Georgie Ross has never forgotten it: 'Ed just got up with his guitar and got them all singing along with him. He was already a real hit with this crowd of young people. He sang "Stan".'

It was a perfect end to the day, although Ed was about to discover that his musical progress would have its downs as well as ups.

4
SPINNING MAN

Ed was very upset. Without warning, his first guitar teacher had decided that teaching wasn't for him. Playing the guitar was crucially important to Ed and this seemed like a hammer blow to the twelve-year-old boy. He took it very badly. His mother recognised that she needed to act quickly to rekindle his enthusiasm or Ed would go back into his shell. She started asking around to see if someone else in Framlingham might take on her son, and discovered that two neighbours in the street were both using the same virtuoso guitarist to teach their children. They spoke very highly of jazz musician Keith Krykant, whom they'd found through an ad in a local community paper, and thought he would be ideal for Ed.

Keith, who was in his early fifties, had only moved recently to the town but, coincidentally, he had already heard of Ed. He had started teaching Richard Croney, one of the children who lived across the road from the Sheerans. One afternoon Keith was walking home with Richard when they saw a ginger-haired boy on the other side of the street. Richard piped up, 'That's Edward Sheeran,' and told Keith that Ed played concerts in the town and was already quite well known locally.

Keith and his wife, Sally Voakes, a jazz singer, had started to play gigs in the area and were building a following themselves. Sometimes it would just be the two of them, the Sally Voakes Duo or, for other nights, they might be joined by three or four local musicians.

One evening they were booked as a duo to play the Crown Hotel, which occupied a central position in Market Square. Imogen and John decided to go.

They were impressed, not just with Keith's playing but also by his calm demeanour. They approached him and asked if he might consider teaching Ed. He agreed to give him a weekly lesson, charging £20 for an hour. The lessons, usually in Ed's untidy teenage bedroom, continued for the next five years and complemented his development as a guitarist and, just as importantly, as a songwriter.

Ed already had a few guitars hanging on the bedroom wall. His rock guitar had pride of place over the bed. He preferred to decorate the orange walls of his room with his favourite instruments rather than posters of footballers or pop stars. When he grew tired of one or no longer played it, the guitar would be banished under the bed.

One of the first things Keith noticed in the room was an Epiphone Les Paul Sunburst guitar. He offered Ed a Bigsby tremolo unit that he wasn't using at the time, and popped it round to the house. By the time of the next lesson, Ed had put it on and was practising using it. Ed and his mum were hugely appreciative of the gesture, which helped teacher and pupil form a bond of mutual respect and the Krykants and Sheerans to forge a lasting friendship.

Keith quickly realised that Ed's playing was 'pretty advanced' for his age and that he also had a great deal of confidence in his own ability. Laughing, he recalls, 'He'd got a little bit of an inflated ego. He once said that I was the only guitarist he'd seen that was better than him. He was only thirteen!'

Musically, Ed was at a crossroads. Like many teenage boys, his initial ambition was to be a rock god. He had his electric guitar, admired Eric Clapton and others, and had formed his own group with two friends from school, Fred and Rowley Clifford. They called themselves Rusty and played heavy-metal covers, mainly Guns N' Roses. Their showstopper when they appeared at the old Drill Hall in Framlingham was the American band's most famous hit 'Sweet Child of Mine'. Ed liked that song but wasn't wild about the rest of the material.

While Fred did his best impersonation of charismatic singer Axl Rose, Ed took on the Slash role of lead guitarist. He relished the solo, meticulously learning every note in his bedroom after school. He didn't sing because he wasn't any good at it. 'I couldn't really hold a tune until I was sixteen,' he admitted.

Eric Clapton's most famous band, Cream, had been a trio, as was the Jimi Hendrix Experience and Rory Gallagher's Taste. It seemed the perfect number to draw attention to the guitarist. 'They took it very seriously,' observes Georgie Ross. As well as various assemblies and low-key school events, they played at the annual charity concert at Thomas Mills, one of the big occasions of the year.

Ed was already getting bored with the band. Keith Krykant observes, 'He was playing this rock but I think was beginning to realise there was other stuff out there. He'd done that. He exhausted it. He was just imitating others.'

Everything changed when Ed discovered the second of the three great musical influences in his life. He was staying up late one night, watching videos on the music channels, when he saw 'Cannonball' by a then little-known artist called Damien Rice. It was very quirky, a series of apparently random images sprinkled with shots of Damien's face as he sang. The almost surreal experience was linked together with a hypnotic acoustic riff.

Ed was immediately hooked. He went out and bought Damien's debut album *O* the very next day, which was later his choice in *Q* magazine's fascinating 'The Album that Changed my Life'. He admired its honesty and rawness: 'It was like he'd reached down his throat, grabbed his heart, ripped it out, stuck it on a plate and served it up to the world.' Ed couldn't wait to share his discovery with his friends. Unfortunately the Clifford brothers thought it was 'shit' so Rusty was hastily disbanded due to artistic differences. The falling-out was an early indication to Ed that he was better off doing it all himself.

Damien was born in Dublin and brought up in the thriving town of Celbridge, about fourteen miles from the city. He was already in his late twenties when he released the album that made his name internationally. He had spent his first years in music as part of a rock group called Juniper, which he had formed with friends from secondary school. Eventually, he became disenchanted with the musical compromises he felt he was making to please their record company. He became his own man and travelled around Europe busking, eventually settling in Tuscany where he wrote many of the songs for *O*.

His first solo composition to be released as a single was the agonisingly beautiful 'The Blower's Daughter', which highlighted his ability to share his emotions with the listener. Ed was entranced by Damien's ability to sing with such passion and share his private and innermost feelings with the world. Some of the songs were inspired by his relationship with the singer Lisa Hannigan, who provided fragile, haunting vocals alongside Damien on many of the tracks. She was his muse, they worked well together and he loved her taste.

Commercially, Damien has yet to top *O*. The *Irish Independent* described the album as 'one of the great Irish cultural success stories of the decade'. Sadly, Damien and Lisa would later split acrimoniously. The notoriously private singer heartbreakingly told the Irish music site *Hot Press*, 'I would give away all the music success, all the songs and the whole experience to still have Lisa in my life.'

Ed had soon learned to play all these poignant songs but he had to wait to see Damien in concert for the first time. That changed in 2004, during the late summer holidays in Ireland. Ed's cousin Laura told him that Damien was playing a low-key gig for under-eighteens at Whelan's in Dublin where she lived. The pub in Wexford Street was widely recognised as the original music venue in the city and was internationally famous for the quality of the acts that had performed there and as a popular location for television and films.

Laura and Ed were able to get tickets that stipulated, 'All adults must be accompanied by an under-18'. The adult, as ever, was John Sheeran. The gig would prove to be highly significant for Ed, one of the most important evenings of his life so far. For the first time he saw a solitary singer captivate an audience by performing his own songs: 'He holds them in the palm of his hands with just songs he has written on his own with a guitar.' Ed stood at the front, unbothered at being surrounded mainly by winsome teenage girls.

Afterwards, John took his two charges into the front bar area where Ed, who barely looked his then age of thirteen, had his first experience of a meet-and-greet where an artist takes the trouble to chat, sign autographs and pose for pictures with members of the audience. This interaction was an essential part of the whole experience of small gigs in pubs and a lead that Ed would follow diligently in the future.

He was lucky in that he was standing next to Damien's cellist, Vyvienne Long, who asked him, 'Can you watch my cello for a bit?' He dutifully guarded the instrument for twenty minutes until she reappeared, this time with Damien and the rest of the band. Ed told Lisa Hannigan he hoped to make a recording soon and she sweetly gave him an address so that he could send her a CD when it was finished. Ed, in a bright yellow T-shirt, had his picture taken with Damien, who was wearing a red hoodie, the same item of clothing that would be associated with Ed when he first started gigging. While not exactly scruffy, Damien was clearly an artist unbothered by image and the need to look like a star every minute of the day.

When he met Damien, Ed thought he was very cool: 'If he had been a dick, I'd probably be working in a supermarket.' He would later admit that it was life-changing – at that moment, he decided that he, too, was going to write songs like

Damien. He was not a teenager who dreamed of doing something: he would go and do it. He would be a singer–songwriter, and one day he would appear at Whelan's with just a guitar. Like Damien, he was destined to write many songs that would never see the light of day. Both were constantly creative.

Fortunately, his cousin Laura shared his enthusiasm. Whenever they got together, Ed would say, 'I'll be Damien, you be Lisa,' and they would record all the songs on *O*, which Ed knew backwards and forwards, in the garden shed at her family's house in Tuam, County Galway. Ed was lucky to have two older cousins, Jethro and Laura, who were inspired by the music he loved.

Back in Framlingham for his next lesson with Keith, he couldn't wait to tell his guitar mentor that he had seen Damien Rice and he, too, was going to be a singer–songwriter. First, though, he needed to find an old guitar. Damien played one from the Lowden guitar factory in Ireland, which looked the worse for wear but had a beautiful sound that filled the room. Keith recalls, 'I turned up one day as usual and he said to me straight away, "Have you got an old acoustic guitar? I don't want a new one. I want an old, battered, characterful acoustic guitar." So I told him I did have one actually, a Dallas model I'd bought for my wife Sally twenty-five years or so before. We didn't use it much anymore so I sold it to him. He wanted to play "Cannonball". And he started generally to get more into acoustic music.' Ed was thrilled to have the instrument as it meant he could practise playing Damien's music and make it sound more authentic. He probably knew the songs better than anyone other than the artist himself. That was part of his extraordinary gift. He was a sponge who could soak up a piece of music, then improvise and experiment to turn it into something entirely new and unique to him.

An additional attraction of *O* was that each song seemed to build slowly from an initial guitar riff and blossom into an emotional climax – something Ed aspired to achieve with his songs from the beginning.

For Christmas 2004, Ed's main present was a Boss Digital Recording Studio, a home studio for his bedroom. He immediately threw himself into recording his first album. He was determined to finish it in the holidays so it would be ready in time for the next term at Thomas Mills. He started work on Boxing Day 2004, and had completed fourteen songs twenty-four days later on 19 January 2005. Although he was proud and excited at the time, he now keeps *Spinning Man* away from the public. It is an amazing achievement for a thirteen-year-old, but it sounds nothing like the Ed Sheeran songs we know today.

For starters it's a rock album, bearing far more of the influence of Green Day, Guns N' Roses and Oasis than the acoustic lyricism of Damien Rice. He seems to have taken the power punk of Green Day's 'American Idiot', combined it with the more traditional rock of 'Sweet Child of Mine', and thrown in a dash of 'Don't Look Back in Anger'.

He had been building up his collection of guitars and wanted to play his best one on the album. He had acquired a striking B. C. Rich rock guitar during his Rusty days. Slash and Axl Rose played B. C. Rich models onstage. You couldn't miss Ed's, which was purple with gold hardware. Keith was impressed: 'It was a really serious guitar with a beautiful bird's-eye maple neck.'

Spinning Man featured fourteen tracks and fifty minutes of music. The album starts with a drum intro and a dirty guitar riff. This is 'Typical Average', one of the first songs Ed wrote. Lyrically, it's not a high point, repeating, 'I'm a typically average teen, if you know what I mean', but it does possess a strangely catchy quality, even if the vocal is distinctly shaky.

The second track, 'Misery', contains another powerful rock solo, setting the tone for the guitar work on the complete album. His first rap is 'On My Mind', which seems to be directed at an unnamed girlfriend and, while it lacks the power of his later, more sophisticated work, it sounds more like Ed than his Green Day numbers. And it was the first Ed Sheeran composition to contain the phrase 'fuck off'.

Even more interesting is 'No More War', which is a protest song about the futility of war. The older Ed would deliberately avoid writing strong political statements so this is a rare song that proclaims, 'Put down your guns because it's not for fun'. 'Moody Ballad of Ed' is back in 'Typical Average' territory and is probably even shakier vocally as he drifts in and out of tune. He sounds a little better on a slower number, 'Addicted', but 'Butterfly' and 'Concord' are more representative of what is basically a rock album. The last consists of crashing chords and a power solo that would have done Deep Purple or Jeff Beck proud *circa* 1970. There's more of that on 'Crazy', which has an even longer head-banging guitar solo, and 'Broken', which seems to reference 'Sunshine of Your Love', a classic Cream track that featured Eric Clapton.

That rock sound continued on 'Celebrity' and 'Sleep', which must have been a precious commodity in the Sheeran household, with Ed on electric guitar in one room and Matthew on violin in another. 'Mindless' was a post-punk homage to Kentucky Fried Chicken before the album ended on a high note with 'I Love You', which was probably the closest track to future Ed Sheeran. The problem with his slower songs was that they exposed more obviously his vocal limitations at the time. As every musician knows, recording the album is only the start of the process. He needed a title and decided to call it *Spinning Man* after a late work by the great surrealist Salvador Dalí. John Sheeran had hung a print on a wall at the house so Ed was very familiar with it and the title seemed perfect for a spinning CD.

To add to the professional feel of the project, Ed enlisted his parents to help produce a proper CD, complete with case and sleeve notes, which proudly declared that all the material was copyright Ed Sheeran and Sheeran Lock Ltd. He asked Alison Newell, a local artist and family friend, to design the cover. She featured his Faith guitar to one side of a black background. Some delicate white spirals, shaped like a prawn, make simple embroidery. The back featured a photograph taken by his father of Ed playing the same guitar on the streets of Galway the previous summer, his first venture into busking. In his thanks, Ed included 'all those who put money into my guitar case'.

He also thanked his cousins Laura and Jethro, his brother Matthew and all Sheerans and all Locks. There are thanks, too, for Mums and Dabs, his pet names for his mother and father since he was a toddler. Among the friends he acknowledges, he mentions Claire – the inspiration for some of the songs, including 'I Love You'. According to Ed, they had a very innocent hand-holding friendship that was over by the time he recorded the album, although he was upset when they broke up.

For his musical inspiration, Ed cites Damien Rice, Eric Clapton and 'Jimmy H' (presumably Jimi Hendrix) but there is sketchy evidence of their influence on the album. There's something of Hendrix and Clapton but *Spinning Man* bears no resemblance to Damien Rice, who really doesn't do solos, big riffs or long instrumentals on an electric guitar. At thirteen, Ed was still searching for his own sound and his first album was really a hangover from his schoolboy band Rusty. He is, though, too modest about the achievement.

Perhaps the most interesting aspect of *Spinning Man* is its maturity, best exemplified by his personal message on the sleeve notes: 'Songwriting and playing the guitar are like having a direct line to my thoughts and feelings. Everyone has strong feelings whatever their age. We can all feel love, joy, longing, pain and hate.' His mother may have used her editing skills to help but it clearly reveals Ed's early self-awareness.

He sent the CD to Lisa Hannigan but wished he had waited when he didn't get a response. The reaction from those he played it to in Framlingham was very encouraging. Nobody wanted him to lose heart by being over-critical of his first recordings, particularly his mother and father. They agreed that if he wanted to make money out of his music, it had to be recorded to a higher standard than he could achieve in his bedroom. He also needed to work on his singing.

When his mum and dad realised how seriously Ed was taking his music, they asked Keith, who had been a television and radio producer, if he could find a local studio to record some of the songs to a more professional standard: 'John said to me, "Give him some experience in a studio."' John was more interested in Ed spending time in a proper studio than in the finished product.

They found the ideal location just a few miles away in the town of Leiston at the renowned Summerhill School, the progressive educational facility founded by A. S. Neill. His grandson Henry Readhead ran the studio there mainly for the school but said that Ed could come with Keith for a session in March 2005.

Keith agreed to waive his fee as producer for the day in return for an hour or two in which John would show him how to improve his business online and make better connections for his own music and performance. John taught him how to build a network of links so that one gig would lead to another. Imogen told him, 'It's the currency of the day.' That system of barter had served Sheeran Lock well and would continue to be useful to Ed as he sought to promote his work.

For *The Orange Room*, named in honour of his bedroom, they chose Ed's five favourite tracks from *Spinning Room* and put them in a different order: 'Moody Ballad of Ed' followed by 'Misery', 'Typical Average', 'Addicted', finishing again with 'I Love You'.

The most striking improvement from *Spinning Man* was the use of acoustic guitar and, generally, a better vocal, but his attempt at falsetto on 'Addicted' needed plenty of work. Occasionally, there are hints of the later Ed Sheeran. Keith remembers doing his best to convince Ed that he needed to tune his guitar all the time because it would show up on an edit even if it was just slightly out of tune: 'He was a little bit lazy about it.'

Ed had turned fourteen and was beginning to stick up for himself musically. When Keith hinted that a vocal was just a little bit out of tune and they should go back and do it again, Ed was quite clear: 'I like that. I want to keep that as it is.' Henry acted as sound engineer and one of his protégées, Megumi Miyoshi, who was sixteen and a promising singer, helped with mixing and some backing vocals.

The Orange Room clearly illustrates the growing influence of Damien Rice, although 'Typical Average' still sounds like Green Day jamming after a heavy night out and is not remotely related to anything from *O*.

Ed saved up and pooled all his resources to have a thousand CDs produced, which was quite optimistic. He proudly took them to school and offered them round for a fiver. Most of them sat around in boxes at home, where they remained until he became famous. Then he had to ban his mum from selling either *The Orange Room* or *Spinning Man*.

In an interview on *The Jonathan Ross Show* in December 2014, Ed played a short segment of a song from his phone. It was 'Addicted' and sounded very average. His guitar work was good but not the vocal, which had cats running for cover. In Ed's defence, his vocal problems were mainly because his voice had yet to break so he struggled with intonation. But as Ed accurately commented, 'You have to learn and really practise.'

5
THE LOOPMEISTER

One evening Keith and Sally Krykant were among a group of friends invited round to John and Imogen's house for dinner. When they arrived, Preston Reed was already sitting at the dining table. Anyone taking an interest in guitar would have known about him, a striking figure who featured often in the serious music press talking about his unique playing style.

Ed had noticed in a guitar magazine that the virtuoso player was offering places on a summer-school venture at his home in Scotland. He would be teaching his percussive method, known in the business as 'tapping', to a few chosen students during the summer holidays. Ed set about convincing his parents that the workshop was vital to his development as a musician.

Preston, it transpired, was playing a gig locally and the Sheerans went along. Instead of grabbing a quick autograph, they invited him to stay at the house; he accepted. Keith was particularly impressed: 'This guy is a world-class international player, who had developed his own style of playing. It was completely different to just changing the tuning.'

Presumably John and Imogen made a deal involving the 'currency of the day' because, during the next summer holidays, Ed set off with his father on a train to Girvan on the Ayrshire coast for a five-day summer workshop. Preston had moved to this beautiful part of Scotland, fifty miles south of Glasgow, from his home in Minneapolis in 2001.

This was not a holiday for Ed, although he and his father managed to fit in a boat trip to Ailsa Craig, the famous granite island in the Firth of Clyde. Preston was impressed by Ed's work ethic, unusual in one so young: 'He was intelligent and quick; he very quickly picked up the things he had come up to learn. Even at fourteen, you could tell he had a real determination and ambition.'

The trip was made more memorable for Ed by the presence of the only other student on the trip, an amazing guitar player from Oklahoma called Jocelyn Celaya, who would develop a strong following in subsequent years as Radical Classical. Jocelyn had arrived with her boyfriend, who told everyone that he used to be a gangster in Mexico. Ed, who was enthusiastic about gangsta rap at the time, couldn't believe he was face to face with a real one and bombarded him with questions. On the last night, everyone got together for a party and Preston played some of his own compositions including 'Fat Boy', 'Metal' and 'Ladies Night'. Ed entertained everyone by making up rap lyrics to accompany the music. 'He just rattled it off,' recalled Preston. 'It was quite funny and impressive as well.'

On his return to Framlingham, Ed was not about to become the second Preston Reed but the interlude helped him view the acoustic guitar as more than just a stringed instrument.

Preston's technical innovations showed him 'the music you could make using the guitar as a source of sounds'. Ed absorbed that lesson from his trip to Scotland and would use it in his own way when he was introduced to an even more important character in his development as a performer.

But, first, he had to go back to school. Ed was fortunate in that it wasn't just his mum and dad who recognised he had a special talent and could make something of his music. The director of music at Thomas Mills, Richard Hanley, realised early on that the teenager was different from his other students and needed a more thoughtful approach. Richard specialised in classical music and was more closely involved with teaching Matthew, but he followed the headmaster's lead and gave all his students the opportunity to flourish. That was the key for Ed, who has always acknowledged the debt he owes his school.

At first, Richard was hoping to persuade Ed to follow his brother and join the school orchestra, but soon discovered he was persevering with the cello on sufferance. Ed was relieved to give it up and concentrate on the guitar. He could often be found in one of the small practice rooms in the music department working on a new song. Richard explains, 'I think the school gave him the chance to be creative, to have the time and space to play and compose and perform.' His passion for his music was all-consuming.

Ed was never going to match Matthew's academic dedication. Even Imogen acknowledged that her younger son was not an exam person and struggled to apply himself to read music properly. In many ways, though, Matthew was the more eccentric of the two talented brothers. Richard acknowledges that Matthew was very creative as well as academic: 'He had some quite avant-garde ideas.' One Easter he composed 'Broken Pavements' for the school concert at St Michael's: 'It was a very atmospheric piece. I can still remember the sunlight pouring through the great east window at the church illuminating the players. It was a magical moment.'

As teenagers, the two Sheeran boys were totally different. They had their own groups of friends and just did their own thing. For a time, Keith Krykant taught Matthew as well: 'He particularly wanted to know about jazz improvisations. He was very mathematical in his music and was very interested in theory. He wanted to know how the notes added up mathematically to give a certain chord.

'He wanted to consolidate some of the things he was doing on the piano and understand how they related to the guitar. He used to compose on a computer and had a much more mechanical approach to that than Ed, who was more interested in getting a song out with a rhythm and a melody.' In his own way, Matthew was just as ambitious as Ed: he wanted to establish himself as a classical composer. The two boys never fell out but, as Keith remembers with a smile, 'They never used to speak to each other in the house.'

Keith was still trying to teach Ed some music theory but he was fighting a losing battle. Every week he would arrive at the house with a careful plan for the lesson with 'Edward' – as he always called him, just as his parents did. He explains, 'I would decide that we would take a piece of music – pure music notation – and I would explain to him how we would get that on to a guitar. It is quite tedious. And we maybe would get five minutes into the theory and he wasn't really interested in it. He would suddenly say, "Oh, Keith, do you want to hear a song that I wrote last night at one o'clock in the morning?" And I would say, "OK." So he would start playing this song. And ask me, you know, "What do you think of this?" And I might suggest that he put something extra in just to bridge the chords – harmony, if you like. And if he liked it, he would light up and go, "Wow, that really works now. Keith, you're a genius!"'

Ed was showing great maturity for his age in what he was listening to and what he wanted to play. His father's taste had rubbed off on him. He still wanted to enjoy his favourite hip-hop artists but, post Damien Rice, he was developing more interest in singer–songwriters such as Ray LaMontagne, whose debut album, *Trouble*, in 2004, had showcased his distinctive vocal style, as well as all-time greats, including Paul Simon. He spent an entire lesson with Keith learning how to play the famous Simon and Garfunkel hit 'Sound of Silence'.

'You could see that he liked songs with strong melodies,' observes Keith. 'Most of the kids at the time were listening to *The X Factor*, which had just started, and following that, but he was appreciating other things.'

Another of Ed's characteristics that served him well as a teenager was his lack of fear. He was appreciative but not overawed by the occasion. He took meeting Preston Reed in his stride. On another memorable occasion John and Imogen had arranged a dinner party where the guests included the local vicar. Keith and his wife were there: 'Edward sang a ballad in the front room in front of the vicar and everybody else in a very, very confident and emotional way. It was very mature because he was only fourteen. It was extraordinary. Most of the children I teach won't ever sing or play in front of their mum and dad. In fact they will play in front of anyone else *but* their mum and dad. But his mum and dad were there and he sang this song and completely held the audience – except the vicar, who can't stand guitar music.'

The priest might not have appreciated being in the audience for a concert at the Shepherd's Bush Empire in January 2006. The modest Sunday-night gig would change the course of Ed's life as a performer. He and his dad had driven to London to see Nizlopi, an unconventional duo who had just had a number-one hit with their 'JCB Song'. He was transfixed, though, by the opening act, an Irish singer–songwriter called Gary Dunne.

Gary used a Boss Loop Station and it was the first time Ed had witnessed how exciting that could be live. Gary built a song that filled the popular venue even though he was alone. He performed five numbers finishing with his 'Amerikan Folk Song', which Ed singled out as the track that had made him realise looping was the way forward for him to create his own individual sound. The musician plays a few bars, then has the loop station play it back while he lays another set of chords over the top. This can be done multiple times building layers of sound. In other words, you become your own band.

Gary did his best at performing the often thankless task of being a supporting act when the audience were standing around chatting and having a pint. He made a point of plugging his album, *Twenty Twenty Fiction*, which was on sale at the merchandise desk in the foyer. He also announced that he did house concerts, if anyone was interested.

Ed couldn't stop talking to his dad about the loop pedal so John wrote to Gary saying, 'My son absolutely loved what you did,' and inviting him to Framlingham for Ed's fifteenth-birthday party in a few weeks' time.

'House concerts' were part of Gary's musical world. They enabled him to earn extra pennies when he was between tours, further spread the word about his music and hopefully sell some CDs. He quoted John his standard deal at the time: 'It was accommodation, a few hundred quid and a six-pack of Guinness. They were simple times.'

The week before his birthday, there was a tragic turn of events. One of his school friends, Stuart Dines, was killed in an horrific coach crash in Germany. Stuart, who was three months younger than Ed, was one of a group of pupils from Thomas Mills on a half-term trip to the Austrian ski resort of Fugen. On the autobahn near Cologne, the double-decker coach got a puncture and had to pull over onto the hard shoulder. A lorry carrying metal rods careered into the stationary vehicle.

Stuart was killed when a piece of metal from the lorry smashed through one of the coach windows.

Ed was not on the trip, but he knew Stuart well and they had been round to each other's houses. Stuart lived in the nearby town of Woodbridge and his elder brother and sister went to school there. His parents, however, chose Thomas Mills for Stuart because he had ADHD and they felt it would better suit their son. That proved to be the case and, just like Ed, he was a happy and popular classmate and not at all an outsider. His proud father Robert recalls, 'Stuart was very outgoing and if anyone was a bit shy, they could latch on to Stuart. He would talk to anybody. He had so much energy.' He also shared Ed's gift of being able to memorise complicated lyrics, which would leave his father wondering why he couldn't do the same with his schoolwork.

The school flag was at half mast when everyone returned after half-term. The headmaster at the time, Colin Hirst, who had faced the difficult task of telling Stuart's parents what had happened, said that the children were 'devastated and shocked'.

Stuart's father Robert remembers, 'Ed was very, very upset, like a lot of the children.'

Ed had to come to terms with the death of someone he saw practically every day. He resolved to write a song about his feelings. He composed, he said, 'whilst I got round to actually accepting it.'

The song that he eventually finished is a breathtakingly beautiful tribute to his friend called 'We Are'. He completed it in time for Stuart's funeral at Woodbridge Methodist Church and the CD recording was played during the service along with some of Stuart's favourite Queen records. So many people wanted to pay their respects that they filled the church and the hall next door, into which they piped the music so that everyone could hear it. Afterwards Ed presented Robert, and Stuart's mother Jackie, with a signed copy of the CD. 'It is a lovely song,' observes Robert.

Before the funeral, Ed's fifteenth birthday party was a chance to cheer himself up, as well as his friends. Ed went to a lot of trouble setting up a PA system in the spacious living room at home and he and his dad drove off to Ipswich Station to collect Gary. This was the first time they had met him. Gary played a hugely appreciated set of his songs to 'Ed and all his teenage buddies, who told me they loved the show'.

He stayed up late talking with John and Ed and a few of his mates. They reminisced about Ireland. Gary is from Portlaoise, fifty miles west of Dublin. His father, also called John, ran a folk club at Kavanagh's pub, which hosted many of the musicians Ed most admired, including Andy Irvine, an original member of Planxty. Gary still has the picture of Andy, his father and a teenage Ed taken there.

Most of the country had seen a loop pedal for the first time when the Scottish singer–songwriter KT Tunstall used one to mesmerising effect on a 2004 edition of *Later … with Jools Holland*. She stole the show when she created a one-woman-band effect for her song 'Black Horse and the Cherry Tree'. But Gary had first become interested in looping two years earlier when he had played at the Lobby Bar, a music pub in Cork. He was on a bill that included the acclaimed American singer–songwriter Joseph Arthur and could scarcely believe Joseph wasn't using a backing track. Gary had marvelled at how he could make all those sounds live through a loop station. The music business is full of such chance connections. That gig in a tiny bar in Cork would lead indirectly to one of the most important ingredients in the development of the Ed Sheeran sound.

By coincidence both Gary Dunne and Damien Rice had supported Joseph Arthur at one time. Ed was thrilled to hear that Gary had also opened for Damien Rice on tour and told him about the gig at Whelan's he had been to with his cousin Laura. Gary observes, 'He was a hardcore Damien Rice fan back then.'

Gary found meeting the Sheeran family a 'very warm and enjoyable' experience: 'In the morning Imogen cooked a big, beautiful fry-up and we went for a walk near by.' Before he left Framlingham, Gary went through the process of looping with Ed. He showed him the Boss RC20 model he used and recommended that Ed try it. It was a simple but rugged piece of equipment that could survive being hauled around by an impatient teenager.

Ed went straight out and bought one, which cost roughly £250. Looping was not a technique you could learn overnight and it took him well over two years of constant practice to feel that he had finally mastered the pedal – he soon found that one mistake could throw a whole song out of synch. The new skill, however, did allow him to improve 'We Are' and turn it into a multi-layered ballad, recognisable as the one he would perform many times in the future.

Gary was happy to offer advice by phone or email and they remained on very good terms. It was a two-way street: Ed had videoed Gary's gig at his house, chopped it into individual songs and put the entire thing on Gary's Myspace page.

Ed was of the generation that appreciated the power of a good live video online. Gary observes, 'I was ten years older and just didn't understand at the time. He was so digital savvy and web savvy in a way that I wasn't and I wasn't really interested in. I remember him telling me, "You've got to get out there." He kind of ran my Myspace for six months.'

Gary and Ed never composed together. He explains, 'Our connection isn't about songs. It's about live looping. I suppose I passed on a craft to him, a way of making music. Of course, he has since evolved massively but the craft remains the same. He is just using it in a much more complex way than I ever did.

'Looping is like playing a different instrument. It's not just getting onstage with a guitar and singing a song. It's getting onstage with your voice and your guitar and creating a sound. You are using a different canvas.'

Gary is proud of his part in Ed's journey to global success: 'When I sit in an audience of 80,000 people and I see Ed do his thing with an acoustic guitar and a loop station, I can hear a little DNA of where he and I connected. It's a beautiful, beautiful thing.'

6

WANT SOME NIZLOPI

As soon as his voice broke, Ed's vocals improved dramatically. The time was right for him to have some lessons. He struck lucky with Claire Weston, a Framlingham-based singer and one of the best-known sopranos in Suffolk. She had been a leading light of the English National Opera before settling back in her home county to teach at Framlingham College and Woodbridge School. She also took on pupils from Thomas Mills.

Claire's favourite piece of music is Verdi's *Requiem*, although she is very partial to Benjamin Britten as well. Neither composer featured on Ed's mixed tapes but she also admitted a liking for The Beatles, a connection shared by many of the players in Ed's journey. Under her expert guidance, Ed's singing began to resemble the familiar style of the future. Still a little shaky in places, he sounded more like *the* Ed Sheeran on his next CD venture, an album he called simply *Ed Sheeran*. The title may seem uninspired but it followed a long-established method in the music business of getting your name in front of the public.

The music revealed a gentler, more thoughtful Ed. He had discovered that he wrote in waves so most of the songs for *Ed Sheeran* have a similar feel. They were pleasant without having the extra ingredient that grabbed you by the throat. He was in proper singer–songwriter territory, with a series of considered ballads including the poignant 'In Memory' and 'The Sea', which reflected a more serious-minded teenager.

In the 1970s this album might have been considered bedsit music – introspective tracks that you would put on the stereo, lie on the bed, gaze at the ceiling and consider the injustice of the world. Fittingly, on one of the catchiest tracks, 'Spark', he says the world is harsh and he is 'stuck in the dark'.

He highlighted his change of mood from *Spinning Man* and *The Orange Room* by calling one of the tracks 'Quiet Ballad of Ed'. The 'moody' song had been banished to history. The lyrics are more mature, although his vocals still sound young. He didn't completely forget his earlier teenage self: the guitar in 'Billy Ruskin' is very reminiscent of his old favourite 'Sweet Child of Mine'.

Perhaps the most interesting track is 'Pause', which fused rap and melody, as so much of his music would in the future. The rap was provided by his cousin Jethro, whose verse – including a name check to Sheeran Lock – fits snugly into a catchy song that included one of Ed's anthem-like choruses.

The next step in the musical education of Ed Sheeran was to make his first video. He went along to Bruizer Creative Film & Video Agency in nearby Woodbridge to make a film to accompany him singing the opening number on the album, 'Open Your Ears', which, unusually for Ed at the time, featured a piano melody as well as backing vocals from his cousin

Laura. She's not in the video, which showed Ed, in a red Nizlopi T-shirt and smart black blazer, gazing upwards at a camera. The whole three minutes is filmed from above with Ed, looking very clean cut with neatly brushed hair, against a spinning backdrop – a spinning man. He is standing on a black paw print, which he had adopted as his new logo and featured on the front of the CD cover. He may have got the idea from the family cat or from the sign by the roadside outside Framlingham for the Earl Soham Veterinary Centre.

The overall effect is inoffensive, but neither the song nor the video hinted at the artist Ed Sheeran would become. He is definitely a work in progress, although it reflected the mind-set in the Sheeran household. Keith Krykant, who continued to be impressed with how they went about achieving their goals, observes, 'His parents took Ed very seriously. Because of their background in media and promotion, they were already treating Ed like a celebrity – quite extraordinary really.'

Part of the necessary process of celebrity was to take Ed out of his comfort zone in Framlingham and into the wider world. He continued to hope that contact with Nizlopi would prove the answer. They were firmly established as his favourite band but he was having no luck in engaging their attention. Ed was among the collection of fans known as the People's Republic of Nizlopi, who knew the words to every song. Damien Rice was not forgotten, but Ed wanted to meet the duo from Royal Leamington Spa who offered so much more than one hit record. While he was enthusiastic about Gary Dunne's looping at the Shepherd's Bush Empire, Nizlopi moved him. He was spellbound by the way they engaged with the audience and made everyone at the venue feel involved.

Nizlopi were two old school friends – Luke Concannon, who sang and played guitar, and John Parker, a beatboxer and double bassist. Like Ed, they both have strong Irish connections. John's mother is Irish and Luke's grandparents were from Kerry and Roscommon, while his dad, Kieron, is an accomplished musician and keen piper. The boys grew up playing in folk-music sessions and festivals, singing in pubs and busking in Ireland. Luke explains, 'It was very relatable for Ed. Our families are really quite similar.'

They also had a musical heritage that Ed could appreciate: 'We had two strands of musical influence. We had the singalong stuff like The Beatles that we used to hear and play in pubs in England, as well as having some rare old times in Dublin. But alongside that, there was also this thing about being a modern young person listening to and playing hip hop. We had to figure out what our music was and so we called it folk hip hop.'

Their background was almost identical to Ed's. He, too, had absorbed the classic Beatles tracks his dad played in the car, loved Planxty and The Chieftains during his trips to Ireland and had embraced the music of Eminem and Dr Dre. Later, when Ed would describe his own sound, he called it 'acoustic hip hop'.

Luke and John needed to find a name for themselves. One afternoon they were sitting with their then band in the kitchen at Luke's home when his mum mentioned to her son that a family friend, Di Nizlopi, was popping around on Sunday. One of the band misheard and asked 'What's a dinizlopi?' thinking it was some weird dinosaur. Everybody laughed, and there and then they decided to call themselves Nizlopi, a Hungarian name. Luke liked the idea in particular because he had a 'lust' for the family's daughter, Nina.

When he left school, Luke studied English at Sussex University and after he had graduated invited John to join him in Brighton. They spent time gigging around the town while writing and rehearsing much of their first album, *Half These Songs Are About You* – a career blueprint that Ed would follow in the future.

The opening track, 'Fine Story', was the first that Ed heard on Myspace. He was hooked by Luke's unique vocal style that seemed to breathe anguish and emotion.

He loved the poetic ballad 'Freedom' and, of course, the unforgettable 'JCB Song'. That breakthrough hit resonated with Ed because it was inspired by Luke's difficulties at school. He didn't have a stutter but suffered from dyslexia. He wrote the much-loved song about those struggles and his nostalgic memories of days out perched on a toolbox beside his dad in his yellow digger. When Ed saw them perform at the Shepherd's Bush Empire, they were coming to the end of their tour promoting the song, which had been number one just before Christmas. Typically of the time, it lost the top spot to an *X Factor* winner, Shayne Ward.

The album was released on Luke and John's own label, FDM Records. Following their chart success, they resisted approaches from major record companies, fearing a corporate approach would change them. They didn't want to compromise – a philosophy that Ed much admired.

During 2006, Ed tried hard to be included in their world, but although he went to more concerts and wrote to them at the label, he didn't register with Nizlopi. That was until he sent them a video of him singing one of their songs, 'Find Me', which contained a line that appealed to his romantic nature: 'You are an angel sent from above.'

Luke recalls how impressed they were: 'He looked like a little choir boy but a bit scruffier. He was very sweet. He was covering this song and doing all the parts himself. He was beatboxing. He played the baseline on the guitar – and it's not an easy part. It's got harmonics in it. He sang and it's got falsetto lines, and then he looped it all up. And we were a bit like "Wow!" I remember us saying that if we had enough money, we would have signed him to our label. But we didn't have enough resources to promote Nizlopi at the time.'

So nothing happened. Undaunted and determined as ever, Ed did not give up. Instead, he shut himself away in his bedroom and wrote his own song for Nizlopi entitled 'Two Blokes and a Double Bass.' He decided to include it on his next recording venture. Ed had boundless energy and had soon compiled eleven songs. The problem would be the recording costs. He wanted to use a studio in London, which would inevitably be an added expense at a time when the Bank of Mum and Dad was running low.

John and Imogen were not parents who watched their children develop while they sat back and did nothing themselves. They worked hard on new Sheeran Lock ideas, particularly those encouraging young people and disadvantaged communities. From their Framlingham base, they combined prestigious work, including a United Nations Millennium exhibition, with pioneering 'cultural identity projects', as they called them, under the banner of Pride of Place. The idea was to involve schools in programmes that focused on creativity and enterprise.

While Ed was working hard on his new songs, they joined forces with the Commission for Racial Equality to launch a national art competition called Young Brits at Art, in which eleven-to-sixteen-year-olds depicted their thoughts on contemporary Britain. John curated an exhibition of the entries, which took place in the autumn of 2006 at the Royal Albert Hall in London. Imogen edited an accompanying book designed by Alison Newell.

The Sheerans' business took a knock when a key sponsor left. They had to close their office in Framlingham and work from home. They certainly didn't have the spare cash to bankroll Ed in the studio. Fortunately, his grandmother Shirley saved the day and lent him £500, which he promised to pay back – and did. He recorded it at the Din Studios in Crouch End over a five-month period from October 2006 to March 2007 under the watchful eye and ear of producer Julian Simmons, who was well known for his expertise with vocals. As a result of his encouragement and ongoing lessons with Claire Weston, Ed's voice on *Want Some?* is a further improvement on the *Ed Sheeran* album.

In little more than three years, Ed's music had matured enormously. That much was obvious from the opening chords of the first track, 'You Break Me'. They were melodious, jangly and acoustic, introducing a song that was more polished than anything that had gone before. He was developing his own individual style, using his guitar as percussion and nimbly displaying his vocal range on 'I'm Glad I'm Not You'.

The lyric for 'You Need to Cut Your Hair' mentions advice from his dad, a recurring theme in Ed Sheeran songs. In this case his father is warning him against giving in to lust to chase an unsuitable girl. She may or may not have been 'Sara', who has blonde hair and blue eyes and is the title subject of the next song. A softer Ed croons, 'May I say you look like an angel today.'

Jethro was brought in to provide the rap on 'Move On', highlighting how easily Ed could move between genres – one minute a romantic ballad, the next spitting hip hop. The guitar work on 'Yellow Pages' reveals how accomplished Ed was on the instrument, while the lyric is a clever description of the agony of telling someone too soon that you love her. Less successful is 'Smile', pleasant enough but more of an album filler than the other tracks.

'Postcards' begins with a strong piano introduction and is an interesting departure from the usual guitar-led numbers. The song that would become the best known on the album was his ninety-second tribute to Nizlopi, 'Two Blokes and a Double Bass'. He managed to include the word 'Nizlopi' in the lyric, which was no mean feat, and he gives a name check to Gary Dunne. The effect is clever and dextrous and you can imagine Luke Concannon singing it. He also mentions 'Flooded Quarry', a song he kept returning to over the years as his favourite Nizlopi tune. He even picked it as his premier Desert Island Disc, because it would always 'make me feel happy and make me feel warm'.

The first recorded cover Ed did was 'The West Coast of Clare', a very challenging yet beautiful Irish lament by Andy Irvine. Ed's vocal is perhaps the least successful on the album, although that may be because he found it more difficult singing to a piano than to a guitar. His new vocal confidence, however, served him well on the last track, 'I Can't Spell', which he sings entirely a cappella. The song was a bold and brave musical statement from a sixteen-year-old.

This time, Ed was responsible for his own artwork and design, although Alison Newell helped with layouts. He again chose a black-and-orange colour scheme. He had drawn a complex maze – lots of random orange scribblings in a block against a black background.

The finished CD was ready just in time for final preparations for his GCSEs, although his parents were anxious about his lack of academic application. Even his dad called him lazy for his failure to do much schoolwork. Ed loved reading and would often have his head in a book when he was taking a break from his music: English, therefore, was not presenting a problem and he particularly enjoyed studying *Of Mice and Men*, the novella by John Steinbeck set in the Great Depression.

Surprisingly, it was art, of all things, in the Sheeran household that was causing consternation. He received a poor mark for one of his final pieces in which he had copied the cover of the Damien Rice album *9*, the follow-up to *O* that had been released in November while Ed was recording *Want Some?*. His art teacher Nicky Sholl explains, 'Basically he just copied the cover instead of moving it around or doing anything with it. I think he'd just changed some of the lettering. Needless to say, he didn't get a brilliant mark for that.'

Nicky and a concerned Imogen discussed how her son could do better. Ed had been brought up surrounded by a talented network of artists so he was in a strong position to rescue the situation. Eventually he produced an Andy Warhol-style self-portrait. Nicky observes, 'I think the idea of fame and self-image really excited him even then.' Ed sailed through art, securing an A grade. Intriguingly, the artwork for *Want Some?*, which Ed produced himself, bears some comparison with the random drawings that feature on the cover of Damien's album *9*.

Ed took time off from studying to take part in a special tribute concert for Stuart Dines, held at Woodbridge School at the beginning of June. Many local acts took part in an all-day festival to raise money for the Kariandusi School Trust, a charity working to aid the education of young children in rural Kenya. The year before Stuart's death the Dines family had enjoyed a wonderful holiday in Kenya; they wanted to support something there that could be a lasting tribute to their son and Ed was keen to help. More than £10,000 was raised and, as a result, a school in the small village of Simba, near Gilgil, in Kenya, now boasts the splendid Stuart Dines Library.

Ed didn't want to sit around and do nothing when his exams were finished. He sent his song 'Two Blokes and a Double Bass' to Nizlopi, and this time followed up with an idea that grabbed their attention. Luke explains, 'He said, "Look, I want to do some work experience with you." He was super-persistent and enthusiastic and we were just like, "OK, we need a work-experience kid." So him and his dad came to a gig we were playing in Birmingham and we met up afterwards. We had a good chat and we got on well with his dad, who's from an Irish family like mine, so the result was Ed came on a run of dates with us.' Ed's father had already been to some Nizlopi gigs with his son and understood that they were hard workers, not 'crazy rock 'n' rollers'.

Ed reported for duty with a copy of the new Harry Potter book in one hand, guitar in the other and his rucksack on his back. The seventh and final novel, *Harry Potter and the Deathly Hallows*, had just been published and Ed had been quick to buy his copy. He had devoured J. K. Rowling's saga of the boy wizard and was loving the last instalment.

Nominally, sixteen-year-old Ed was a guitar technician for the summer holidays but he was more interested in watching what happened on tour. He was treated as a member of the crew and shared a room with the sound technician. Luke laughs, 'He did do the guitar stuff but he did it with the minimum level of concern – probably the way ninety per cent of teenage boys in England would do a job. It was, like, "I've done that, now I'm just going to do what I want to do."

'I remember our tour manager saying that Ed just watched us play and didn't do anything. But I think he just wanted to soak up as much as he could and learn about being a musician, so he just didn't give much of a feck about making sure things were plugged in at the right level or that there was water on the stage. That wasn't his thing.'

Ed was in his element, brimming with enthusiasm to make the most of his opportunity. Luke observes, 'He was like your little brother's friend who was just so excited to hang out with the big kids. I remember that the sense on tour was that he was a really sweet kid but he was more interested in being a musician than being any good with the tech side.'

Ed was fascinated by Nizlopi's engagement with their audience. They encouraged responses and would invite members of the audience to sing or rap with them. Luke would shout, 'Are there any MCs in the audience?' and get them onstage. He and John would improvise. They would write something before they went on and then just play it.

Luke explains, 'I think there was something quite different about what we were doing. And we were talking about real shit – songs about sexuality, about family, politics and spirituality. There was passion. I think that's maybe why he was so intense about us.'

One of Ed's first gigs with them was in July 2007 at a festival called Sheep Music at Presteigne in Powys, just over the Welsh border. The event coincided with some of the worst summer weather for many years and, as a result, many of the roads were impassable. Normally this would have been a bore with the van almost reaching the site and discovering a whole set of road closures and having to go back and try another route. Ed, however, kept everyone entertained. Luke recalls being challenged to a rap battle in the back of the van. 'I'm enthusiastic for that sort of thing too. So it would be like "Hey, Ed, you're hair is red and you didn't go to bed and I bet I could slap you until you're dead." Both of us were white middle-class boys with no real hip-hop pedigree.'

Occasionally, specialist hip-hop artists would join Nizlopi on tour and Ed was always keen to challenge them, too. They liked him because he was quick to learn their songs and embrace their music. Everyone was impressed by how quickly Ed could just listen to something and then have it in his head. Luke observes, 'He could play all of our songs – and there were about fifty of them around.'

At the very muddy Sheep Music site, another singer made a lasting impression on Ed. His name was Foy Vance and he possessed a magnificent moustache and probably the purest voice of any of the artists from across the Irish Sea, which so influenced Ed. He was already in his early thirties and had slipped under the radar of mainstream music. Ed was enchanted and asked the Nizlopi crew who he was. Unfortunately, the answer was lost in translation as they, too, were Irish and Ed thought they said 'Five Ants', which seemed like a cool name.

His efforts to trace 'Five Ants' on Google came to nothing but eventually he arrived at Foy Vance, who was from Bangor in Northern Ireland and whose debut album, *Hope*, had just been released. Ed bought it immediately, listened to it constantly and, as was his usual practice with something he liked, learned all the songs. He was particular struck with the hauntingly beautiful 'Gabriel and the Vagabond' – seldom has the singing of the word 'Hallelujah' sounded so emotional.

While he gained invaluable experience of touring, Ed was quietly forging his own path with live gigs. They were only small and he didn't stray far from Framlingham but every single one helped him become more accomplished. He started taking part in acoustic nights in the basement of a Cambridge café – an ideal outlet for him because it was relaxed and friendly and the music came first.

The nights, which were known as 'The Living Room', were run by a local promoter, Phil Pethybridge and his friends. Every other Thursday, they hired the basement of CB2 in Norwich Street and transformed it into a space with atmosphere and ambience, where twenty or so people sprawled on cushions and rugs, puffed cigarettes and pipes and listened to the best local music they could find.

The Living Room was a cosy evening, providing artists with an environment in which their music could be heard properly, not drowned out by noisy wooden floors and customers yelling their drinks order across a crowded bar. The musicians were asked to play stripped-down sets, which suited Ed and his loop pedal, performing songs from *Want Some?* and his *Ed Sheeran* album.

Phil had first spotted Ed just down the street playing a few numbers in the Man in the Moon pub and asked him if he would like to play at his venue. That would be the blueprint for Ed's live work over the next few years – one gig would lead to another. Phil had remembered Ed as an enthusiastic young member of his 'street team', a modern way of gaining publicity for up-and-coming acts. Ed had discovered street teaming from school friends and asked if he could tag along. He came to love it because taking part meant he would be given a badge and a free ticket to a gig. He was developing a keen eye for merchandising through his mother and liked collecting badges in particular.

There were two separate strands to street teaming: first, taking care of existing fans by sending them CD samples, posters, stickers and badges and encouraging them to share those gifts with friends. Phil explains, 'What you find is that fans who love an artist and share their love with other people are likely to be a better, more proactive influence than someone just reading about an act in the *Guardian*.' Second, the street team engages with people at a show who might never have seen an artist before and finds ways of contacting them afterwards, usually by getting their email address. Ed was particularly good at this and would come away from a concert with pages of email addresses. By taking part, he was able to watch, among others, Kate Nash, Jack Penate, One Night Only and The Horrors. Ed, as he always did, filed street teaming away as something that might be useful to him in the future.

The Living Room was obviously the archetypal smoky basement, but that changed in the summer of 2007 when the smoking ban was introduced. From then on, Ed would join everyone for cigarette breaks outside and smoke a roll-up or two. Sometimes his father would drive him over to Cambridge or, on other nights, he would be joined by his first serious girlfriend, Alice Hibbert, a radiantly pretty brunette and one of the most attractive girls in school. As one friend confides, 'He was punching above his weight there.'

Alice, who lived in a village a few miles from Framlingham, was a highly intelligent girl who was not especially musical but was a talented artist. She and Ed became well known around the town as a team. Phil was appreciative of her low-key approach: 'Alice was like Ed's right-hand lady at the time. She would always be quite placid about things and let it happen. She wouldn't actively get involved in things like gig set-ups. She would just be there, chilling out and chatting to people. She never caused any issues or anything like that, which is quite nice, actually. She just supported Ed in doing what he was doing, really.'

Alice was there when Ed played his first festival, the Secret Garden Party, on a site near Huntingdon, the week after he had been stuck in the mud at Sheep Music. Phil invited him to play in The Living Room tent, a large Indian marquee that held about four hundred people. Alice was always pleasant and willing to help, but she would never interfere. As Phil observes, 'Sometimes when an artist brings family or close friends along, they get in the way. I think Ed had realised that if you don't cause any problems for people then you get invited back.' After Ed had performed, he and Alice stayed on to relax and enjoy the rest of the festival.

Ed formed a friendly relationship with the promoter he referred to as Phil Living Room. For his part, Phil always found Ed easy to get along with and amenable to cover for someone. 'I phoned him up the night before one concert and he was having dinner with Alice. I told him so-and-so had pulled out and asked could he do it? He just said, "Yeah, what time do you want me there?"'

7

ED STAGE LEFT

Ed was trying to make up his mind whether his future lay in music or in acting. He wasn't sure what to do, even though he was making such good progress musically. During his time at Thomas Mills he had enjoyed being involved in the annual school productions that Georgie Ross put together but had never been cast in a leading role.

His first acting venture was in *West Side Story*. He was twelve when he played Officer Krupke, alongside his brother Matthew, who was cast as his boss, Lieutenant Schrank. By the time Thomas Mills staged *Grease* two years later, in 2005, everyone knew that Ed was the school's young guitar maestro, so Georgie created a character that would give him the opportunity to sit on the stage and play. Ed, who had grown his mop of ginger hair quite long, was Roger, guitarist of the T-Birds. She recalls, 'It was wonderful. Everyone worked together brilliantly. I've got a really nice memory of going backstage at the end, into the drama studio, and Ed had his guitar and got everyone to sing "Hey Jude" but changed it to "Hey Miss Ross", and it was like "take a bad play and make it better". I started crying.'

Ed thrived on being part of a group. Many of his best friends were in the cast, including Fred Clifford, Nic Minns, Felix and Lily Hunter Green and Briony Gaffer – and his brother, of course. Even when Ed's commitments outside school life were growing, he would still seek out Georgie and tell her that he wanted to be in the school play. He missed *My Fair Lady* the next year but assured her he would be back when he started his A levels. He loved the camaraderie of it all – such a contrast from the hours of lonely guitar practice.

Before he had agreed his work experience with Nizlopi, Ed had decided he wanted to broaden his theatrical experience and applied for a summer course with the Youth Music Theatre UK. The YMT, which was only a couple of years old, had been set up when the National Youth Music Theatre ran into financial difficulties. The idea was to give talented young hopefuls the chance of some professional stage work. It was most definitely not a holiday camp or something to fit in after double maths.

Ed auditioned in May in Norwich and was told he would be in the cast of *Frankenstein*, a new stage musical that the YMT would be putting on in Plymouth that August. Although he was earning a little money from his music, he needed help from his family to pay the £800 fee for the two-week-long course.

As usual, Ed did not land a leading role. He wasn't cool – he didn't try to be – or conventionally handsome and he had never had a dancing lesson, other than what he had learned for his school productions. Perhaps more importantly, he didn't really have a stage-musical voice. But he was full of enthusiasm, which was the principal requirement for being an ensemble player.

The new production of *Frankenstein*, with music by the composer and theatrical agent Jimmy Jewell, was a grisly piece described as a 'Gothic horror musical' and an 'unstoppable voyage into the darkest recesses of the human soul'. The stage production was a very loose adaptation of the classic novel. The monster created by Frankenstein wants to be loved; when he is rejected, he embarks on a gruesome killing spree. Ed was one of the few cast members who stayed alive. This was not a light frothy musical in the style of *Grease*.

The producers had big plans for the show and assembled everyone for a pre-rehearsal long weekend at a West Country boarding school that everyone thought resembled Hogwarts. As usual, Ed was noticeable because of his hair but he did not push himself forward. Nobody had any idea at that first encounter of how much Ed had already accomplished musically.

Katie Kalil, who met him through the YMT, recalls, 'Ed was so humble. He hadn't talked about his music and we had no idea that he was writing his own stuff. At the time everyone was on Myspace so we all went home and everyone added each other on Myspace. And then I added Ed and I'm like "Wow! He's a musician."'

Katie played his songs to her friends back in Newcastle and they were equally impressed. 'I was just like blown away. I listened to his music almost every day. When we went back for the main event at the beginning of August and got together again, a lot of us already knew the words to all his songs because we listened to them so much.' Katie barrelled up to Ed and told him, 'What the fuck! I can't believe it – you never let on you were so good.'

Ed and Katie were part of a friendship group of half a dozen teenagers during the two weeks in Plymouth. They all stayed at a large house within walking distance of the centre, although they were too young to go out drinking. Katie was fifteen and Ed was sixteen and a half. She had a much bigger part than Ed, playing Frankenstein's sister who ends up, in true horror fashion, getting burned to death. The lead role was played by the dashing Matt Brinkler, who would later become a good friend of Ed's when they were both based in London.

The first occasion the entire cast witnessed the extent of Ed's talents was when they had a talent show one night and he got up, rapped and sang. The next day he was back singing in the chorus, playing a villager or 'a dude on a ship'. He did his best at dancing, although he was not a natural by his own admission.

They were a typical bunch of teenagers escaping school and parents in summer. The girls shared one room as a dorm and the boys another. They would hang out together during the lunch break or in the evenings. 'We just thought we were the coolest kids, smoking roll-up cigarettes and flirting with each other,' Katie laughs.

Some of the teens paired off for the equivalent of a holiday romance but Ed was not one of the lucky ones. 'It's a dog-eat-dog world when you're a fifteen- or a sixteen-year-old boy,' says Katie. 'He would talk to girls but he was kind of shy. After listening to his music, it was clear he was very romantic and had been in love.'

As usual, Ed seemed more confident when he had a guitar in his hand. The gang used to sit around in a circle and Ed would make up a song that included lyrics about each one as he went round. It wasn't Dylan but it was fun to be part of an Ed Sheeran original even if it was only 'Anna, she has a flower in her hair.' Most of the time, there was serious rehearsal to be done, although everyone went out for dinner in Plymouth and on one occasion saw Wayne Sleep star in a revival of the famous Cole Porter musical *High Society* at the Theatre Royal. They all thought it was really cheesy.

Finally, the big evening arrived when *Frankenstein* was premiered at the Barbican Theatre in Castle Street. It was very well received. Ed had been nervous, just as he was when he performed live for the first time singing 'Layla'. He said, 'You kind of get through.' Most of their parents travelled to see the show and everyone agreed that the whole experience had been 'super fun'. Certainly Ed did. When he became famous, he was happy to be a patron of the YMT. He explained, 'The thing that I gained from YMT was friends, definitely friends. The experience helped me with what I am doing now through confidence – getting up in front of people.' He meant it when he added, 'I think young people should audition for YMT if they are into singing, or if they are into dancing, or if they are into acting. Or if they just want to meet like-minded people who like the same things.'

The YMT has literally dined out on Ed's minor involvement for the past ten years. His picture is at the top of their home page online. But he doesn't mind because he had a great time. By an amazing coincidence, three days before *Frankenstein* in Plymouth, the theatre staged a production of *Oh! Carol*, based on the music of Neil Sedaka, at Queen's University in Belfast. One of the cast was a very young-looking Sam Smith, one of Ed's few musical rivals in the UK.

The producers were so pleased at *Frankenstein*'s reception that they set up a London performance at the Cochrane Theatre in Holborn. Katie says, 'I remember us all thinking that this was a really good show. At our age going to an off-West End theatre was the coolest thing ever.' Disappointingly, Ed couldn't make it as by now he had committed to going on the summer tour with Nizlopi. He surprised his new friends, though, when they were taking a break from rehearsal and getting some lunch. They turned round and Ed was there. He had taken the trouble to join them for fifteen minutes and wish them good luck. Katie recalls, 'We were impressed he came to meet up with us. He was really busy and we were like "He's really doing it!"'

Ed continued to adopt a scatter-gun approach, pressing on with his songwriting and performing while keeping his acting options open. His biggest ambition seemed to be an overwhelming desire to be famous. It prompted him to audition for a new TV series called *Britannia High*, an attempt to transfer Disney's *High School Musical* into a British setting. The show, set in a London theatre school, was based on an idea by the choreographer Arlene Phillips, who was best known as a judge on *Strictly Come Dancing*.

Ed passed through several rounds of auditions purely because of his singing ability. After he made the final forty, he said, 'I'm very surprised because I can't dance.' He stood out as a talented musician and came across as articulate and well spoken. There was no phoney Estuary English with Ed.

He didn't dress up for the finals held over two days at the Granada Studios in Manchester but, wearing a modest green top and blue jeans, he impressed with a version of 'All My Life', one of his favourite Nizlopi songs. He made it through to the next round when just sixteen hopefuls were battling for the six main roles. The show's singing mentor, Chris Neill, who produced the Céline Dion number one 'Think Twice', thought Ed was 'great' and a 'quirky folk singer'. He commented that he would sign him.

Gary Barlow, the star name brought in to write most of the soundtrack for the venture, was less impressed. When he popped in to cast an eye over the talented youngsters, he singled out three hopefuls as having the best voices. The man who would become the chief judge on *The X Factor* failed to spot Ed, although he did notice Pixie Lott. Ed's dancing was literally the main stumbling block: 'Ed hasn't got a clue,' said Arlene. Even he had to admit, after his efforts in the group dance, 'I messed up. I got kicked in the face by accident.'

He didn't progress to the last round of six – two definite, and four maybes, who included Pixie, an accomplished dancer. She was the same age as Ed but had the advantage of being a scholarship student at the Italia Conti Academy of Performing Arts in the Barbican, London. In effect, she was already attending a sort of *Britannia High* at the age of eleven. The majority of the boys and girls at the auditions were stage-school students, which placed Ed at a disadvantage from the start.

Pixie was much further along in her career, with West End musical experience and a record deal. She didn't yet sport the vivid blonde hair that was almost a trademark when she became a number-one artist in 2009 with the catchy 'Mama Do (Uh Oh Uh Oh)'. She and Ed became instant friends when he turned up for the first audition wearing his Nizlopi T-shirt. She was also a fan of the group and was very impressed when he told her he had been with them on tour. They were never romantically involved but were buddies who encouraged each other's efforts to build their careers. Pixie would often cheer him on at open-mic nights in London. In the end, she, too, missed out on *Britannia High* because Arlene and her fellow casting judges thought her acting was too weak.

Pixie and Ed caught a lucky break by not being chosen. The series was part of ITV1's autumn schedule the following year and there were high hopes it would become essential viewing on Sunday evenings. Disappointingly, it tanked and ran for just nine episodes. A viewing audience that began at 3.55 million had slumped to 1.3 million by the finale.

The whole experience was educational for Ed, although he knew that the show was not right for him. He explained his feelings to Georgie Ross when they spoke about it. 'He was very mature,' she says, 'and it was not the right direction. He had his own strong sense of who he was and what he wanted to achieve. He had the strongest sense of self of anyone I have ever taught.'

Ed had experienced an amazing summer for a sixteen-year-old – onstage in Plymouth, performing at his first festival, auditioning in Manchester, on the road with his favourite band. Now, it was time to go back to school and start his A levels.

8

ACCESS ALL AREAS

Ed learned early on that, if he wanted to be noticed, he had to push himself out there. Nobody was going to beat his door down in Framlingham. He might not have made the final six for *Britannia High* but he had made some connections with some fellow artists, including Pixie Lott, whom he could call friends in the future.

He continued to watch for opportunities. He spotted that the Norwich Playhouse was organising a Young Bands Night, which aimed to give local teenagers the chance to perform on a proper stage. The theatre's director, Caroline Richardson, was concerned that the new premises licence had meant that many pubs, which had previously hosted live music, stopped doing so because they were worried about serving alcohol to under-eighteens.

She attracted local sponsors including City College, Norwich Arts Centre, Plug Studios and, most importantly for Ed's future, Access to Music. Ed submitted some of the tracks from *Want Some?* and waited to hear if he would be selected to appear at 'Play the Playhouse'.

Caroline didn't want to choose the young artists herself and instead asked Ian Johnson, then manager of the city's Access to Music college, if he would pop in as an independent expert, have a listen to the entries and help finalise the line-up for the concert. He went for a couple of local bands but thought the singer–songwriters all sounded a little similar. Eventually he said, 'Why don't we give it to the youngest?' That was Ed, and based on that highly scientific approach, he won the opportunity to appear.

Ian had forgotten all about Ed until he walked onstage at the concert in October 2007. For the occasion, Ed, a very skinny teenager, was dressed in a neatly pressed beige shirt and blue jeans. He wore his favourite choker around his neck but, more interestingly, he had various wristbands, including a Liquorice Allsorts bracelet his mother had made. Imogen had begun to design and make her own distinctive jewellery, which would soon be part of the Ed Sheeran merchandising. On the inside of his left arm he had scrawled in red marker pen the running order for the six songs he would perform, including 'Two Blokes and a Double Bass', 'Sara', 'You Break Me' and 'I'm Glad I'm Not You'. Intriguingly, on the outside of his right hand, he had drawn a large red + sign. Instead of his usual Faith guitar, he played a teardrop-shaped Martin Backpacker model, which he could fit into his rucksack. The guitar, which resembled a large ukulele, would become his faithful companion in the future when he was travelling from gig to gig across London.

Ian, who had seen hundreds of young acts starting out in music, was immediately struck by Ed's performance: 'The theatre was packed full of young people. I didn't have any thoughts about what to expect. Then on came this young man and he very quickly managed to get those in the front row of seats interacting with him onstage. And I thought he was incredibly confident for a sixteen-year-old.

'He asked one girl her name and then he put her name in the next song when he rapped in the middle. It was very polished. He just had the audience in the palm of his hand – he sort of sang to them personally even though there was something like a hundred young people sat watching him.' In effect, Ed was putting his own spin on what he had seen Luke Concannon do many times at his concerts. Ian was so impressed that he emailed Ed, saying that he would try to find him other opportunities.

Being out in the big world, performing in front of an appreciative audience, did not motivate Ed to give his full attention to analysing Beethoven and Mozart for his music-theory course at Thomas Mills. Yet he did not take for granted the freedom his teachers, Richard Hanley in particular, gave him. He still wanted to participate in their events, especially if his friends were involved. He would take part in school concerts and took them just as seriously as public gigs. In return, they trusted him, even if it meant putting something vague in the programme, such as 'Ed Sheeran: Song from Latest Album'.

He joined the other A-level music students for an autumn concert in October 2007 at the listed Church of St Andrew in the picturesque village of Marlesford, five miles from Framlingham. Richard still remembers it with pleasure: 'It was lovely, lots of different styles – a perfect evening in a country church.'

A very talented classmate, Tom Rose, who is now an award-winning composer, played two Bach preludes, Polly Virr, who went on to become a professional cellist, performed *Allegro Appassionato* by Saint-Saëns. Ed sang 'Gabriel and the Vagabond' by Foy Vance. Another student, Dan Chapman, a close friend who is still part of Ed's inner circle, had bagged Nizlopi's 'Freedom'.

Ed was a furiously busy schoolboy. Ten days later, he was back in Norwich appearing at the Castle Mall with other local artists in a day-long festival. Just a few weeks after that, he joined his friends to take part in the annual school musical, *The Sound of Music.* Georgie Ross recalls, 'He was busy with auditions outside of school but he still came and found me and said, "I want to be in it." He didn't have time to learn much of a part but was happy to accept a minor role as a German soldier for three nights in November 2007.'

Tucked away in the chorus, Cherry Seaborn would become hugely significant to Ed in the coming years. She was popular and always included in anything that Ed's group of friends were doing. Georgie observes, 'In terms of drama she was quite shy. But she was very clever.' She was also good at sport, not something Ed bothered with much. He had been drawn to her during their school years, but any attraction between them had never gone further than a few shy glances followed by a rapid look in the other direction.

Not everything about his A-level course was as uninspiring to Ed as Beethoven. He enjoyed making a guitar from scratch. It was more woodwork than music. He made a copy of his Backpacker guitar because the flat edges were easier to shape than the rounded surfaces of his other guitars. He took the fingerboard from an old guitar and persuaded his mum to send off for a pack of veneers so that he could choose the right timber for finishing the headstock. He was rightly proud of the finished instrument, although he decided against playing it in concert.

Public gigs continued to be offered. Ian Johnson had been true to his word and secured Ed some bookings in connection with the Norwich Fringe Festival he was running. They included a Young Person's Night at The Workshop, a pizza parlour on the Earlham road in Norwich.

More significantly, Ian provided the link between Ed and the next important figure on his journey, an enthusiastic A&R scout from London called Jono Ball. He had sent an email to Ian, asking if had come across any new talent. Jono had only recently started with Crown Music Management, which was based in Parsons Green close to the Chelsea football ground. At university, he knew he wanted to work in the record business and had done many months of work experience at EMI and Virgin Records but hadn't been taken on. He continued to try to get a foot in the door while working in telesales, but it wasn't until he was advised to meet with music lawyers that he found a way in.

He secured an interview with Sarah Stennett and Mark Hargreaves, the two lawyers who had formed Crown in 2000. He told them how hard he was prepared to work for them. They decided to take a chance and see where his enthusiasm would lead him. They gave him a desk and let him try to find a star. When he joined, the leading act on the books was Sugababes, the girl group at the top of the charts with their fifth studio album *Change*. Another up-and-coming artist they were marketing was the Australian singer–songwriter Gabriella Cilmi, whose debut album was scheduled for release in early 2008, when she would be on tour supporting Sugababes. She was only sixteen and was actually younger than Ed.

Left to his own devices, Jono sent out a blizzard of emails to public schools, stage academies, Butlins and Blackpool seaside clubs in the hope they might recommend someone. He also tried the Brit School and Access to Music. In return he received literally hundreds of possibilities, which he went through laboriously. Ed's link stood out from the half-dozen or more that Ian sent. Jono wasn't interested in image: 'I've always just listened to the music or the voice so everything ticked the box with Ed. I kind of picked up in particular on "You Break Me".' Jono contacted Ed through Myspace Messenger and they left it that Ed would send him *Want Some?*.

Jono was encouraged by what he heard. He already knew he liked 'You Break Me' but now enjoyed 'Yellow Pages', 'Need to Cut Your Hair' and 'Two Blokes and a Double Bass.'

The problem he faced moving forward with Ed was that, as the most junior in the office, trying to engage decision-makers higher up the ladder was a constant battle. The general opinion at Crown was that Ed's material was not strong enough: 'I wasn't thinking like that. I was just thinking that I love all these songs. I wasn't experienced enough to be thinking in terms of a breakthrough song, then a follow-up and then a big hit.

'"You Break Me" was the first one that everyone latched on to and said, "That's a cool song, but you probably need two or three more like that to get this off the ground."'

Jono needed to see Ed live, to meet him but also to reassure himself that the teenager on the CD could actually perform. He helped to arrange a small gig upstairs at a renowned music venue, the Bedford pub in Balham, south London, one of those where the audience of half a dozen or so is made up of family.

Ed was joined by his father and beforehand they all sat down for a chat. Jono recalls, 'I introduced myself as the gateway into Crown Music and said I could take Ed in to meet the managers. It was a very light chat. His dad was really nice and obviously a big fan of Ed and the music. I was only twenty-four myself and didn't have all the chat. There wasn't a lot of talking. Ed got up with his mini guitar and performed a set with his loop pedal. I thought it was just fantastic.'

They left it that Ed would come into the Crown offices for a chat with a manager. That turned out to be Oxford-educated Chloe Roberts, the elder sister of the Welsh singer–songwriter Jem (Jemma Griffiths). Jono remembers Ed thought that was 'awesome' and was equally excited to learn that Chloe managed another of his favourite acts, Get Cape. Wear Cape. Fly, the recording name of a twenty-one-year-old singer–songwriter from Southend called Sam Duckworth. Sam, who was signed to Atlantic Records, had recorded most of his first album, *Chronicles of a Bohemian Teenager*, in his bedroom, an encouraging precedent for Ed.

Chloe agreed that she would deal informally with the management side of looking after Ed, while Jono kept an eye on things day to day. Crucially, Crown never offered Ed a contract. According to Jono, he broached the subject once with Sarah and Mark but was told the company didn't need one for Ed. The decision had been made that if Ed moved to London, Jono would place him with other songwriters in the hope that the collaborations would strengthen his material.

Ed's problem was that nobody had heard of him in London. That was not the case in East Anglia, especially not in Framlingham where his personal following was growing. He agreed to help his mum with a fundraising gig for St Michael's Church. They booked the Sports Bar at the local Railway Tavern, the pub where Ed used to sit and play his guitar with his friends from school, even though he wasn't old enough to order a drink. Later, he would serenade the landlady, Gemma, with a song to get a beer on the house.

The landlord at the time, Neil Pascoe, let them have the room for free and they charged a small fee on the door. He recalls, 'He filled the place. You couldn't get in the door. There were a hundred people – maybe more.'

Many of the local fans would travel to see Ed when he was appearing at venues all over the region, including Ipswich, Cambridge and Norwich. That following gave him the confidence to badger Nizlopi for a support spot. He would still go along and help when he could and they were always happy to see him. They weakened when they were booked to play the Norwich Arts Centre one Monday evening in early April 2008. Ed was on first, followed by an acoustic group, Lewis Garland and the Kett Rebellion, then Nizlopi. Ed made good on his promise to bring in a crowd and, again, at least a hundred people turned up just to see him.

Luke Concannon stood next to John Sheeran to watch Ed: 'He was looping, he had strong songs and his voice was good.

It did seem he already had a package. I turned to his dad and said, "Wow. He's good!"'

Afterwards, they went back to the house in Framlingham and enjoyed the Sheerans' wonderful hospitality that naturally included one of Imogen's full English breakfasts complete with Ed's favourite sausages.

Ed was elated at how well the show had gone. He would never be slow in giving Nizlopi the credit they deserved for helping to shape his career: 'Without realising it, I learned how to perform live and sing, project my voice and write songs just by being around them.'

The experience was a dream come true for Ed and afterwards he had no desire to go back to school for another year of A levels. He didn't want to follow his brother's example and go on to university. Matthew had won a place to study music at Sussex. His father backed his younger son, but his mother was less convinced. Imogen wanted him to secure some qualifications so that he would have something to fall back on if his musical ambitions were unfulfilled. Fortunately, with the help of Ian Johnson, a compromise was reached that suited everyone.

Ian was on friendly terms with the family, partly due to his East Dulwich connection. He had grown up in that area of south London and his mother used to take him to the Picture Gallery every week. Imogen had phoned him one day to thank him for putting Ed in touch with Jono Ball and to let him know Ed was leaving school. She was clearly worried that he was 'jacking in his education, moving to London and didn't really have any support group there', but Ian immediately came up with a solution: he suggested Ed join the Artist

Development Programme at the Access to Music college in Stratford, east London. Ian explained: 'Two days a week, he's with other young people so he can make a social circle of friends his own age and he can still get some education – UCAS points. So if it all goes wrong for him then he gets a qualification.'

Access to Music was designed to help young people who did not necessarily fit into the conventional way that music was taught in schools with the emphasis on classical and the rules of theory. They would go home and learn the drums, guitar, or practise making music on their computer, none of which would be recognised in school. The idea of ATM was what it said on the tin: to provide students with access to the music world they wanted to join.

The teachers, like Ian, were experienced professionals in the music business – not professional educators. He himself had originally been a punk rocker who became a chief buyer and manager for the HMV store in London's Oxford Street.

Ed was a perfect example of someone who didn't need a traditional musical education. John and Imogen were elated when he was offered a place but downcast when they realised how much it was going to cost. Ian helped them secure some government funding, which would cover accommodation and tuition costs.

His mother was happier, if still a little apprehensive. Ed also had to reassure Alice that he would be back regularly. Like so many young couples of their age, they would have to cope with one going off to continue their education. In any case, Alice would be applying to university soon. They split up. It seemed for the best. They got back together the next day.

After all, it wasn't as if he was going to the other end of the country – Ipswich to London Liverpool Street was just over an hour on the train. And he would be home frequently. During their very brief time apart Ed was inspired to start the achingly beautiful song called 'Sunburn', one of his most heartfelt lyrics, about the misery of a teenage break-up. He explained his motivation: 'Every single girl that I looked at, I was kind of like, "But you're not her!"' The song is the only one that contains Alice's name.

At Thomas Mills they took his leaving well. Georgie Ross observed that his year was made up of a strong group of people that really moulded together. As a final hurrah, Ed joined the other music students on a summer trip to Salzburg, the birthplace of Mozart. Richard Hanley recalls that after each day of sightseeing and touristy things, they returned to the youth hostel where they were staying and the group relaxed outside in the early-evening sun. 'Ed would get his guitar out and entertain us all. And we would all sing along with him. That's a really lovely memory to have.'

Ed has always been appreciative of Richard, still calls him Mr Hanley, and says that he was the teacher who never doubted what he was trying to achieve. The Salzburg serenades would be the last time that Ed entertained his peer group as a schoolboy, although he did return to Thomas Mills the following spring to take part in a charity concert organised by the sixth form.

The time had come to leave Framlingham on the next leg of his adventure, but it would always be home.

PART TWO

THE NEXT BIG THING

9

SINGER-SONGWRITER

Ed was extremely nervous. He had performed lots of gigs but this one was different. He desperately wanted to win The Next Big Thing competition in Norwich. He had seen the announcement for the contest on Myspace while still at school and had won through heats and a semi-final at the Brickmakers pub to make the final, which was being held at the UEA (University of East Anglia).

His ultimate failure at *Britannia High* had put him off TV talent shows, which is why he never entered *The X Factor*, but this was different. He was going to be judged on his live performance and that was what he did best. He wouldn't have to dance or try to do justice to other artists' material that didn't suit him. He just had to sing his own songs. For the final in November 2008, watched by 500 people, Ed drew the short straw. He was going to be on first.

It was so nearly a disaster. During his second song, two of his guitar strings broke. He battled on. Even worse, another two broke in the middle of his third and final number. Inside, he was panicking, but nobody in the audience realised as he quickly set about reharmonising. He literally had to think on his feet. Ian Johnson, who was there, remembers it well: 'He just carried on. Everything broke but he did it. And of course he won. All the judges thought he was worthy of winning. They could see the potential.'

The broken-strings disaster probably worked in Ed's favour because his performance in overcoming adversity was the most memorable of the evening. He was also the only finalist to use a loop pedal and to mix hip hop with folk. He stood out. Afterwards the judges praised his ingenuity and his sheer determination to carry on. His success was particularly galling to one local band that the majority of the audience thought was sure to win and would have little trouble seeing off the 'young ginger lad with a guitar'.

Ed's prizes were worth more than £1,000, and he said all the right things when he won: 'I know it's a cheesy thing to say but everybody should be the winner tonight. They are all the next big thing.' It was a gracious comment, but one that would not prove to be the case.

Afterwards, Imogen phoned Keith Krykant to tell him the good news and thank him for instilling in her son the determination never to give up and an innate sense of harmony that meant he could cope with having to ad lib when his strings broke. Ed went home to sleep. He had been gigging all week in London and was shattered.

He didn't have much of a chance to unwind. He had to be in college on the Monday. Two weeks later he was back at UEA, this time opening for the British R&B singer Jay Sean, who was promoting his hit album *My Own Way*. He would break America the following year with 'Down', his first single release there, which topped the Billboard chart. The song featured the superstar rapper Lil Wayne, a collaboration that instantly gave Jay credibility.

Second on the bill was Magnet Man, the hip-hop singer from Barbados. Ed was billed as the 'Next Big Thing Winner 2008'. Performing alongside such popular urban acts was giving him far more relevance than singing a couple of songs to twenty people at an open-mic night: the focus had to be on getting the name of Ed Sheeran out to as wide an audience as possible. From that point of view, the gig was probably a better reward than any of the actual prizes.

Ed settled into a weekly routine while in London. He was at Access to Music on Monday and Tuesday and enjoyed hanging out with young people with the same ambitions as him. For the rest of the week, he would be taking advantage of Jono's offer to fix up songwriting sessions in the day and then, hopefully, be gigging in the evenings. Ed's philosophy at the time was simple: he would not turn down any opportunity to play. He was available. He would often recount a conversation he had with his father who mentioned he had read that singer–songwriter James Morrison had played something like 200 gigs in a calendar year. Ed vowed he would beat that. And he did.

His first gig in London was in November 2008 at Liberties Bar in Camden High Street. The eighteenth-century pub used to be called The Camden Head – it is again now – and was well known as a music venue in an area that many saw as the musical centre of the capital. Gary Dunne lived two minutes away and was topping the bill, so at least there was a familiar face to encourage Ed. His dad came along, too, to offer his support.

The evening was organised by promoters Kevin Molloy and Nick Ward under the banner IK-TOMS, which stood for Internet Killed the Open Mic Session. They were fed up with the self-promotion and impersonal nature of Myspace and wanted to build a thriving community of live acts in the London area. This was perfect for Ed, who so enjoyed being part of something.

After the show, Gary had to tell Ed off. The seventeen-year-old, in his enthusiasm, had been giving away copies of *Want Some?* for free. Any old hand on the circuit knew this was a bad idea; selling CDs was their means of surviving in their world. Earning a few pounds in that way each night enabled the lowest tier of performers to buy food and travel for the next day. Ed quickly learned that lesson.

To begin with, Ed shared a depressing flat in Finsbury Park, north London, with two girls, but he quickly decided he was better off staying on a friend's sofa or in a sleeping bag on the floor. Fortunately, Matt Brinkler from his *Frankenstein* days lived near by and was happy to oblige when Ed asked if he could sleep on his sofa for a week or two. Matt laughed, 'Three months later, we had to throw him out.'

Ed's policy over accommodation was simple. He was always upfront about asking for a place to stay and had no embarrassment about it. Perhaps it was one of the advantages of having such an open house at the family home in Framlingham. One evening after playing a gig at the Ivy House in Holborn, he started chatting randomly over a cigarette outside to one of the audience, Daryl Snow. He invited Ed back to watch TV and sleep on the couch. Daryl became one of Ed's most loyal friends, always happy to offer the young musician somewhere to stay. Ed has never forgotten his kindness and in 2015 was best man at his wedding.

Jono Ball, meanwhile, was gamely trying to turn Ed into the next big thing for real. The master plan was to put him with various songwriters and see what developed. For the most part this proved a success. His first suggestion was Gordon Mills Jr, who was already on Crown's books. He was the son of Gordon Mills, the renowned manager of Engelbert Humperdinck and Tom Jones, who had co-written the latter's debut hit 'It's Not Unusual'. Gordon Jr, a multi-instrumentalist, was making a name for himself in this world, too. He had co-written the unashamedly romantic falling-in-love 'Dream Catch Me', a big hit for the singer–songwriter Newton Faulkner, who had been flavour of the month in the music business since his debut album, *Hand Built By Robots*, topped the charts in 2007.

Ed appreciated Gordon's relaxed attitude to songwriting. They sat in the garden of his home in Weybridge and smoked Marlboro Lights, talked about music and the world, and kicked around some ideas for songs. Ed thought it was a great day and left to sleep on Jono's sofa in Fulham, firmly of the opinion that songwriting was 'the best fucking job in the world'. None of the songs from that first session would make it on to an Ed Sheeran recording but subsequently they co-wrote 'This', one of Ed's most intense love songs.

Next up, Jono put Ed with Si Hulbert, another songwriter Crown were managing, who had co-produced many of the tracks on the Sugababes new album *Catfights and Spotlights*. Jono told Si, 'I've got this young guy who is absolutely brilliant.

You should do a session.' Si, who was in his mid-thirties, was encouraged but understood that you needed to make a quick connection in this world or the day would be wasted.

Ed caught the train to Si's home studio in Chislehurst, a town in Kent he already knew from visiting family there when he was a boy. Si put the kettle on and the two chatted about music over a mug of tea. They hit it off straight away. 'I was expecting a little folk guy,' recalls Si. 'He wasn't like that at all. He was dressed like a hip-hop guy basically – baseball cap, big glasses, carrying his little travelling Martin guitar. I remember that because it was beat up with lots of scratches and paw prints.'

As they were chatting, Ed noticed a ukulele that Si had just been given. He sprang up and asked if he could have a go as he had never played one before: 'He's very enthusiastic. His brain runs at a million miles an hour. We started working our first tune there and then.' Si soon discovered that Ed was not like any other musician he'd met. He explains, 'His brain is like a filing system – you can almost see him kind of rifling through it and thinking, This will work, or That will work. He just pulls out chords and lyrics. They just appear.'

On that first day, they developed a song called 'Miss You' and had completed the beginning, the middle and the end during their first session together. In basic terms, the song was about missing somebody you love but Si suggested to Ed that they make it very open for people to put their own interpretation on it: 'I said leave it ambiguous so it could be someone who died, somebody who'd moved country or moved schools.'

This was an important piece of advice that Ed would heed in the future. Each song told a story that people could relate to in different ways – Ed would prove a master at this. He was also very quick to realise when something wasn't working. Si explains, 'Ed would simply say, "Let's try something else,"' and they would move on. Si also grasped early on that Ed was not a one-trick pony where songwriting was concerned, happy to use his knowledge of rap and urban music to change the character of a track: 'It's very unusual to have somebody who is basically a songwriter on a guitar to do anything other than melancholic, inward-looking stuff. And it takes a lot of skill to do that.

'Because of his knowledge of rap, he was able to change lyrical tempo and stuff like that. And I thought his rapping was just brilliant. Nobody else does it quite like him. It was very natural and would just flow. Even when we were just playing around with an idea, he didn't make any mistakes. There wouldn't be a wrong chord being hit or any of the normal stuff without any prep or rehearsal.' Ed would be in the middle of a melodic ballad when he would suddenly change tempo just by the rhythm of his guitar-playing. 'He used to do a lot of drumming on his guitar and create different beats and we would record all of those so we could integrate them into the songs we were working on. He was very skilled.'

After their first session, Si was straight on the phone to Jono, telling him they needed to put some more dates in the diary with Ed. They saw each other frequently over the next six months. Ed enjoyed the break from his busier life in London. The house in Chislehurst was a family home, not a noisy flat on a London street. He also got on well with Si's then partner and their little boy, and was always a welcome guest if he needed to stay over. He usually had a bed but they bought him a sleeping bag to use if the house was full.

Even though Ed was leading a nomadic lifestyle, he thrived on domesticity and the comforting routines he missed from home. He would find them again in his next important collaboration with a talented songwriter. This time he had to leave the comfy confines of the Home Counties and catch the train to South Wales to meet Amy Wadge for the first time.

Amy was originally from a small village near Bristol but had studied across the Severn Bridge at the Royal Welsh College of Music & Drama in Cardiff. In many ways, her early career was similar to Ed's. She had started writing songs, playing guitar and making records as a schoolgirl. Her inspiration had been the acclaimed singer–songwriter Tracy Chapman. Not long before she met Ed, Amy had released her third album, *Bump*, which she recorded when she was eight months pregnant with her first child, Mia. She had married the actor Alun ap Brinley in 2001 and moved to Church Village, just outside Pontypridd. Motherhood prompted a career rethink – less gigging and more writing in the garden shed she had converted into a studio. Ed was the first artist Amy was asked to work with when she joined the publishing company BDi Music as a songwriter. BDi, which had been started in 2004 by senior A&R executive Sarah Liversedge, had formed an alliance with Crown in which clients could be matched for their mutual benefit.

Amy met Ed at the nearest train station in Treforest, the mining village where Tom Jones had grown up after the Second World War. She was in her early thirties and was apprehensive when Ed and his mini guitar arrived: 'When I picked him up from the station, I thought, What on earth will we have common?' In no time at all she was completely won over by the teenager.

They sat in her kitchen and he played her one of his signature songs, 'You Need Me, I Don't Need You', complete with rap and trademark anthemic chorus. She immediately got it – the fusion of two musical genres that Ed was striving for in his music. She knew from that first cup of tea that Ed was destined for great things. Amy endearingly recalled, 'I kept running into the room and saying to my husband Alun, "Oh, my God, this boy is unbelievable."' During the two days, Ed spent at her house, they wrote nine songs together. She was amazed at his abilities but later recalled giving him one piece of advice at the time: 'Enjoy your life now because it's going to get crazy.'

Ed caught the train back to London, promising to return soon. He could write a book about all the railway stations he has visited in pursuit of his musical ambition. His next stop was back in the Home Counties when he popped on to a train to meet Jake Gosling, the next important figure on his journey to success.

At Crown, Jono Ball was dealing with BDi executive Lesley Scott, who thought Jake, one of her clients, would be potentially a good person for Ed to meet because of his hip-hop credentials. Jake had already heard of Ed. He had seen some demos on Myspace including a rough one of 'You Need Me, I Don't Need You', which he particularly liked. He was enthusiastic, therefore, when Lesley suggested they might try a songwriting session together. Ed was duly booked to travel down to Jake's studios in the wealthy village of Windlesham on the Surrey border with Berkshire.

Jake picked Ed up from nearby Sunningdale station. Like Ed's other collaborators, Jake was already in his mid-thirties but that never bothered Ed where music was concerned. Jake had been studying for his A levels at the prestigious Bryanston School in Dorset when Ed was born. Crucially, perhaps, he was part of the music scene that most excited seventeen-year-old Ed. He had just finished producing a new album, *See Clear Now*, by the east London rapper Wiley, one of the leading figures of the UK grime scene. He told Ed he had been working with other grime artists including Wretch 32, Kano, Ice Kid and Scorcher. Ed was desperate to be more involved in that world so perhaps Jake could help.

Despite the age gap, they had very similar tastes and liked what was going on in music. Jake was impressed with Ed's musical knowledge. He wrote online, 'The main thing I liked about Ed was that he had so many ideas about his music and what he wanted to do but also had a real love of urban underground music and had so much respect for these artists – and from his appearance, you never thought he would!'

They started working on songs the moment they got back to Sticky Studios, which Jake, who was brought up in Windlesham, had originally set up in an old summer-house in an orchard in the village. Those sessions didn't cost Ed anything, which was lucky because he didn't have any money. Jono Ball explains, 'No money needed to change hands. When writers are co-writing they've got a publishing cut so if anything does blow up then they know they'll get paid one day.' People like Jake, Amy Wadge, Si Hulbert and Gordon Mills Jr had their own home studios so it was only their time they were giving for free.

The first track that emerged from his sessions with Jake was one called 'The City', which is based on Ed's observations of London. 'It felt like we had created some magic,' said Jake. He had appreciated that Ed was different and was a talent worthy of nurturing: 'He needed to be directed and told that what he was doing was right and to stick to it and not just sell out.'

Ed had found a kindred spirit, someone with whom he was in tune, not just for writing songs but also for producing the finished sound that best represented what Ed was trying to achieve. He hadn't produced a new CD since *Want Some?*, back in early 2007. Now was the right time for some new Ed Sheeran.

10

IN THE CITY

'The City' is not a love letter to London. The song is unlikely to reach the iconic status of 'Waterloo Sunset' by The Kinks or Adele's unforgettable 'Hometown Glory', the teenage blend of anger and nostalgia she wrote at fifteen. Instead, Ed's song considers what it's like for a seventeen-year-old boy trying to find his feet in the 'city that never sleeps'.

Where to sleep became a preoccupation for Ed when he decided to stop paying rent in London and hop between generous friends, songwriters or people he hardly knew, just to find a place for the night. He discovered that he could close his eyes anywhere, which was invaluable when he took a few trips around the Circle Line after a heavy night.

Ed was definitely the person you did not want to sit next to on your morning commute into work. He invariably looked rough and often had no place to wash properly. Even he admitted that his personal hygiene was not what it might have been. One of his friends, who used to put him up, observes, 'He was a seventeen-year-old kid. I don't think showering was high on the list.'

Another said, 'You wouldn't want to be downwind if he took his shoes off onstage because his feet stank.'

One evening, he fell asleep next to a heating duct with a view of Buckingham Palace. He was too tired to wander around trying to find a bed for the night so decided to stay where he was. It wasn't the worst spot in the world. At least he was dry and warm, although goodness knows what his mum and dad would have thought if they had known at the time.

Ed was never homeless. He had a safety net of friends and family so this experience was more like a camping trip than a desperate situation. He stayed there another night because it inspired him to write a song. He only had the poignant lyric as he gazed up at the stars and thought of Alice: 'It's not a homeless life for me; I'm just home less than I'd like to be.'

Left to his own devices, Ed was not looking after himself properly. He was existing on a diet of beer and chips and, as a result, putting on a lot of weight. He was drinking too much, particularly when he had finished playing for the night. Sometimes, instead of cash in hand, he would play a few numbers in a pub for a beer or two, just as he used to do in Framlingham. His consumption would inevitably increase if he was rushing to make three gigs in a night.

At least he made it a rule never to drink before a gig, following a poor performance at the Ivy House one night. Afterwards, a member of the audience came up to him and told him how disappointing it had been. Ed was mortified and resolved never to let that happen again.

He had no trouble passing James Morrison's total when he managed an estimated 312 gigs in 2009 alone. Often those might be evenings when he played just a couple of songs before moving on to the next. Some were regular, like singer–songwriter sessions at the Regal Room in the Fulham Palace Road or the World's End pub in Finsbury Park, where he became great friends with Irish singer–songwriter Kal Lavelle, who hosted acoustic nights there under the banner of 'We Love Sundays'. She is one of the many people who helped Ed on the way up whom he would not forget. 'She is one of the most wonderful people in the world,' says a friend.

He didn't confine himself to London. Although it's true that he left home when he went to college, he was back and forth to Framlingham most weeks to see his family, take his washing for his mum and catch up with Alice, of course. He also continued to gig relentlessly around East Anglia, especially in Norwich, Ipswich and Cambridge. In Norwich alone, he did more than 100 gigs over the years. Alice tended to join him for more local appearances but seldom went to London, which seemed to be a part of his life that Ed kept separate. Jono Ball met her just once: 'She was lovely – a really nice, kind girl.'

College was a welcome diversion for Ed from the relentless gigging and travelling. Its location in east London was ideal. He could hop on a Monday-morning train from Ipswich straight into Stratford. The first lecture was always the same, a general discussion about music, led by Luke Hannam, the course director. One week it might be about Radiohead, the next time Bowie, Rihanna or, Ed's favourite, grime.

Luke was a popular and respected figure with the students. He had been the bass player in nineties' bands Emperor's New Clothes and Gramme, before opting for a career in education. Ed was one of about twenty musical hopefuls in the class but he was by far the most advanced in terms of the number of gigs he had performed and the contacts he already had. One of the students, Clare Nicholson, from Norwich, remembers the very first time Ed walked into the classroom: 'There was no one else like him. He had charisma, big-time. It oozed out of him. He just looked like a star with his T-shirt and scruffy red hair.' As ever, Ed enjoyed being able to hang out and socialise on the building's roof terrace, smoking his favourite roll-ups between lectures.

As the academic year rolled on, Ed had commitments that meant he couldn't always attend college but he was still ticking off enough modules to pass the Artist Development Programme. The students would often showcase their talents at the Gramophone Club in Shoreditch. For the majority it was a big deal but for Ed the evening was just another gig. He only turned up once but appreciated the chance to play for his classmates and friends. He sang 'We Are', his saddest song about loss, and received rapturous applause, not least for his looping skills, which by now he was making look ridiculously easy.

Ed played for his peers again at an Access to Music Awards evening at the Mermaid Centre in Blackfriars. He sang 'You Need Me, I Don't Need You', which was already on its way to becoming his signature tune live. Many well-known faces on the London music scene were in the audience, including Goldie, the multi-talented DJ and actor, who had been a pioneer in the many kinds of urban music Ed enjoyed. Afterwards, Goldie was asked what he thought of the acts he had seen. He responded, 'I was really impressed with that kid Ed. I think he is going to be giant. I would actually produce that kid. He has a raw talent.' He was asked what three words of advice he would give the student hopefuls: 'Must have patience.' Ed was going to need lots of that as he continued to strive for a breakthrough.

Access to Music also entered Ed for a national talent competition run by Island Records to mark their fiftieth anniversary. The first prize was the release of a single. For the record company, the contest provided the chance to sign some undiscovered talent. It seemed like a golden opportunity for Ed. All around the country, music colleges and universities were submitting their best acts. ATM put forward Ed as being from Norwich even though he was now based in London. As a result, two acts from the course made it through to the grand final at the Gibson Guitar Building in Tottenham Court Road – Ed and an indie band called The Interpreters.

Ian Johnson went to the final to support both acts. He was worried when Ed took a call from Crown on his mobile just before he was due to go on: 'He looked a bit despondent. I asked him what was going on and he said, "They can't make it but they told me not to do the rap in one of the songs that I was going to do." I told him, "No, no, no, that's mad because that's how you rehearsed it. If you do it differently now, you're going to do it wrong."'

That was good advice because Ed went ahead as he had planned. Ian recalls, 'I looked across at the Island staff and they were all responding and tapping their feet. I could see that there was something. And he won.'

Ed was jubilant, believing he was now on his way as a recording artist. That proved not to be the case. Island had a good working relationship with Crown but the company seemed strangely lukewarm about Ed. Jono Ball pressed for a proper record deal, not just the one-off single prize, but got nowhere, even though the label was already home to both the Sugababes and Gabriella Cilmi.

Ed's prospects with Island were not helped by a meeting that the UK chairman, Darcus Beese, had at Crown's offices with Sarah Stennett and Jon Shave from The Invisible Men production team. Jon and his co-writers had been responsible for many of the hits of the Sugababes and Gabriella, and were generally considered to be the go-to producers at Crown.

The meeting took place in a studio on the ground floor. While they were there they noticed Ed outside, apparently peering through the window and grinning at them. Jono wasn't involved, so only heard about it second-hand: 'They are meeting the head of Island Records and Ed is grinning through the window, as he does, because Ed is beautifully awkward and that's how he's gotten into the groups of people he has – just by not being afraid to approach people.' On this occasion, Ed's approach seemed to do nothing more than make the others uncomfortable. Eventually he had a day's session with The Invisible Men to try to work up a song but, for once, it didn't come together for him. Jono observes, 'The song was crap.'

Ed was becoming more frustrated at the lack of progress in securing a record deal. Jono Ball was equally exasperated with what he perceived as a lack of imagination at Crown when it came to Ed. He rightly feared they were failing to recognise his potential: 'The feedback I was getting was that Ed was a ginger white kid who wanted to be a rapper – and who's going to sign that?'

Ed's relationship with Crown deteriorated further in April 2009 when he played an event called The Big Secret at the Ginglik, a hot and sweaty underground venue in the middle of Shepherd's Bush Green. The club used to be a Victorian toilet but had been transformed into a comedy spot that also held acoustic events. Ed shared the bill with other aspiring singer–songwriters, including Kristy Gallacher and Moray McLaren.

Ed, still only eighteen, was particularly excited that night, because Sarah Stennett was finally due to come and see him perform live for the first time. He was now playing 'You Need Me, I Don't Need You' as his final number. It was a tour de force. The beauty of it was that he could introduce new verses, add people's names or take them out whenever he wanted to. It was the sort of number, the ultimate loop-pedal song, that built into a crescendo of excitement.

Jono was there: 'He did the most incredible set. He was playing songs that he had been writing in the co-writing sessions. Sarah never showed.' It was finally dawning on them both that they were never going to get the attention of senior management. Jono explains wistfully, 'I was devastated. I just didn't know what to do to get her there.'

Afterwards, they sat on a wall in the middle of the Green and smoked a cigarette. Ed was very upset and basically tore into Jono, which was not like him. The attitude at Crown, it seemed, was not going to change. They didn't think Ed was there yet. Jono observes that they continued to be confused by his raps in the middle of songs and thought he needed to find more structure. The industry as a whole seemed to agree.

The evening wasn't entirely wasted for Ed. In the audience that night was a young producer and songwriter, Jay Brown, who lived locally and had popped down to listen to some music. She loved his performance: 'He instantly captivated me.' They started chatting and she told him she used to write songs hanging around skate parks in London. She discovered that Ed, as ever, needed a place to stay that night and offered her sofa. He stayed a few days and they wrote a song together.

Better than that, though, they chatted about music, their dreams and ambitions. 'I remember feeling inspired by the conversation,' said Jay. 'Persistence is key.'

For the most part, the songwriting was going well. Alice had a place at Reading University and was moving on with her life. Being apart was proving to be inspiring for Ed, who wrote some of his best songs during this period of missing her, including 'So' and 'Be Like You', which he put on the *You Need Me* EP. His own college course was winding down. He had accumulated enough points to pass and could go on to study at a university if he chose to do that. His mum was happy, so job done.

He appreciated the freedom that Access to Music had given him and has continued to support the organisation. He was happy to oblige when Ian Johnson asked if he would become a patron. He posed in a college T-shirt and gave them a dream quote to use on their website: 'It was a wicked course. It gave me the final push and I loved the freedom. They understood that half of the learning you need for the industry was outside the classroom with gigs and studio time.'

During the year, he continued to play gigs in East Anglia on trips home but in 2009 he missed the Secret Garden Party because Phil Pethybridge was less than impressed with his new material and felt it wasn't right for the tent. Phil wasn't the only critic of *You Need Me.* They preferred the more acoustic Ed when it was just him. He had to admit, 'Not a lot of people were keen on that.' The general opinion was that he was a loop-pedal person and that was what he did best. Ed was very much his own man but he did take that view on board when planning his next CD. A couple of years later in 2011 he would re-release it as an acoustic record.

Ed went along with Alice to the Secret Garden Party anyway, just to listen and enjoy the festival atmosphere. He saw Phil, who recalls they spoke about the new music: 'He had some tickets so he just came to say hello. I just said I didn't think it was as good. And he agreed. He said it was probably going to come to an end with his management company. He wasn't really keen on what they were trying to do to him either because he was getting feedback that actually people liked what he was doing, rather than what was trying to be forced upon him essentially. That's the feeling I got anyway.'

Ed was very clear about his image or lack of it. He explained his thinking in his first ever television interview, made by Chinacake Productions for BBC Blast – the corporation's initiative to help young people launch themselves in the creative arts. Ed had it all worked out at the age of eighteen. He was articulate and thoughtful when he explained, 'I would like to convey an image of just a regular person rather than being very glossy. I would like to look like someone's kids or someone's mate or someone's brother rather than someone that you wouldn't ever meet.'

He was clearly happy in his skin and didn't want to change into somebody he wasn't. Perhaps the final straw with Crown was a notorious conversation he had with Jono Ball. By now Jono was at his wit's end about what to do with Ed to take him forward. He was still getting negative feedback about a ginger-haired boy trying to rap. Jono would like the ground to open up and swallow him when he remembers their chat: 'I had to give him that kind of feedback and now I have to live with it. It was literally a five-second thing. I said, "Listen, I've got a ginger-haired friend who likes to put blonde highlights in their hair. Is that like something you would do?" And he was like, "No." It was a stupid thing I threw on the table. I was just trying to think of something we could do. We were just getting nowhere.

'It really cut deep with Ed when it wasn't meant to. I regret saying it now because it affected him so much. I would always suggest stupid things but I was only trying to help. He was ticked off and maybe it was one of the nails in the coffin.'

Everyone seemed to agree that what Ed needed most was time to continue his development. Even he was finding the London gig scene repetitive. Perhaps a degree course would be best, after all. Both Jono and Chloe encouraged him to enrol at the ACM (Academy of Contemporary Music) in Guildford. Newton Faulkner was a former student, as was Amelle Berrabah, one of the Sugababes, so there was already a Crown connection. Jono and Chloe travelled to the campus with Ed to look around. He duly signed up for a degree course beginning in the autumn term of 2009. He had found his own student flat in the town and was all set. On the very first day, he realised the course was not for him. He turned up with his acoustic Martin guitar and was promptly told that he should have brought an electric guitar for lectures that day.

The prospects for a happy time at university were not good. Ed was already thinking in terms of his next CD with Jake, had performed literally hundreds of gigs since he had left school, and here he was being ticked off for having the wrong guitar. As his former teacher Keith Krykant said to Ed's mum at the time: 'I think you're wasting your time because he's already ahead of those guys.'

Ed didn't stick around long. He was given a huge helping hand by Just Jack, who needed an opening act for his nationwide tour in late 2009. According to Ed in his book *A Visual Journey*, his college was not supportive and told him his place would no longer be there if he left to take this new opportunity. He chose to leave.

Subsequently, Ed has been outspoken about his attitude to university, calling it a mistake – at least for him. He believes you should take a degree only if you need it to find the job you want. He didn't need it: 'If you want to be a singer then make sure you go to a lot of shows of people you really admire and study how they do it.'

He would often return to his theme about academia; that many students go to university with no sense of purpose or expectation of what they might do when they leave: 'If I wanted to be involved in a film, I'd drop out of school, go and work on a film set and work my way up as a runner.'

Ironically, Ed wrote a touching song called 'U.N.I.' which is nothing to do with his views on further education. Instead, it's about the inevitable sad parting when one's teenage girlfriend goes off to university, obviously referencing his relationship with Alice, who had started her degree and moved away from Suffolk. They had soldiered on when he became busier but, as the lyric states, he was on a tour bus and she was in halls of residence. They hadn't officially split yet but the sentiments in 'U.N.I.' were universal.

Tellingly, Ed has never endorsed the Academy of Music in Guildford. He has praised the Youth Music Theatre UK, Access to Music, and Richard Hanley and his team at the Thomas Mills High School in Framlingham, but nothing for ACM. Rumour has it that his record company later requested that ACM did not use his name as an endorsement – a move that may or may not have originated with Ed – but that has not been confirmed. He is pictured on its website as one of its famous alumni but, seemingly, has never had a good word to say about the place.

The relationship between Ed and Crown limped on for a while longer before Ed received an email from them that basically suggested now was the time for an amicable parting of the ways and encouraging him to have a think about it. A few days later, Ed responded that, yes, he would like to leave amicably, and that was that. There was no contract to terminate.

At the time, Jono believed Crown had made the right decision: 'I was like, OK, cool, so Ed is never going to work. So, it is the best thing to walk away.'

The music business is awash with stories of the one that got away, from Decca failing to sign The Beatles to the countless record labels that didn't recognise Ed Sheeran had something. Jono Ball did his best but, realistically, was too junior to make it happen for an artist he believed in. His own prospects improved when he was promoted from A&R scout to assistant manager. He would have the chance to learn how to manage from Chloe and others by observing how they handled campaigns for VV Brown, Jessie J and Ellie Goulding. He could only gaze in wonder at Ed's future progress and the success of his next management team. 'There is always a guy before the guy,' he says philosophically.

Ed is happy to acknowledge that his former management company were instrumental in him finding the right songwriting partners, but he doesn't look back fondly on their desire to change him. If Ed had listened to Crown, he would have been just one more singer–songwriter, and there are literally hundreds of them struggling off the tube with a guitar and an amp for another deflating gig in front of half a dozen people and a dog. Ed knew he was different and was determined to prove it.

He was about to get the chance.

11
LOOSE CHANGE

Finally, Ed fulfilled one of his big ambitions. He played the Shepherd's Bush Empire in November 2009. He wasn't headlining, but the first time he'd seen Nizlopi there, nearly four years earlier, he had turned to his dad and told him he was going to perform there one day, and now he had. He was so excited that after his set he ran down the front row high-fiving everyone.

Understandably, it was by far his favourite date on the Just Jack UK tour that moved Ed's career out of first gear. He happily acknowledged how much he owed to the Camden Town musician who agreed to let an unknown singer–songwriter open for him. Just Jack is the stage name of Jack Allsopp, who, ironically, considering Ed's views on university, had studied for a degree in furniture design before abandoning that in favour of rap and electronic hip hop. He released his first album, *The Outer Marker*, back in 2002 but only reached a wider audience in 2007 following his television debut on *Later ... with Jools Holland*, a programme that has launched so many careers. His single 'Starz in Their Eyes', a blistering observation of the price of fame, only just failed to make number one and was nominated for an Ivor Novello Award.

He described his music as 'meaningful': 'There's not a lot of meaningful music out there. It's all about drinking and partying. I try and make my songs about issues, without being preachy.' While he wouldn't repeat the level of success of his first hit, 'The Day I Died' was a top-twenty single in the summer of 2009, which helped to sell tickets for his autumn tour promoting the album *All Night Cinema*.

Ed had been suggested as a support act to Jack by another north London musician, Lester Clayton, a well-known face on the capital's music scene, leading his own band and promoting various nights. He had booked Ed for a number of shows across town during the last year and appreciated that he was a cut above the run-of-the-mill singer–songwriters. Jack rang his manager, Stuart Camp, who worked for Elton John's company, Rocket, to tell him about Ed. Stuart recalled the conversation: 'He said, "I've found this kid from Suffolk, he's only got his guitar and this crap pedal and he says he'll do it for free." Free you say? Fine.' Ed was booked.

He still had time to fit in more gigs before the tour. Ed was back at The Living Room in Cambridge in October 2009 when he met the singer–songwriter known as Passenger for the first time. They were part of a four-act bill. Ed was first on at 8.30 for half an hour, then a local group called Ed Hope and Friends, followed by Passenger and finally Megan Henwood, then a Radio 2-nominated young folk musician.

When he appeared at The Living Room, Passenger was playing songs from his first solo album, *Wide Eyes Blind Love*, which he was releasing on his own label the following month.

In real life he is Mike Rosenberg but he decided to keep the name when his group '/Passenger.' split up at the beginning of the year. He was reinventing himself, going back to busking and playing smaller venues to get started again.

He and Ed became instant friends: 'We both watched each other's set and we just hit a chord with each other.' Over the next couple of years Mike spent much of his time recording and touring in Australia, but whenever he was back in England, they would meet up in London, try to play a venue together and 'just hang out'. Mike was another artist who Ed became friendly with on his way up and didn't forget when he had the chance to offer a helping hand.

The Just Jack tour was only a short one – five dates, beginning at Newcastle's O2 Academy. For the first time, Ed received some proper reviews. A couple of songs at an open-mic night might prompt a line on someone's Facebook page but was unlikely to generate much interest. This was different. Sammy Allen, writing online for Brum Live, said, 'The support came from the overwhelmingly talented and all-round fabulous Ed Sheeran.' Sammy was a little unsure as to how to describe Ed's sound but opted for 'indie acoustic with a rather large smattering of pseudo rap and beatboxing (but with a tinge of folk)'. That seemed to cover all bases. He played 'The City', 'Homeless' and 'We Are' before completely wrong-footing his audience with a traditional Irish folk song, 'Wayfaring Stranger'. He sang it a cappella with the help of his loop pedal, which allowed him to be his own backing singers.

His last song was a powerhouse version of 'You Need Me, I Don't Need You', for which he managed to involve the crowd in a singalong. He threw in a line or two from 50 Cent's classic rap song, 'In Da Club', as well as a reference to smoking weed. The performance was accurately summed up as 'kickass'.

The online review on the Soulside Funk site was equally enthusiastic, noting slightly humorously that he had started 'gingerly' before leaving to rapturous applause: 'He's the good guy living the dream and you cannot help but root for him.' That observation went straight to the source of Ed Sheeran's universal appeal.

Ed was already proving to be savvy where merchandising was concerned. Just before the Just Jack tour, he had supported the Noisettes at the UEA in Norwich, which was like a hometown gig for him. It was a big crowd and Ed took along several hundred copies of the *You Need Me* EP for the merchandising desk. They had all been sold by the time the headline act went on.

His mother Imogen was the driving force behind his merchandising. She understood its importance, not just for making some cash but also for reaching a wider audience. Her PR experience was proving invaluable. She didn't travel and look after things on tour, leaving that to the team who went on the road. After he had finished his slot on the Just Jack tour, Ed would march straight offstage to the 'merch' desk and stay there for as long as he was needed, posing for pictures and signing copies of the CD.

One person who was particularly impressed with Ed was the star of the night. Just Jack rang his manager to tell him how amazing his opening act was and that he should come and see for himself. Stuart Camp dutifully hopped on the train to catch him at the O2 Leeds Academy one evening. He immediately agreed with Jack and enjoyed a few beers with Ed after the show, which helped to break the ice between them. They got along. Stuart was already an experienced and successful manager, looking after James Blunt as well as Just Jack. He preferred a paternal, low-key approach to business, believing you didn't get anywhere in this world by shouting at people and behaving badly. Ed could relate to that attitude. But, like Ed, Stuart's affable manner concealed inner steel. That suited Ed too.

He was originally from Bury St Edmunds in Suffolk, under an hour's drive down the A14 from Framlingham. He was another of Ed's contacts who had gone to university and, while studying at Leeds, had decided he fancied a career in the music business. He had been earning some extra money helping out at the Town and Country Club in the city, which later became the O2 Academy where Ed had just played. Just as many students do, Stuart had sent out a flurry of letters hoping to find a job and, to his surprise, was given work as a general assistant (tea boy) by Korda Marshall, a legendary figure who became his mentor. Korda had originally been at the Infectious/Mushroom label, then had gone across to East West Records, which later became part of Atlantic.

In the small world of music, this was a connection that would ultimately benefit Ed greatly. Stuart sought to imitate Korda's calmness in his own career, which finally took off when he was responsible for a series of rock acts that included The Darkness, who were arguably the most famous Suffolk act before Ed. His big breakthrough came when he recognised the potential of James Blunt, then little known and trying to generate some interest in his first album, *Back to Bedlam*. Stuart ended up as product manager on the release, which became the biggest-selling album of the decade. James was one of those Marmite artists you either liked or loathed. Fortunately, eleven million people worldwide liked him enough to buy the album. The best-known track on *Back to Bedlam* was 'You're Beautiful', a wistful song of love and regret that Ed might have written. James described it as 'kind of miserable'. The lyric describes seeing his ex-love on the tube in London with her new man, whom he didn't know existed: 'She and I caught eyes and lived a lifetime in that moment.' Stuart left the record label to become James Blunt's full-time manager at Twenty First Artists, the management company that became Rocket Music. He literally never looked back.

In the first instance Stuart had quite enough to do with managing James to devote too much time to Ed. But he was always available for a chat if Ed was in west London, slipping out of the Rocket offices in Brook Green for a beer and to give his opinion on Ed's plans. They had no formal agreement and there was never a suggestion that Stuart had in any way poached Ed from Crown.

Ed and Stuart discussed a master plan: to put out a series of CDs of varying styles to gather as many different fans as possible with a view to getting signed by a major label. By the turn of the year, he had it all worked out. 'You Need Me' had been the first; then it would be 'Loose Change', which he had mostly recorded and was practically ready to go, followed by a folk EP and then one that would be a collaboration with a number of MCs. He explained, 'I just want to make different sounds but that's not me trying to be different – it's just what I want to do.'

Ed was in no mood to take it easy when the Just Jack tour ended. Just before Christmas 2009, he accepted an invitation to play a seasonal event in an East End warehouse for the homeless charity Crisis. He was asked if he would play some cover versions that everyone knew, so he dusted off some classics including 'Sweet Child of Mine' by Guns N' Roses. This turned out to be the favourite song of one of the people there, a young woman called Angel.

They talked a little about music and Ed enjoyed meeting her. He was struck by her fortitude: she was one of the very few girls among so many homeless men. He thought little more about her until he chatted later to one of the organisers who told Ed the full, distressing story. Angel was addicted to smoking crack cocaine and had taken to street prostitution to fund her habit. Ed was profoundly affected by what he heard. He had enjoyed a very sheltered upbringing in Framlingham and, while he had been in London for more than a year, he hadn't experienced such grim reality as that faced by Angel, and others like her, every day. He was, after all, still only eighteen.

That night he went back to his student flat in Guildford and sketched out the lyrics for 'The A Team', the song that changed everything for him. He only met Angel once and soon lost track of her whereabouts, although he did hear she had moved on to a centre off Tottenham Court Road. Her plight, and that of the many others surviving in such bleak circumstances, would prompt Ed to 'give back' to charities like Crisis. When he could, he popped into its centres up and down the country and held a workshop to help some of the young clients with their songwriting.

Despite the upsetting subject matter, the song turned out to be memorably melodic and an easy one to whistle, which, strangely, made its message more powerful. The 'A Team' of the title is a reference to class-A drugs. Not so subtly, he sings of her selling love to another man. The inspiration for the track is herself, immortalised in the lyric, 'It's too cold outside for Angels to fly.'

Ed quickly arranged to visit Jake Gosling to make the recording. They had come to an agreement that for each CD Ed made he would pay Jake £1,000 to cover his time and production costs. They had moved on from the informal publishing arrangement and Jake had bills to pay like everyone else. Two weeks into the New Year, they had finished the song and the new EP was ready to go. Ed thought it sounded 'wicked' – one of his favourite words – and they celebrated with a trip to Pizza Express. After much deliberation, they decided to call it *Loose Change*, a phrase used in the second verse of 'The A Team', which Ed decided would be the opener. The second track, 'Homeless', also contained those words, which was a neat touch.

While 'Homeless' had been inspired by the couple of nights he had spent on the streets, the finished song turned out to be more one of regret about the time he was spending apart from Alice. The tone was wistful with a contrasting jaunty melody and had none of the biting observation of 'The A Team'. He had completed it with Anna Krantz, another aspiring singer–songwriter.

Anna, a brilliant pianist, had been even more precocious than Ed. She had starting writing songs at the age of eight. By the time she met Ed, she had recorded an album, *Precious Time with You*, at the famous Abbey Road Studios in north London and had been the support on Will Young's 2006 arena tour. In 2009, she had signed a deal with EMI Publishing Ltd and, like Ed, was being placed with other artists in the hope that the collaborations would bear fruit. It was an inexact science but she was instantly impressed with Ed's music. The first time they met, she told him, 'You don't need me but let's write some songs.'

They wrote half a dozen together, including 'Homeless' and 'Sofa', the fourth track on *Loose Change*. This is a simpler song reflecting whimsical feelings about staying in all day with Alice. All he wants to do is lie on the sofa with his sweetheart, drinking tea and watching TV. A characteristic of Ed's songs is that he references everyday things that are relatable. In this case, he sings that they kick off the day watching *Friends* on T4 – something many couples did.

'Little Bird' is another deceptively deep love song. Once again the rather cheerful rhythm contrasts with the sad subject matter. Ed makes light of it when he talks about the song. According to Ed, his inspiration was the time that he and Alice were on a summer bike ride and came across an injured chicken on their way back to her place. Alice, who was studying animal sciences and specialised in poultry, wanted to nurse it back to health but Ed wasn't interested and, tired from days of gigging, needed a cup of tea and bed. In the morning the chicken is dead and Ed tries to kiss his girlfriend to make it all better. He cannot be sure of her love, he says.

The revelation that the little bird was a chicken and not a robin or a chaffinch was a blow to the romantic vision of the song. Ed explained that he was trying to write love songs that were a little different. He didn't want them to be 'I love you songs' but more 'You buy me chips and cheese'. His mum Imogen designed a lovely necklace as part of her Ed range. Her bird did not look like a chicken.

So much was happening in Ed's life at the start of 2010. As well as writing his most important song to date, he linked up with an ambitious young video-maker and entrepreneur, Jamal Edwards, who was destined to become one of the most influential figures in music. He had started the ground-breaking online channel SBTV from the kitchen of his mum's house in Acton, west London. For Jamal, it had all begun with a Christmas present. He received a video-camera as a gift in 2005 when he was fifteen. He was already the annoying boy in school who filmed everything on his phone, but now he had some serious kit to turn his ambitions into reality. He left school at sixteen to work in his local Topman shop but would spend every spare moment making videos of his favourite grime artists and posting them on his new YouTube account. He called his fledgling business SBTV after his rap name, Smokey Barz.

His mother, Brenda Edwards, had finished fourth in the second series of *The X Factor* in 2004 and went on to achieve success in West End musicals. He would joke that she didn't really understand the grime scene that he liked so much, and she thought he was going to spend the day at the zoo when he said he was going out to film Chipmunk. His philosophy was that his media platform in the digital age proved that you did not have to be in a reality programme like *The X Factor* to achieve success in music today. You can build an audience online. In many ways Ed Sheeran would be the living proof of that.

Jamal had to work in Topman for four years before he started making any money from YouTube. He came across Ed online after he was recommended to watch him singing a version of 'The City' recorded at Jake Gosling's studio. They exchanged Twitter messages and met up at a few urban nights across London before Jamal suggested they make a video together.

Jamal was keen to work with Ed: 'He was so different. When I first saw him, I thought This guy is sick – he's rapping, singing, playing the guitar, beatboxing, everything. I need him on the channel.' He had pioneered an F64 film – a 64-bar round of rap music – and wanted to film Ed for his new concept, an A64, which basically would be the acoustic equivalent. Ed would be the first person on SBTV who was not an MC or a rapper.

Jamal already knew Jake, so it seemed sensible to go to Windlesham and film there. On the day in February 2010, they filmed three songs. Ed sang 'The A Team' while sitting on Jake's brown leather sofa that he had slept on a time or two. He was wearing a sensible pullover as if he was playing the song for his mum and dad before tea. He stood in the studio to perform 'You Need Me, I Don't Need You'. This was Ed at his best, looping and producing a powerful vocal on a number he had already sung a hundred times. He had the ability to make it sound fresh every time he played it.

On the way home, they slipped into the waiting room at the local train station to film Ed performing his version of

Nizlopi's 'All My Life'. He displayed just a hint of embarrassment as he sang the line about drinking 'Evian from your pants', perhaps hoping that no commuter would wander in at that precise moment.

'You Need Me, I Don't Need You' proved to be by far the most popular of the three clips when Jamal posted the day's work on SBTV's YouTube channel. This was the song that best reached out to his site's core audience. Within a week, 4,000 people had watched it. By the end of the month that figure had grown to 20,000. In 2018, the video had passed ten million hits.

Most significantly, exposure on SBTV gave Ed the credibility he needed in the grime genre. Artists, who probably hadn't even heard of him, were getting in touch suggesting they might do something together. As Jamal rightly observed, 'It helped me and it helped him. It was a good partnership.'

Jamal features, but is not named, in the up-to-date verse of 'You Need Me, I Don't Need You'. The well-known line talks about when Ed played the Enterprise in Camden Town 'and some fella filmed me'. That was Jamal. The next line in his original version was 'Just a singer–songwriter. Fuck Gabriella Cilmi', which wasn't meant literally but as a dig at singers who didn't write their own songs. Sensibly, he had changed the F-word for 'like' by the time it came to finishing the *You Need Me* CD, but not before Gabriella's boyfriend had made it clear that he wasn't too happy with the original lyric. Although he had first written verses for 'You Need Me, I Don't Need You' at the age of fifteen, it really summed up Ed's determination to succeed. Everyone can dream of sticking two fingers up at the world, which perhaps explains why the song proved to be such a popular anthem for closing his concerts.

The success of his collaboration with Jamal was an unexpected bonus. More people were recognising that Ed Sheeran was not just your average singer–songwriter. He was genuinely crossing over between the folk and urban scenes. Even the record companies showed a glimmer of interest when he started to attract attention online.

Not everything went smoothly. He played the opening of the Noir Bar in Queen Street, Norwich, towards the end of February 2010. Ed had helped to bring in a large crowd on the night but they were a noisy bunch. One member of the audience trying to listen to Ed remembered, 'They were especially rude. The louder he played, the louder they talked. Eventually Ed turned it all off, got up on a table and started to play an acoustic set.'

12
A FINE EXAMPLE

As usual Ed was juggling about six balls at the same time. He had hoped that Amy Wadge would travel from Wales to Sticky Studios to help record his folk EP but she was heavily pregnant with her second child and unable to make it. He had seen her perform several times when she had gigs near London and thought she had a perfect voice for some of the songs they had written together.

The tracks he planned to record at Jake's were songs he and Amy had written together in her shed so she knew them well. Instead he asked another singer–songwriter, Leddra Chapman, to handle the backing vocals. She had released an album the previous year on ALC Records (Anna Leddra Chapman) that was well received by the critics, but made few commercial waves. She had a clear folk voice that suited the five simple but grown-up love songs that Ed planned to feature on his new CD. Her tone complemented Ed's soft vocals. 'Fall' is a proper soppy love song. 'Fire Alarms' has an Alice-inspired lyric that questions whether the object of his affection really loves him – he references carrying schoolbooks in their arms and dodging classes. 'Where We Land' asks if it's love. 'Cold Coffee' is about waking next to your love in the morning. The last track, 'She', is a reflective, more jazz-oriented ballad, in which he's considering whether or not to leave his love.

Ed rang Amy to tell her that the EP was ready and she was thrilled to learn that he had decided to call it *Songs I Wrote with Amy*. The collection is one of the undiscovered gems in the Ed Sheeran discography, full of gentle guitar and undemanding lyrics more suited to a picnic by the river than a night at a club. The CD was a striking contrast with what had gone before.

Before its release, Ed had organised a songwriting trip to Los Angeles. It was part of the grand plan and was not a spur-of-the-moment decision. He wanted to experience another music scene, fearing he was in a rut in London. He was already talking about it in online interviews. He didn't know that his visit would become one of the great pop stories – a certainty for one of those TV comedy-dramas in the future.

He tweeted just before he left in April 2010: 'I'm off to sunny Los Angeles for a month on Monday. Can't wait!' He knew he had somewhere to stay when he flew into LA for the first time: a friend in London had made an introduction to John Hensley, the man behind Flypoet, a series of monthly spoken-word and music showcases that had built up a loyal following in the city since he had launched the evenings in 2000. John adopted a realistic approach to why his shows were proving so popular: 'They come for the music and discover the poetry.' His mission was to provide the means for poetry, which he loved, to reach a wider audience. He hoped to make his nights attractive for couples on a date, who wanted a cocktail, some great food and to be entertained – a modern equivalent of the old smoky jazz clubs.

John was a poet himself and took promoting this particular literary genre in modern culture very seriously: 'Poets don't just entertain people. They inspire them.' Urban music and R&B were the ideal crossing point between music and the spoken word. Ed, therefore, was the dream artist for him. Normally, he wouldn't book artists without seeing them in person, but he decided to take a chance on Ed because of the passion of their mutual friend, a poet living in Finsbury Park: 'I took her enthusiasm to heart and said, "What the heck!".'

Ed duly arrived. He had paid for his flight from the sales of *Loose Change* and was determined to make the most of his trip. John showed him the sights, bought dinner and settled Ed in before his US debut the following evening.

The poster for the event is a collector's item. Ed sneaked in at the bottom after 'profound speaking artist' Steve Connell, 'wordsmith' Ise Lyfe, 'performance painter' Norton Wisdom, a regular, and Thea Monyee, a poet and therapist who was described as 'super, feminine, energy and fire'. Ed was billed as 'the hottest thing on the London music scene in his first LA appearance'. Martinis were just $5.

Ed had come to LA prepared. As usual, he travelled light – his luggage consisted of a rucksack, his trusted mini guitar, some copies of *Loose Change* to sell and his loop pedal. He was introduced onstage at the Savoy Entertainment Center in Inglewood as nineteen years old, all the way from the UK. He performed a nine-minute version of 'You Need Me, I Don't Need You'. The audience loved it. He invited people to come up onstage and rap as everyone cheered and hollered.

John could only marvel at the positive reaction Ed received and promised to help fix up other appearances around LA. For the next week or two, Ed travelled back and forth across the city, playing at any night that would have him. As John put it succinctly, 'He murdered every stage we put him on.'

One of the gigs was an R&B night at the Key Club on Sunset Strip in Hollywood. By his own admission Ed looked 'fucking weird'. Ed recalled, 'I was boozing and I was very chubby with wild hair.' He was also the only white man in the place. Undaunted, he won over the audience, which on that particular night contained Marcus King, manager of Jamie Foxx, one of the very few stars to have won both an Academy Award and a Grammy.

Marcus chatted to Ed after his spot and invited him on to Jamie's radio channel, the Foxxhole, which featured the latest in hip hop and R&B alongside some uncensored comedy. When he heard Ed's music, Jamie was impressed enough to invite him to his open-mic club night. Jamie Foxx was hilarious on *The Graham Norton Show* in 2017 when he described the scene: 'There was a dude up there rapping and he was sweating and he was black. There was another girl, she came up and sung and she was black. And they were singing blackness, it was incredible. And so all of a sudden, I said, "Ladies and gentlemen, Ed Sheeran," and it was like "pop", he pops out, his little red hair and a ukulele. One of my homies – who's an incredible guitarist – was just like "Yo, Foxx, what's this man? What you doing to the room right now? You gotta respect the room." And it was just like a movie. I said, "Well, let's see what the kid has."' After twelve minutes, according to

Jamie, Ed got a standing ovation. He said he invited Ed to sleep on his couch, where he stayed for six weeks. It was brilliant television by a master storyteller but probably had a large dose of artistic licence.

Ed's sofa surfing is the stuff of legend but he had to admit he spent just a few nights at Jamie's Hidden Valley mansion, although he did have time to work on some songs in Jamie's home studio. Even so, he was staying with an A-list Hollywood star, which was definitely worth bragging about, and news of his adventure soon reached record-company ears in the UK. Ed's credibility was rising rapidly.

When Ed had become a number-one artist, Stuart Camp commented in an interview with Music Business Worldwide (MBW): 'You know you're big when Jamie Foxx is bullshitting about you!' Ed described his month in LA as 'life-changing'.

For his part, Ed was always grateful for the exposure he received from hooking up with Jamie. 'He's just a really, really nice dude,' he said, in his customary understated way.

As far as Ed was concerned, everything began to go right when Stuart Camp started looking after him. It didn't happen overnight. They didn't yet have a formal agreement, but when he came back from California, he needed somewhere to stay, as usual, and Stuart's white-leather sofa became his bed of choice. Ed thought it was the most comfortable he'd ever slept on.

Stuart and his team at Rocket were clearly a better fit for Ed than his previous management: 'They're just wicked,' he said. 'They're like, "You do your thing and we'll do our thing and we'll meet in the middle", rather than telling me what to play, what to wear and what to sing.' He also got on famously well with Stuart's partner, Liberty Shaw, who made the finest cheesecake he had tasted. He looked upon their place in Balham as his second home, called them Lib and Stu, and was even known mischievously to refer to them as Mum and Dad – although not usually to their faces. Liberty took it all with good humour: 'I cut his hair, clothe him, wash him, feed and shout at him and he treats me like crap … so just like a parent really.'

Liberty was a professional make-up artist and stylist. Sensibly, she didn't try to change Ed. Both she and Stuart realised early on that the image that best suited him was already in place. He could scrub up when necessary but he was a young lad making his way in the world, not a boy-band pin-up.

Superficially, nothing much had changed since his trip to Los Angeles. He was still gigging as much as possible, mainly in East Anglia and London, while working with Jake. Finally, he cashed in his prize with Island Records. There was no point in it going to waste. At one time, the plan had been to use 'The City' but that had ended up on an EP. Instead he released 'Let It Out', a sweet song about missing Alice. He had made the video to promote the track the previous year, enlisting the help of a Norwich-based photographer, Sylvie Varnier, as director. She had worked at the Waterfront venue in Norwich and had taken pictures of many of the acts that played there. In her film, Ed is walking through Norfolk countryside while imagining the girl he is missing. He looks young and endearingly awkward as he walks towards the camera. It's simple but effective. The production, which featured powerful drums, was much lusher than the normal stripped-back Ed Sheeran and seemed more a leftover of his time with Crown. Perhaps the song wasn't strong enough to make an impact as a single and the Island saga finally fizzled out.

The video for 'The A Team' was a much more successful venture. The simple black-and-white film perfectly captures the bleakness of the song's message. Ed was already friends with a young actress, Selina MacDonald, who had asked him if he had a song that a director could use to make a music video. She knew someone who was just starting out and they wanted to put something together. Ed suggested 'The A Team' and Selina, who already knew the song, asked if she could play Angel. She arranged for Ed to meet the director, Ruskin Kyle, and Ed gave them the go-ahead: 'They said, "We need to buy a crack pipe and some fishnets." So I gave them £20.'

The video has now gone down in folklore as the one that cost £20 to make, which is a slight exaggeration, but it was produced on a shoestring. They made it over a week, mainly outside Angel tube station in north London, which was chosen to emphasise the name of the tragic heroine. The film, which Ruskin shot in black and white, begins with Angel's friend discovering her dead body and then, for the next four minutes, we learn how she got there. She is sleeping on a park bench, selling the *Big Issue*, begging for 'loose change', sitting on the pavement with a sleeping bag and an empty takeaway coffee cup. She makes the decision to walk the streets as a prostitute and is picked up by a man in a BMW, who takes her back to a hotel room where the fishnets have their moment. The money she earns pays for a little plastic pouch of crack, which she smokes, fatally. The video is a very obvious interpretation of the song but effectively presents Angel's wretched tragedy.

Selina MacDonald has a face that seems made for sadness and the video would have been far less memorable without the close-ups of her desperation. Ed makes a brief cameo appearance as someone who buys a magazine and chats for a moment. Nobody involved could have imagined that, just eight years later, the clip would have been watched more than 287 million times on YouTube.

Ed posted the video on YouTube as part of his ongoing campaign to get his name out there. He had to be patient, as Goldie had advised, and continue with what he was doing while hoping that Stuart could make some progress behind the scenes. He continued to play as many gigs as he could. For the most part he enjoyed them. He played The Living Room tent at the Secret Garden Party again in 2010, showing that there were no hard feelings about being turned down the previous year. At the event, he saw Phil Pethybridge, who had been running street teams for a variety of acts, including Scouting for Girls and Paloma Faith, as well as Ed's new friend Passenger. He suggested that Ed should have a proper team helping him for his next tour, which would be with the rapper and singer Example. As a result of being organised with merchandise and street teaming, Ed reached thousands of potential followers. This was how you built up a fan base. There was no point in just turning up, playing and going again.

Ed had reached out on social media to Example, who had just broken through as a chart act in 2010. Ed and Example were quite similar in that they were both intelligent and articulate white men progressing in a world of urban music dominated by black artists. Neither was conventionally good-looking but they both had charisma. Example was the stage name of Elliot Gleave, who had grown up in Fulham, south-west London. As a boy he was diagnosed with Asperger's syndrome, displaying signs of mild autism, including a photographic memory and an advanced facility with numbers. He enjoyed rap battles in the playground of his high school in Putney and loved the R&B music that went with the urban scene. It's easy to see why he and Ed would get on so well, even though he was eight years older.

He had decided to call himself Example because his initials were EG. Rather like Ed, he had been gigging for years before finding success with his second album, *Won't Go Quietly*. When they met, he told Ed that he had played something like 600 gigs on his way up, to which Ed countered that he had done a thousand. Example was already in his late twenties when he had his first top-ten hit with the album's title track. He followed it with an even bigger hit, the exuberant 'Kickstarts', a very personal song. At the time, the fashionable description for his brand of music was EDM, which sounded like a pill available in clubs, but actually stood for Electric Dance Music. He later described his sound as 'uplifting rave tracks'. It was a winning formula but not something that Ed particularly aspired to so the two artists were not musical competitors. Instead they became great friends.

Example was impressed with what he saw on SBTV but Ed was originally booked for just one show, at the Waterfront in Norwich in May. The gig is best remembered now for Example and Ed getting together in the car park for a freestyle rap that became known as the Nando's Skank. It's just a couple

Ed always loved the camaraderie of stage work: he was fourteen when he was given the role of Roger, a guitar-playing member of the T-Birds in *Grease* at Thomas Mills High School.

Just to be sure he knew what he was playing, Ed scrawled the set list on his arm when he performed in his first competition at the Norwich Playhouse when he was sixteen.

Ed's father, John Sheeran, liked to keep a record of Ed's progress and took this picture of his 15-year-old son after his first looping lesson with singer-songwriter Gary Dunne.

The 2008 final of The Next Big Thing competition in Norwich was nearly a disaster when four guitar strings broke, but Ed still won.

Playing songs for students at the Access to Music College in Norwich in 2010. When he made it in the industry, he became a patron.

For once, Ed put his guitar down and relaxed on the grass outside a Cambridge college to have his picture taken a few months before he signed with a major record label.

Looking far too serious celebrating his record deal in January 2011 with mum Imogen, brother Matt and dad John at the Station Hotel, Framlingham.

Famous friends… Harry Styles became great mates with Ed on their way to global stardom: they chat happily at the 2013 Teen Choice Awards in Universal City, California.

Elton John welcomes Ed to the annual Oscar night party for his AIDS foundation in 2014. Jane Fonda sits beside Elton while Ed's manager Stuart Camp keeps an eye on things.

Justin Bieber clinks glasses with Ed at the 2015 MTV EMAs in Milan. They took home seven awards between them.

Close pals… Hanging out with singer-songwriter Foy Vance.

Ed shared one of his finest hours with songwriting partner Amy Wadge when they collected the Grammy for 'Thinking Out Loud' in 2016.

Attending the Q Awards with Example, who's been a buddy since Ed supported him on tour in 2010.

Embracing Stormzy after they performed 'Shape of You' at the 2017 BRITs.

Some guys have all the luck … paddleboarding with Taylor Swift near her home on Rhode Island.

Ironically, Ed was playing 'Thinking Out Loud' on the catwalk when supermodel Adriana Lima paraded past at the 2014 Victoria's Secret Fashion Show in London. No doubt what he was thinking...

Ed had prepared for the fashion show by eating a sausage roll in his dressing room – not a tasty treat recommended for the Victoria's Secret 'Angels'. And, at the end of an exhausting evening surrounded by supermodels in their lingerie, Ed still gets to go out to dinner with his then girlfriend, Athina Andrelos.

Ed always knows how to behave: calm and patient between his dad and Stuart Camp at the BRITs.

Respectful: receiving his MBE from Prince Charles at Buckingham Palace in 2017.

Happy and smiling: with producer Benny Blanco collecting a Grammy for 'Love Yourself'.

Yee-hah!!! Jumping for joy; collecting the Best Male Video award with Emil Nava for 'Sing' at the MTV Video Music Awards.

From worst-dressed to best-dressed…well, very nearly. London street look 2011,

Super casual; performing at the SXSW Music Festival in Texas 2012.

Nice green hoodie for the German Radio Prize gala in Hamburg later that year – fashionably long in the arms.

Super smart, winning the Global Success Award at the 2018 BRITs.

Ed poses happily with Chris Martin in front of 60,000 people in Central Park, New York, for the Global Citizen Festival dedicated to ending extreme poverty by 2030…

But does not want his picture taken, strolling home after dinner in Notting Hill with fiancée Cherry Seaborn. Smiling broadly, she eventually gives up, but Ed is still determined to stay incognito.

of guys messing about but went viral when they posted it online. The highlight was probably Ed singing 'my tongue is on fire' to the tune of 'Sex on Fire' by Kings of Leon.

More than four million have watched the rough-and-ready recording. While today many would find their way to the clip because of Ed, back in 2010 it was Example who was the attraction. A lot of Ed's early fan base came from his fans.

Ed finished that first tour with Example and, mostly, it went well except for a gig in Manchester when the audience just wanted to rave and weren't interested in Ed. He was very down about it and sulked all the way to London where they were next due to play the Islington Academy. Not every gig was going to be fantastic, and Ed had to pick himself up quickly and give a great show the next night. He did.

Example booked Ed to join him on his autumn tour around some small UK venues in September and October. One of the stops in Glasgow provided the unwelcome inspiration for the song 'Drunk'. Ed apparently missed the tour bus the following morning after he had put away one too many vodkas mixed with orange squash.

The second act on the bill was the grime artist Devlin. He and Ed would enjoy rap battles on tour including one memorable backstage session when they both demonstrated their skills at the O2 Academy in Sheffield. Devlin was a vocal athlete while Ed was more melodic.

After the tour was finished, Example presented Ed with a bottle of whisky and a card that said, 'When my career is on its uppers and you're selling out stadiums, can I support you, you talented bastard. Love Elliot.'

13

A BIG DEAL

Ed appeared with a band for the first time at the Rhythm Factory in Shoreditch. The place was small, hot and sweaty, but satisfied Ed that he could perform seriously with other musicians. Realistically, it was a dress rehearsal for what he had planned later in the year: a live CD and DVD. The crowd wasn't huge, just large enough for him to divide up the room to sing various bits of 'Homeless', which he planned to do at the second, more important, gig. He introduced 'The A Team', saying, 'This one's for the ladies.' He wasn't being serious – just parodying some ghastly Vegas patter or a compère bringing on a bunch of male strippers. His band for the night was The Remedies, members of the Music Is Remedy collective that offered their musical support to different performers around London, including spoken-word and hip-hop artists. They had all come across Ed in the previous couple of years. He posted on Facebook: 'I'm not gonna play with a band again for a long time, so come and enjoy the new shit.' That wasn't strictly true as he would be doing just that a week after the Example tour ended.

The Bedford in Balham had never seen so many people crammed in for a gig. More than 300 Ed enthusiasts crowded into the back room where music nights were held to watch him perform. Ed had now signed a formal management agreement with Stuart Camp and the prospects of a major record deal were getting closer every day. This gig at one of the premier venues on the London gigging circuit that Ed knew so well was a showcase to reveal how accomplished he now was as a live performer. Stuart had been particularly keen for him to demonstrate that he could play with a band if he needed to.

Ed took to the stage to play 'The A Team' with The Remedies, who kept everything low key, which enabled Ed to shine. While it was not rock 'n' roll, the set rattled along. He had changed his travel guitar for a full-sized one more in keeping with fronting a band. He no longer looked like the lone troubadour.

Playing the Bedford was just like performing at his local for Ed. Stuart lived quite near by and they would often pop in for a drink or to listen to some music. Tony Moore, the promoter at the venue, was always happy to book Ed because he knew he could count on him. On one occasion a band he had booked failed to turn up for a local Balham street fair, so at the last minute he called Ed, who was staying with Stuart, and asked, 'Can you get here?' Ed simply said, 'Yeah, of course', put on his red hoodie, went straight over and played in the rain.

'He always came with a generous soul,' says Tony. He had thought Ed was destined for a bright future the very first time he watched him perform 'You Need Me, I Don't Need You' with his usual gusto: 'I was hearing someone playing the acoustic guitar, doing something astonishing.'

The Bedford was one of Ed's favourite venues around London because Tony, who at one time had been a keyboard player with, first, Iron Maiden, then eighties chart band Cutting Crew, always put the musicians first. None of the acts was paid so there was never commercial pressure to bring in an audience. At his first venture in London, the Kashmir Klub in Holland Park, he played host to early concerts by Nizlopi, Damien Rice and KT Tunstall, which was a good precedent for Ed. Tony had in fact met John Sheeran a few years before at an Indigo club night at the O2, when Ed and his father had gone to see Nizlopi perform. Tony recalls, 'His dad was a really nice chap. He told me, "My son is into music!"'

Ed called Tony to ask him if he could hire the Bedford to record a live CD and DVD. Tony told him he could have it for just £100, the cost of the engineer for the evening. They agreed on the date, Sunday, 17 October 2010, and Ed charged £5 on the door to help with his costs. Everyone had to pay, and that included the executives from Atlantic who had come along to see him. Early on in the show, someone shouted, 'Why on earth aren't you signed?', which might have been Stuart having a laugh. The loud response was 'Blame his management!', which would have been a neat answer from the record-company bosses.

For the show, The Remedies were joined by backing singer Sophie Pringle. They all wore the black Ed T-shirts with a large orange paw print on the front, which were on sale at the merchandising desk.

In all, he played thirteen songs but only seven with the band. He stood alone for 'U.N.I.' and you could have heard a pin drop until he broke into a rap and everyone started cheering madly. Leddra Chapman added the harmonies for the numbers from *Songs I Wrote with Amy*. He also presented 'Wake Me Up', a song he said he had written in LA that is arguably his most personal love letter to Alice. He later explained that he had picked out every little thing he had liked about her and put it into words. The list includes the number of times they had watched *Shrek* together (twelve), the fact that she hates smoke but can match him drinking, and how he had carved a brooch for her when they went to the beach. That was apparently a trip to the Suffolk seaside resort of Southwold one New Year's Day. The lyric is Ed at his most poetic, with no embarrassment at describing how beautiful she is. He had developed an uncanny ability to blend personal details with universal sentiments. He also mentions that her younger brother could beat him at computer games. They were good pals. Rick Hibbert filmed and posted online one of Ed's party tricks – playing the James Bond theme by tapping a kitchen knife on different wine glasses. He didn't repeat it at the Bedford.

For a change he didn't finish with 'You Need Me, I Don't Need You', although that number did feature an energetic cameo from special guest rapper, Random Impulse. Instead, he unplugged and stood on a chair in the middle of the floor to perform two ballads, 'She' and 'Sunburn', which inspired the young female element in the audience to gaze ahead wistfully. Perhaps the highlight was a stunning version of 'We Are', which seemed to grow as a song with a backing band and some gentle harmonies from Sophie. The executives from Atlantic were particularly impressed. In the future when he played it, Ed would refer to it as 'the song that actually got me the record deal.'

The experiment of playing with a band was a success. Soulside Funk, the online site that seemed to have adopted Ed, noted that he was performing 'like a seasoned pro many years his senior'. The risk of playing with a band made for an 'even more engaging and enjoyable gig'. Ed actually played twice more with the band this year – at Cargo in Shoreditch and at the Waterfront in Norwich. But in the end he followed his dad's advice, which Stuart backed, that he didn't really need them. 'It was an irrelevance,' commented one of Ed's team.

Live at the Bedford was not a great commercial breakthrough. That would come later for Ed, but it increased the buzz surrounding him. Ed was thrilled, however, that it reached number four on the iTunes singer–songwriter chart. He observed, 'It's mental', although he was soon absorbed in a more demanding and ultimately more satisfying project. He was joining forces with some of the leading grime artists in the country.

Ed revealed that he had signed a record deal when he played the Waterfront just before Christmas 2010. He made the announcement at an informal lunchtime gathering in front of an invited audience ahead of the main gig in the evening. Ed was already playing the PR game to a certain extent. He did not reveal the identity of his new label but whetted his fans' appetite by saying all would be revealed at a champagne signing in January. That, of course, would mean another round of media and online coverage.

Much of the buzz around Ed Sheeran had been created online, so it was perhaps fitting that the lunchtime guests had entered a Facebook competition to win their place and travelled to Norwich from all over the country. He played a few songs and took questions. It seemed that the following twelve months were already worked out. He told the audience he would be heading into the studio in the New Year to start recording the first album. 'I'm just really keen to make a good one,' he added modestly. He said the first single would be released in May 2011 and would be his fans' favourite: 'You Need Me, I Don't Need You'.

Ed said that he was still sleeping on sofas, which was not strictly the case as he now had his own bedroom at Stuart's. He also said he dreamed of owning his own flat and a house in Suffolk, a dream that would come true very quickly. He took the opportunity to plug the new CD. *Collaborations* was the final EP in his five-point plan to create a big-enough buzz that no label could ignore. The full title was *No. 5 Collaborations Project* and featured a who's who of grime, including his touring pal Devlin, Wiley, Random Impulse, P Money, Ghetts and JME. He chose the title because it was the last in the series. He explained, 'That was kind of a full stop.'

The idea was simple enough – Ed's songs interspersed with some venomous rapping. Individually, perhaps, the tracks offered nothing new, just an extension of the trusted formula employed on his childhood favourite 'Stan', in which Eminem had spat angrily while Dido sang prettily. What made *Collabs*, as his fans called it, special was its ambition – an unsigned artist persuading some of the trendiest figures in music to appear alongside him. It was a testament to Ed's standing in London's contemporary-music scene.

While he had long harboured the ambition to record with the capital's leading MCs, he did not have enough credibility as a new boy on the circuit. That had changed, thanks primarily to his connection with SBTV. Jake Gosling provided another important link to the artists. He produced the record alongside Ed, who received a co-producer credit for the first time. The recordings, which had taken place throughout the summer, had been a logistical nightmare – it was hard to arrange for ten busy artists to travel down to Windlesham for recording sessions.

One of the most striking features of the CD was the original artwork on the cover by Phillip Butah. The artist had long been a family friend of the Sheerans. When he was sixteen, in 1998, Phillip had been the youngest prize winner in a national young artist competition. He subsequently completed many portraits of the Prince of Wales. He was also a judge for the Young Brits at Art competition alongside John Sheeran, who curated the accompanying exhibition. Over the years he had sketched Ed many times in Framlingham. He respected Ed, whom he described in his blog as a 'modest, down to earth, kind friend whose humility makes him all the more endearing'.

For the *Collaborations* project, Phillip went down to Sticky Studios to discover that Ed had been up for twelve days. He observed, 'He was shattered.' Phillip sketched while Ed recorded, but his first offering didn't receive a positive response. It was a full-face drawing that the subject didn't like, perhaps because he was tired and felt he wasn't looking his best. They compromised with an atmospheric one that hid most of Ed's face behind his hand and that was the one they used on the cover.

Ed was tactful when he was asked by online hip-hop and grime site Blatantly Blunt which his favourite track on the album was. He managed to name practically every song as his first choice. He admitted that the one to 'grow on him' initially was 'Family' with P Money, which was actually recorded last. Ed's contribution is arguably the most melodic on the album while P Money raps powerfully about a near-fatal car crash.

Next Ed decided that the opening track with Devlin, entitled 'Lately', which depicts problems with insomnia, was growing on him, and then it was the Dot Rotten contribution 'Goodbye to You'. He seemed to like every other track as well. He didn't mention the one song that proved to be the most popular. 'Lively Lady' was the contribution from Mikill Pane, the rapper from Hackney who was probably then the least-known artist involved. Mickill confessed that he felt a bit of an underdog when he saw the list of the other names that had taken part, until his remix of 'The A Team' became the most downloaded.

Mickill's lyric was certainly the most provocative, the harrowing tale of a young girl sent by her mother to live with her uncle in England in search of a better life. She is farmed out to men and eventually murdered by her vile relative. At the end of the song we discover that it is her thirteenth birthday. The power of 'The A Team' was that it clothed a grim story in a mainstream pop classic. 'Lively Lady' took that premise several steps further. Mikill did not write it especially for *Collaborations*: he had devised the lyric a couple of years earlier and recorded it as an entirely different track – but it fitted Ed's song perfectly. One of Ed's friends recalls, 'The first time I heard it, I had to stop the car and pull over. When you discover at the end of the song that she was thirteen, you go, "Oh, shit."' 'Lively Lady' is unlikely to be heard on the radio, because of its cheerless themes of heroin, violence and underage prostitution – and not least because it contains the C-word.

No. 5 Collaborations Project was released a week into the new year of 2011. For the first time, one of his independent records was reviewed properly online. *Allmusic* thought the tracks 'effortlessly fuse harsh urban rhythms and quick-fire MC skills with gentle acoustic folk-pop and tender poetic lyrics'. It was as if Ed had brought together the elements of a Flypoet night in LA in one 35-minute burst. Henry Yanney of *Soul Culture* observed, 'The folk-meets-indie-meets-poetry format seemingly encourages/forces the guests on board to produce more reflective, thoughtful lyricism than per usual.'

The project made Ed cool. For fashionable teenagers, it was now OK to admit you liked his music. The proof was in the sales. Stuart Camp still laughs about the phone call he received from his client when *Collabs* reached number thirty-six on iTunes. 'We'll never do better than this,' shouted Ed, excitedly.

A couple of weeks later the album reached number two and even entered the main chart, for one week only, at forty-six. Well-known names, including Tinie Tempah, Pixie Lott and footballer Rio Ferdinand, were tweeting about it.

A few days after it's release, Ed was back in the tranquil surroundings of Framlingham for the official announcement that he had signed a six-album deal with Asylum, an imprint of the Atlantic label. Stuart came down from London with the two key executives at the record company, Ben Cook and Ed Howard, who had brokered the deal. Other record companies were interested, which is always helpful for securing the best terms – rather like footballers being pursued by a number of clubs. In reality, Atlantic, which came under the umbrella of the giant Warner Music Group, was always first choice. The story goes that the two Eds had met a few months before at a

Bruno Mars gig at the Notting Hill Arts Club in west London. Bruno, another act signed to Atlantic, was enjoying his breakthrough year and performed early hits 'Millionaire' and 'Just the Way You Are'.

Apparently our hero didn't know who the other Ed was when they started chatting but happily went along when the A&R boss suggested they should adjourn to his house so that his wife could hear the singer–songwriter's material. She turned out to be Miranda Cooper, one half of Xenomania, the songwriting team behind many hits of Girls Aloud and Crown's top clients, Sugababes and Gabriella Cilmi.

Ed stayed the night on the sofa and was surprised the next day by a call from Stuart telling him that Ed Howard liked his music. He confessed he didn't know who the man was and had to be told that he'd slept on his sofa the previous night. All good fun but it seems unlikely that Ed's music was not already known to Miranda and her husband during the Crown years. It's a great story, though, and all part of the new hype surrounding Ed.

Funnily enough, Ed doesn't mention in his memoir that Miranda wrote for the Sugababes and Gabriella. He also doesn't mention a meeting that Jono Ball had with Ed Howard and Ben Cook when Ed was with Crown; it didn't lead to anything but he was certainly on their radar for years rather than months.

Things were immediately different when Ed linked up with Atlantic. *The No. 5 Collaborations Project* was an end and a beginning. Ed alone had created a buzz about Ed Sheeran, almost entirely single-handedly by his own work ethic, intelligence and determination. As soon as he signed on the dotted line, the buzz turned to hype. His publicity got off to a flying start when it was revealed that Elton John, his manager's boss, had rung Ed personally to congratulate him on the success of *Collaborations*.

In basic terms, buzz is created from the bottom – street teaming, for instance, creates a buzz. Small gigs in pubs create a buzz. Hype, however, comes from above. Imagine a movie star moving between talk shows and telling the same story, laughing at the same jokes just to fulfil their hype obligations to a studio publicising their latest blockbuster.

At Atlantic, Ed had a high-flying bespoke marketing manager, Stacey Tang, whose team relentlessly pushed the same lines about Ed – the Jamie Foxx story, the sleeping-on-sofas angle, the disadvantage of having ginger hair, the influence of Damien Rice and Nizlopi. The stories weren't made up but they were embellished where necessary to endorse the right image for Ed. In every interview he seemed to be answering the same questions because that storyline was now the regular brief.

On the day he signed his contract in Framlingham, everyone met up at John and Imogen's before heading to a local pub, the Station Hotel, where Ed and his mates liked to drink in the back room. Ed thought it all 'really cool'. His mum said, 'I used to worry about him when he first went to London. But he gained a second family through music who look after him and let me know he's all right.'

The local paper was invited to photograph the celebration, which wasn't with champagne after all – Stuart, Ben and the two Eds were pictured toasting the deal with brimming pints of beer. Much more Ed Sheeran.

14
WAYFARING

The local pizza place in Camden Town had never seen a day like it: 200 young people queuing down Ferdinand Street at ten o'clock in the morning for an evening gig at the Barfly. They were there to see Ed Sheeran. It was the first indication of Edmania and he had yet to release his debut single. Delivery guys wandered up and down the line all day, taking orders for pepperoni pizza and calzone. At the end of the night, the restaurant owner told one of the doormen, 'We're all going on holiday now.'

Ed had announced the free gig on Twitter. He said it would be first-come-first-served, and would start at 7 p.m. He added that he would try to play to as many people as possible but couldn't promise anything. On Facebook, he told everyone that he would say hello after the show.

The evening was a record-company initiative to demonstrate that Ed was becoming popular among teenagers following the latest trends in music. Here was a young singer crossing the line from folk clubs to hip-hop nights. Even the *Guardian* was interested and sent a reporter along. Equally important, the event was demonstrating to the BBC that Ed should be played on Radio 1.

As the day drifted towards evening the crowd grew to more than a thousand and the police were hovering, concerned that numbers might get out of control if more teenagers turned up to see what was going on. The Barfly holds about 200, so Ed ended up playing three consecutive 45-minute sets but even then there were many disgruntled 'Sheerios' outside. One of the problems was that fans hid in the toilets between performances so that they could sneak back in and catch the next one.

In the end, the venue had to close and there was talk of an extra gig in the Morrison's car park but, wisely, this idea was abandoned. Ed did come out with his guitar and give an impromptu performance of 'The City' and 'You Need Me, I Don't Need You' to those left outside. It was time for everyone to go home because good humour was evaporating when the final few realised the doors had been closed for the night.

The odd can was chucked at passing cars and a few punches thrown but fortunately that fizzled out and the evening was applauded as a resounding success. The *Guardian* had a crystal-ball moment, predicting a top-three hit for Ed's debut single in June: 'If his "indie" followers stay with him now he's signed to a major, he'll be massive.'

Ed's springtime gigs in 2011 were part of the advance campaign. He had spent the first couple of months of the year at Sticky Studios. When he signed his deal, it was decided that Jake would be on board as producer for the first album. They worked well together, and neither wanted the album to be the greatest hits of his five independent releases.

Early plans for 'You Need Me, I Don't Need You' to be the lead single were soon abandoned as it became clear to everyone that 'The A Team' would be a more commercial choice. Surprisingly, the former track proved to be the most troublesome to record, even though it was the first Ed had written back when he was fifteen and had already featured on his *You Need Me* EP. They couldn't get it right despite recording at least twenty versions, and, at one point, an exasperated Ed was going to leave it off the album altogether. They decided another set of ears might help and approached Charlie Hugall, the producer of Florence and the Machine's 2009 number-one hit 'You've Got the Love'. He suggested they use a live drummer and that made the difference.

The song was still a cornerstone of Ed's live gigs when he went on the road as a headline act. This sounded grander than it actually was. Most of the venues were small and Ed and his crew shuttled between gigs in a Mercedes Splitter van, the most popular form of transport for low-key tours. Ed travelled with a small crew, including Kal Lavelle, who was opening for him. She was the first example of Ed not leaving his friends behind, especially those who had helped him in the past. One of his team put it succinctly: 'Ed leaves the ladder down.'

Ed's close companion on the *A Team* tour was another cousin, Murray Cummins, a budding filmmaker who kept a video diary of everything Ed did. The two shared a room, usually in a cheap and cheerful Travelodge. Murray would sort out the day's filming while Ed, in the days before Netflix, watched box sets to unwind. He liked *The OC* and *The Wire* and, of course, *The Simpsons*. It was not exactly sex, drugs and rock 'n' roll.

Murray was five years older than Ed and had known him all his life. He had started filming him in 2008 when Ed first moved to London, more as a means of self-tuition than with any grand design in mind. He had realised his cousin had a special talent when he'd listened to Ed, then a boy, reciting Eminem raps word for word and playing guitar parts that he had only just heard. They used to joke around on tour that Murray was filming a big documentary, although after the record deal was signed, it began to dawn on them that Ed was doing 'really cool stuff'.

Small gigs up and down the country continued to build a core fan base but the most significant event for Ed before the release of the single was his first appearance on national television. He sang 'The A Team' on *Later ... with Jools Holland* for broadcast on the day that Prince William married Kate Middleton, Friday, 29 April 2011. He had only been confirmed for the show with three days' notice. The other guests were the usual eclectic mix, including a Swedish singer Lykke Li, folk group The Unthanks and Avery Sunshine, an American singer-–songwriter. Best known was the indie favourite PJ Harvey.

The star guest did not sing – instead Ringo Starr chatted amiably to Jools about his upcoming tour. Ed was sitting at the next table with his mum and dad – as ever, he'd wanted them to share this special occasion in his life. Imogen couldn't stop grinning the whole time Ringo was talking. All those long car journeys listening to The Beatles and now there he was, right next to them.

Jools introduced Ed: 'A marvellous new artist from Suffolk. Let's welcome Ed Sheeran.' He looked carefully styled, wearing a new black Fly53 T-shirt with his mum's jewellery designs on his wrists and his faithful choker around his neck. He was clean-shaven, which he admits is the quickest way to look twelve, and his hair was in its usual backcombed state, described by one critic as 'artfully scruffed up'.

He admitted that he was 'shitting himself' because it was such a big show. He certainly seemed a little nervous singing 'The A Team' but was more relaxed for his second song. This time he had ditched the guitar to perform singer–songwriter Jamie Woon's version of 'Wayfaring Stranger'. He began with some beatboxing, then expertly demonstrated the effects of his loop pedals. Ironically, considering the previous battles he had fought with Crown, he chose not to perform any raps. But the showcase, which would never have happened without powerful label backing, was perfect for a mainstream audience who needed a break from William and Kate's celebration.

Ed, meanwhile, was straight back on the promotional trail. Not everything went smoothly. At the Hare & Hounds in Kings Heath, Birmingham, the PA system didn't work so Ed simply unplugged and played his entire set standing on a table. The venue has a big reputation in the city as the place where UB40 played their first gig. Ed was in a room upstairs, in which space was at a premium and there was just enough space to breathe out. Many of his songs are well suited to intimate venues, and he casually introduced less familiar numbers, like 'Small Bump', as being 'off the new album'. For once, this was not a lyric written from personal experience, nor was it about Alice, whom he had seen only a couple of times during the year.

'Small Bump' was written from the perspective of a young mother enduring a miscarriage in the fifth month of pregnancy. Listeners often believe every Ed song is autobiographical but sometimes he writes about another's experience from their standpoint – something that requires great sensitivity from a young man only just leaving his teens.

Ed was able to perform that ballad with just his voice and guitar because he could play properly, sing in tune and not suffer any embarrassment when performing. 'It was an incredible show,' said one of the lucky ones who witnessed Ed unplugged. He plugged back in for the encore – and 'You Need Me, I Don't Need You' left everyone going home singing to each other at the top of their voices.

Ed had rescued the evening, and the build-up to the release of 'The A Team' could hardly have gone better. As well as the television and the live gigs, he was doing plenty of radio interviews between concerts. Ed knew all his songs so well that he seldom bothered to rehearse. He didn't have a set list on this tour and just played what he liked.

'The A Team' was officially released on 12 June 2011. The cover was another inspired sketch by Phillip Butah taken from the video image of Selina McDonald in the park, stretching her arms out wide as she embraces a view of London. The song had been around for so long, it seemed like an old friend. Ed had played it live countless times, as well as on TV and radio. The video had already chalked up a million hits on YouTube. He had even posted an acoustic version in May to widen its exposure.

In its first week of release, the song was involved in a three-way battle for the number-one spot, competing with Example's

'Changed the Way You Kiss Me' and 'Bounce', the latest offering from master DJ Calvin Harris (featuring Kelis). Example won but Ed sold more than 57,000 units even though he was number three.

Ed was in Cornwall, preparing to play the Princess Pavilion in Falmouth, when Stuart Camp texted him the news. He observed, 'Having a song about a heroin-addicted prostitute get mainstream success is a really cool thing, I think.' He celebrated by drinking a milkshake on the beach.

He had the satisfaction of comfortably beating both Example and Calvin in the end-of-year charts. He was placed eighth with sales of more than 800,000, the highest of any debut single that year. The only minor irritation was that Adele's classic 'Someone Like You' was the biggest seller with 1.3 million. Ed, being a very competitive person, would be looking to sell more than her one of these days. He would use the continued success of the Tottenham powerhouse as the benchmark for monitoring his own progress. For the moment, she was always a step ahead.

When 'The A Team' charted, Ed was in the middle of a summer run of open-air festivals, including Oceanfest, on the north Devon coast, and Beach Break Live, where, as Ed put it, 'Twenty thousand kids knew my songs.' They were all leading up to Glastonbury, the biggest event of the summer. Ed had dreamed of this: 'You grow up and you're like "One day I'm going to play Glastonbury."'

That year he already knew many of the performers. Some of the 'collaborators' were there playing the East Dance Stage, including Devlin, Wretch 32 and P Money. The headliners for the three nights on the main Pyramid Stage were U2, Coldplay and Beyoncé. Ed was appearing in the BBC Introducing Tent on the Friday. 'Glastonbury, how ya doing?' he asked, as if he performed there every year. It had been raining, of course, and Ed played his thirty-minute set in his faithful old red hoodie and a pair of muddy white socks. He launched into 'The City' and everybody knew the words, particularly the host of teen-age-girl fans who had now adopted him as their favourite.

He played 'Wayfaring Stranger', 'Small Bump', 'The A Team', then announced 'You Need Me, I Don't Need You' as his next single. He came back to perform an encore of his 'favourite song of the moment', which turned out to be the Bob Dylan classic 'Make You Feel My Love'. The song had reached a wider audience when Adele had included it on her debut album *19* in 2009. She sang it as an emotional ballad. Ed's interpretation was much sweeter and gentler.

He might have sung it for Alice, who had joined him in Somerset that year. The two of them had planned to stay on for the duration and watch Beyoncé on the Sunday evening. Instead, they split up. A friend observes, 'She was incredibly self-conscious about the fact that the new album was very heavily about her. Her boyfriend was the Ed Sheeran she went to school with and now it was something completely different. She wanted no part of fame.

'They just were one of those couples who had got together at school and would go through the rest of their life together and grow old together. She caught up with any kind of worries that he had and was so comforting and friendly, and genuinely one of those people who would talk to people and be nice. She cared greatly about him. She is a lovely person and drop-dead gorgeous. They were wonderful together.'

Four years was a long time, even if they had seen less of each other after Ed signed his record deal. He had to pick himself up after the break-up to play some welcome concerts back on home turf in East Anglia. He was the first act to play three consecutive nights at the Waterfront, the Norwich venue that had always looked after him so well.

Latitude in Suffolk was like a homecoming in mid-July, even if rain was lashing down. Ed was making his first appearance on the main stage at a festival. He called it the crowning moment of his career. He was first on in the afternoon and only Paolo Nutini, who was headlining that night, attracted a bigger crowd. One veteran rocker came up to Ed and his entourage afterwards and congratulated them. Everyone politely thanked him, believing him to be a punter, and thought no more about it until later he was introduced onstage by blues singer Seasick Steve as John Paul Jones, the legendary bass guitarist of Led Zeppelin.

Ed's favourite festival, however, remained the Secret Garden Party. He had such happy memories of his times there with Alice. He wasn't expected to play at the event for the simple reason that they couldn't afford him, but he didn't want to miss out and asked his new booking agent, Jon Ollier of Free Trade, to sort something. Jon arranged for Ed to play a secret gig at the Secret Garden, which was a neat touch. Making it secret meant that the festival could not use his name to advertise the event.

Ed was booked under the name of Angel but ruined the surprise when he tweeted the day before: 'I'm playing a secret show tomorrow at secret garden party. Shhh, it's a secret.' Phil Pethybridge, who had organised the appearance with Jon, recalls, 'The tent was rammed – absolutely heaving.'

Poignantly, at this point Ed and Alice were no longer speaking – and didn't for some time afterwards. Eventually, Ed acknowledged that the break-up had been difficult. He explained, 'I think she'll be a bit embarrassed about an album being written about her.' Their split, though, did not mean a last-minute change to the inlay of his debut album + (*Plus*). Poignantly, he thanked Alice for her love, and the times that she had been there for late-night phone calls when he'd wanted to pack it all in – and for 'being the only girl that all of these songs are about'.

15

PRECIOUS MOMENTS

Bus passengers going by the World's End pub in Finsbury Park pointed excitedly when they recognised Ed. He was talking to Pixie Lott among a lively bunch of people who were waiting to be let into the pub. As he had predicted years before, his distinctive looks meant he was easy to pick out in a crowd. He had to get used to being pursued in the street – the fans didn't bother him; it was the photographers who were a nuisance.

He and Pixie weren't queuing for a gig; it was the launch party of Ed's long-awaited first album +. The friends who had helped him along the way were there, including Luke Concannon, Tony Moore, Jamal Edwards, Wretch 32 and the imposing figure of Mikill Pane, who had featured on *The A Team* tour when he strolled onstage to perform some verses from 'Little Lady'. As well as record-label executives and music-business figures, Ed made sure he asked his old school friends from Framlingham to join him. Naturally, his cousin Murray was on hand with his trusty camera.

Songwriter Si Hulbert arrived in a cab. He hadn't seen Ed in person for about six months and had marvelled at how his career was progressing: 'He was the new big thing, and you never know if somebody is going to have the time of day for you when things start changing for them. There was a huge group of people around him, all wanting a bit of attention. I got out of the cab and he saw me and he literally came out of the group of people, straight across to me and gave me a big hug and started introducing me to everyone. And I just thought, That separates people. He wasn't changing.'

Towards the end of the party, so many people had turned up that everyone spilled out on to the street again. Ed, as if by magic, produced a guitar and started playing for his guests. They were treated to 'Ed Sheeran: Live on the Corner of Stroud Green Road'. Tony Moore recalls, 'The crowd was calling for songs and he was just playing them. We were jamming on the street!'

Ed had already battled through a long day, signing copies of the new album in HMV, Oxford Street, as well as performing a song or two for customers and passers-by. That was part of a well-organised campaign around the HMV stores. More than a thousand turned out in both Ipswich and Norwich, some of them bringing their guitars for Ed to autograph. The majority of the crowd were screaming teenage girls. He admitted, 'I haven't got used to that.'

While Edmania might not have matched the hysteria that had surrounded pop stars of previous generations, Ed was well on his way to being a teen idol – and he hadn't even been photographed with Harry Styles yet. Ed would say modestly that he was not exactly boy-band material, which was, of course, part of his appeal.

On the back of the success of 'The A Team', Ed had been able to secure a lucrative deal with the giant Sony/ATV company, arguably the number-one music publishers in the world. He had signed the contract, rumoured to be worth £300,000, over a pub lunch at the World's End. This was entirely separate from his record deal with Atlantic. It was part of his new business plan. The first one – his five self-financed CDs – had achieved everything he had wanted. Now it was time for a second strategy that would expand the brand.

He enjoyed the whole process of composition so it made sense to extend this side of the business by writing songs for other artists. As well as being very lucrative, it would link him with the fan base of other popular acts. One Direction seemed a good place to start, especially as they were signed to Simon Cowell's Syco Records, a Sony company.

Ed was introduced to Harry Styles by guitarist and songwriter Chris Leonard, whom he had known since Crown days and had become a good friend. Chris had been in the punk band Son of Dork, which had a top-three hit with 'Ticket Outta Loserville' in 2005. He and Ed enjoyed many happy and productive times working at Jake Gosling's and would often meet up in London for music, beers and nights out.

Harry was staying in London while One Direction were working on their debut album, *Up All Night*. He asked Ed if he had any songs he wanted to put up. Ed always had songs, so a meeting was arranged with Tyler Brown, then head of A&R at Syco. Ed went in to see him and left some tracks for consideration. They included a song called 'Moments' that he had written early on with Si Hulbert, who was horrified when he mentioned it: 'It was probably the shoddiest demo I've ever done with him, if I'm honest. I was just throwing stuff together. It actually started off as a drum and bass track. I went cold when he told me and then I get a text from Ed, a phone call from Stuart Camp and then an email from Tyler saying they wanted it. Ed was busy with promotion but Tyler is very good at A&R so he told me what needed fixing – take out the drum and bass stuff, basically. I totally changed it into a boy-band sort of epic ballad.'

One concern Si had when preparing the track for One Direction was whether the content was suitable for a boy band. Not every Ed Sheeran song is about him or his own experiences. 'Moments' was actually inspired by the sad death, aged fifteen, of Si Hulbert's younger sister. The song is about missing her: 'If we could only have this life for one more day,' Si recalls. 'I did say to Ed, "Do they know what this is about?" And he said, "I don't think so." This is where Ed's exceptional talent lies. He's able to put it in such a way that connects with everybody on different levels. If you are a fourteen-year-old girl, it's about losing your boyfriend.'

'Moments' did not make the final main listing on the album but was a bonus track and available on deluxe editions worldwide. The song is also one of the most cherished among devoted One Direction fans, performed by the band on all three of their world tours. Band member Louis Tomlinson said it was by far his favourite track on *Up All Night*.

At this stage, the most popular boy band for a generation was actually a step behind Ed. They had placed third in the previous year's *X Factor* when Matt Cardle won, but Simon Cowell had identified them as the act that would break out into stardom. In some ways, an association with Ed Sheeran made them seem much cooler than Saturday-night prime time. They had yet to release a single at a time when Ed had managed two top-ten hits. As he had promised at Glastonbury, 'You Need Me, I Don't Need You' had followed 'The A Team' and made number four in the charts. The song was a publicity penalty kick because it was easily interpreted as a two-fingered salute to his first management team at Crown, who, it was said, had tried to change him and eventually let him go. Ed played along with that storyline even though he had written the original song aged fifteen.

The reviews were mixed, which would often prove to be the case with future Ed records. The critic in the *Irish Times* had not borrowed the *Guardian*'s crystal ball: 'Ed Sheeran is hugely popular right now but I bet in two years' time even the Simon Wiesenthal Centre won't be able to track down anyone who admits to liking this track.' Interestingly, the *Sunday Mail* in Glasgow compared the song favourably with the 'groove and sass' of Justin Timberlake and described Ed as Britain's current king of lyrics.

More important than the reviews, however, was the video. Ed worked for the first time with director Emil Nava in what would turn out to be a long-standing collaboration that was important to both men. Emil, who had left school at sixteen, shared many of the same fundamental principles as Ed: 'I never went to college or uni. I always thought that doing it was the best way of learning it.'

Emil's father was the renowned Mexican artist José Nava, who famously painted hundreds of pictures in a converted shed in Kentish Town. Emil grew up in the peaceful surroundings of Bridport on the south-west coast after his parents split and his mother, journalist Gill Capper, left London for Dorset. Originally, Emil trained as a chef before realising where his true vocation lay. He moved back to London, following in the footsteps of his elder half-brothers, Zadoc and Jake, who were both making a name for themselves as directors.

He moved up from being a tea boy on film sets to becoming a PA and then an assistant director on some famous pop videos including 'Rehab', an iconic song of Amy Winehouse. He struck out on his own with 'Get Sexy' by the Sugababes and a string of Jessie J tracks, including her debut hit, 'Do It like a Dude'.

Ed appears only fleetingly in his video, shot effectively in black and white. We see him occasionally strumming a paw-print guitar. The star is teenage actor Matthew Jacobs Morgan, who performs the song evocatively in British Sign Language (BSL). Ed was continually looking to produce something new and interesting so that his work would be talked about in the morning line for takeaway coffee.

At last, it was time for his debut album to be released. After nine months of hard work, + was in the record stores on 9 September 2011. Expectations were already high but they were exceeded. The first-week sales of 102,000 copies placed Ed at the top of the album charts. By the end of the year it had sold 791,000 copies and ended up ninth in the annual list. He still had quite a way to go, though, to match Adele's sales of 3,772,000 for *21*.

Ed celebrated his success with a second tattoo. Until now he had only one, a black paw print on the inside of his left forearm. He simply chose a + sign to go with it. He persuaded all those involved in the record to follow suit – as if they were members of a secret cult. Amy Wadge travelled from Cardiff to London just to have hers done.

Ed already had the concept of using mathematical symbols in his head. He couldn't choose actual numbers because Adele had already adopted those with her albums *19* and the follow-up *21*. The idea of + was that it 'added' some new songs to his better-known tracks from his earlier EPs.

His starting point therefore was a selection of familiar favourites, including 'The A Team', 'The City', 'Wake Me Up' and 'You Need Me, I Don't Need You'. They were mixed with tracks that he had been playing live for ages – 'Small Bump' and 'U.N.I.'. New songs blended in easily. Some were obviously about Alice. 'Grade 8', for instance, reveals when he fell in love. The Grade 8 in the title is a reference to the highest grade in music exams – something, ironically, he didn't achieve.

Arguably the most romantic track was 'Kiss Me'. It's unashamedly slushy and one that any couple might want as the first dance at their wedding. That's exactly why it was written. Ed would tell the story often at his concerts. His godparents, who had originally been married to other people, became engaged while drunk on the train home from his mum's birthday party. They asked Ed to write a new song and perform it at their wedding. He agreed. His long-time friend from Norwich days Jon McClure, the lead singer with Reverend and The Makers, described it as 'sexy baby-making music', which might have been a bit premature for a wedding reception.

Surprisingly, considering how many times he had played it live, he didn't include 'Wayfaring Song'. Instead, as a hidden track at the end of the album, he sings 'The Parting Glass' a cappella, just as he had done drunkenly at Gary Dunne's thirtieth birthday party and at many family gatherings, especially in Ireland.

Gary was just one of the acknowledgements on his CD inlay. Ed was generous with them, thanking practically everyone who had helped him on his journey, from the early days in Framlingham to the top of the charts. Among the many names, he remembered Claire Weston, Keith Krykant, Mr Hanley, Ian Johnson and all at Access to Music. He also slipped in a thank-you to Alice's parents and her brother 'Ricky Hib'.

He mentioned his inspirations: Luke and John from Nizlopi, Foy Vance, Eminem, Van Morrison, Bob Dylan and Damien Rice. He named the collaborators he was 'honoured' to write with: Amy Wadge, Jake Gosling, Chris Leonard, Si Hulbert, Gordon Mills Jr and Anna Krantz. He didn't forget those who had helped him in London, including Tony Moore and everyone at the Bedford, Kal Lavelle at the World's End and his 'best mate Jamal'. He mentioned the friends, including Daryl Snow, who had let him sleep on their sofa, the MCs from the *No. 5 Collaborations Project*, Just Jack and Example. He even mentioned Chloe and Jono at Crown. He sent his love to his cousins Jethro, Murray and Laura, his brother Matt and his grandparents. He gave a special mention to his dad for the moral support and to his mum 'for the rule that you should always smile and make the best of a bad situation'.

Separately from the acknowledgements, the record is dedicated to Stuart Camp, about whom Ed writes unselfishly: 'None of this would have happened without you.'

Ed remembered to thank Phillip Butah for the album's artwork. As well as the notable orange front cover, the record's notes are interspersed with original drawings of Ed and his family. In one, Imogen is making her distinctive jewellery. John Sheeran, meanwhile, is sketched reading the June issue of *RWD* magazine, which featured Ed on the front cover with the headline: 'Ed Sheeran, Hitting All the Right Notes'.

The critics didn't mention the artwork. They seldom do. Some liked the album. *Wales on Sunday* called it a great debut that 'delivers an inspired mix of gospel, rap and lyrical tracks'. The *Irish Times* called it 'remarkable'. Some critics didn't care for it so much. The *Observer* mentioned 'half-rapped banalities'. Alexis Petridis, the renowned *Guardian* music writer, was given a Twitter pasting by Ed's fans – the Sheeranators – for awarding the album only three stars out of a possible five. The review, in fact, was well balanced but that did not satisfy devoted fans. Alexis was unimpressed by 'Wake Me Up', which he likened to a grisly Match.com ad: 'A listener who can keep their last meal down during that, however, might note that apart from his teen appeal, Sheeran's strength is his melodic ability, a way with a really strong, radio-friendly tune like "The City" or "Grade 8".'

Ed just had to try to ignore the unflattering reviews and was scathing about the writers, who had probably 'listened to my album once or twice' but felt they could make assumptions about the meaning of his lyrics. They clearly rankled with him: 'Everything I do is for my fans. I don't make music for the critics. They didn't spend a tenner on my album; they haven't come to see my shows for the past few years. Well, I don't care what they think. If a fan came up and said they didn't like what I'd done, then it would hit me and I'd take it in and think about it.'

Looking to the future, the most interesting comment came from Adam Woods in the *Mail on Sunday*: 'At this stage, Sheeran still belongs to the kids but + indicates his everyman charisma will work just as well on their mums in the supermarket CD aisle.'

Inevitably, when he set about promoting the album, Ed faced questions about Alice, whom he had named as his creative muse. He deftly swerved them most of the time by saying that he was focusing on his career at the moment. 'If I couldn't make it work with someone I've gone out with for four years, then I shouldn't go out with anyone else just now.' He even spoke optimistically of them ending up being married one day. At the age of twenty, he was talking of settling down and having kids.

Ed was outspoken about the reputation of Mick Hucknall, singer with Simply Red, who had previously been the most famous ginger-haired man in music. Ed did not want to become known for dating lots of girls. 'He did it and now he's known as a sleaze.' Ed thought that being a one-woman man was much cooler than being a player.

Alice and Ed had already broken up when he came across Nina Nesbitt, a very pretty Scottish singer–songwriter. Nina had just turned seventeen when she met Ed, who was making a rare visit to Scotland for the Belladrum Tartan Heart Festival near Inverness. In an adventurous move that would have reminded Ed of himself, she approached him after a radio interview, introduced herself and asked if she could play him some songs.

Her ambition impressed him as much as her playing. She was born in the West Lothian town of Livingston but brought up in Balerno, a small village near Edinburgh. She had no musical background – her father, Mike, was employed by an electronics firm while her Swedish mother, Caty, was a childcare worker. She had started writing songs on the piano at the age of ten and moved on to the guitar at fifteen, posting her material on YouTube. While still at school, she was a model and a competition gymnast but decided that a career in music suited her best. She had already placed online a moving version of 'The A Team' when she met Ed.

She posted on Twitter a picture of her 'havin' a wee sing' for Ed Sheeran, who, she said, was a 'lovely guy'. Ed certainly seemed to be paying attention. He was sufficiently impressed to invite her to play at a couple of his shows on the + tour. She grabbed the chance.

She was certainly noticed when she came onstage in a black mini dress and a matching pork-pie hat at the Shepherd's Bush Empire to duet with Ed. He introduced her as an amazing talent and declared, 'I will let her voice speak for itself.' He asked sweetly if she was all right before they launched into a cover of one of his favourite songs, Leonard Cohen's unforgettable 'Hallelujah', which had been reworked sublimely by Jeff Buckley. The whole world had seemingly had a go at singing it, but Ed and Nina's quiet interpretation was memorable. Emily Jupp, writing in the *Independent*, thought Nina, whom she described as a 'tiny, fluffy haired creature in a pork-pie hat', stole the show: 'The song wasn't ideally suited to her voice but she twisted it to fit her style and created some beautiful harmonies with him.'

While there was obviously some chemistry between Ed and Nina, it was too soon after the break-up with Alice for him to become involved with someone else. He was still coming to terms with what had happened. For the most part he kept his true feelings to himself. On one occasion, though, even the ultimate professional struggled. As part of his album tour in late October, he was playing the Sub 89 club in Reading and Alice was supposed to turn up. She didn't show. An eyewitness at the gig observes, 'Ed was incredibly upset that she wasn't there and did one of the worst gigs of his life. It culminated with him slamming his guitar down during the encore and walking offstage.'

After + went to number one, Ed took himself off to Hamley's, the famous Regent Street toy store, and bought a number of gifts for friends. For himself, he chose a Lego Star Wars Millennium Falcon. He had loved Lego since he was a child and still found building it the best way of unwinding on tour, if there was nothing he fancied watching on TV. Lego is often thought of as a useful tool for children who have ADHD (Attention Deficit Hyperactivity Disorder). Ed was never diagnosed but has admitted that his family always thought he had the condition.

Johnny McDaid of Snow Patrol, who would become a great friend and co-writer, had his own method of dealing with Ed's notoriously short attention span. He would have some Lego in a suitcase and bring it out when they were writing a song together to keep Ed 'in the room'. Ed would sit quietly and make something with the Lego: 'He would kind of get lost in the world for a second, and then come back and come up with this moment that was everything.'

Once Ed even took a new kit on a date. He told Graham Norton on his BBC chat show that the evening did not go well. He built the toy, admired his work, then went home. He also discovered that Harry Styles was a devotee and the two would assemble tricky models together. Harry bought him an Imperial Star Destroyer and the pair of them stayed up until 3 a.m. until it was complete.

The news that Ed was a Lego lover neatly coincided with the release in November of 'Lego House', his third single from the album. The track was an old song he had written with Chris Leonard in the Crown days. Originally he had called it 'Love You Better Now' after another line in the lyrics, but 'Lego House' was a more memorable title. The single reached number five in the UK chart – a commendable result for the third release from an album.

The video continued Ed's policy of trying to be as inventive as possible. Again, he was only on screen fleetingly. The idea that he and Emil Nava came up with seemed simple – Rupert Grint would play Ed. At the time, thanks to his role as Ron Weasley in the Harry Potter films, Rupert was probably one of the very few better-known ginger-haired stars. Ed didn't know him but was able to make an approach through their mutual friendship with Tom Felton, who played the villainous Draco Malfoy in the films.

Ed liked the thought of the actor playing him because of his love of J. K. Rowling's saga. The final film was much more than a simple impersonation, though. It was a ginger *noir*. Rupert, in a red hoodie and with a Liquorice Allsorts bracelet, is filmed strolling by the Thames, composing the lyrics to the song, relaxing in the tour bus and making Lego. In a nice twist, it turns out he's not Ed after all. He's his crazed stalker, who has broken into the bus. He's not composing the lyrics:

he's copying them from the album cover. He walks onstage and takes the applause of cheering fans before literally being tackled by security and strong-armed away. He passes the real Ed coming out of the lift.

Ed turned up to watch some of the filming and meet Rupert for the first time at the Forum Club on the University of Hertfordshire campus in Hatfield. Emil's film is so much more effective than a tired video of Ed and a random actress exchanging meaningful glances while sitting in front of some Lego. Rupert is actually seen smashing Lego, which is not something Ed was ever likely to do.

The success of 'Lego House' marked the end of a dream year for Ed. He even won his first award when he was named Best Breakthrough Artist at the Q Awards, run by the influential music magazine at the Grosvenor House Hotel in Park Lane, London. He was cautious about the future: 'One step at a time,' he said at the ceremony.

The challenge now was to build on the breakthrough.

PART THREE

THE SHAPE OF THINGS

16

ON PATROL

In the New Year, Ed took Nina Nesbitt for a break in Venice. She had been away touring with Example in December but that had finished before Christmas. Since she had met Ed, her life had become almost as chaotically busy as his, so this was a welcome diversion for both of them.

Even abroad, though, Ed had become easily recognisable. He wasn't too delighted when they were snapped strolling near a canal. They featured in a report in the *Daily Record*, which was a little over the top in describing Nina as his new love and claiming they had gazed into each other's eyes over lunch. The newspaper said they had been dating for a month. Apparently, she had been spending a lot of time with Ed at his flat in London.

The story was not exactly the scoop of the century but Ed was far from delighted. He mentioned it indirectly when he was interviewed by Alexis Petridis a month later. He complained that he had been papped 'with a girl who was just a friend, which was quite a shit thing to happen'. His main concern was that Alice might see the picture. There had been very little contact between them since the break-up: 'I've not really spoken to her since and the first thing she sees is me in the paper with someone else.'

Rumours about Ed and Nina were fuelled further when she featured in the video of his new single 'Drunk', the fourth track to be released from + and another top-ten hit. Nina plays the girl he is drinking to forget. She was not the star, though – that role was taken by an adorable talking cat. For the first time Ed was the central character in the storyline, drinking beer, playing computer games and strumming the guitar with his pet. Then he takes the tabby to the pub and it all goes downhill as they knock back shots and eye up sexy girls. Eventually, the cat gets into a fight and is thrown out, so they all go back to Ed's for a party.

Nina was nowhere to be seen when Ed attended the BRIT Awards at the O2 in London towards the end of February. He took his mum and dad and wore an expensive blue designer suit with a white shirt and a black tie for the occasion. He had been nominated for four awards, including Best British Album, but had already correctly predicted that Adele would win.

The night belonged to Adele, not just because she won the top award but also, more notoriously, for her reaction when the host James Corden interrupted her during her acceptance speech. She had only just begun, saying, 'I'm so proud to be flying the British flag for all of you,' when he cut her off because they were over-running on TV and Blur were waiting to finish off the evening with a medley of their hits. As she turned to leave, obviously furious, Adele flipped her middle finger towards a table of executives. Ed had won two awards – British Breakthrough Act and British Male Solo

Artist – but his triumphs were rather forgotten in this jaw-dropping exchange.

Ed had changed out of his suit into an unflattering green T-shirt to sing 'Lego House' but was back looking smart to collect his awards. He knew what he wanted to say but appeared under-rehearsed when, haltingly, he thanked his family, friends, fans, the promoters who had booked him, the radio DJs who had played him, and his label. 'I'm really bad at this,' he added.

Second time around, he remembered Stuart Camp, who was sitting at the table with John and Imogen. Modestly, he acknowledged his manager: 'He's the person that took me – a spotty, chubby, ginger teenager – to up here tonight.' In the space of just thirteen months Ed had gone from signing his record deal at the Station Hotel in Framlingham to standing onstage collecting BRIT Awards. Afterwards, when the TV cameras had gone, it was time to move on to his record label's after-party at Two Temple Place just off the Embankment. On the way to his car at 2 a.m. he needed to stop for a crafty pee, shielded from view, he hoped, by his driver. Needless to say, he was spied by an 'onlooker', who told the papers that Ed had splashed his trousers in his haste.

Earlier in the evening, Ed had missed out on the award for Best British Single for 'The A Team'. That had been won by One Direction for their romantic ballad 'What Makes You Beautiful', their debut number one. Ed was almost old news next to the surge in popularity of the all-conquering boy band.

After the success of 'Moments' and his growing friendship with Harry Styles, he set about writing some new songs for the band before he left to go on his first proper tour of the US. He had his own follow-up album to write, but Syco were planning to bring out the second One Direction album in 2012, well before the next from Ed Sheeran. He came up with 'Little Things', which turned out not to be a new song at all. He had written it with Fiona Bevan, a singer–songwriter from Suffolk. Like Stuart Camp, she had been brought up in Bury St Edmunds, but didn't come across Ed until they had both moved to London. In those days they had shared open-mic nights – part of that small club of ambitious musicians hoping to get a break. They were also both featured on a CD specially produced by IK:TOMS to help publicise new acts. Ed had contributed 'Let It Out'.

Fiona was struggling to pay the rent from small gigs alone and had turned to songwriting to boost her income. After Ed had signed his record deal, she invited him round to tea at her flat in Dalston in the hope that they might compose a song for his debut album. They hadn't co-written before but Ed was always enthusiastic about working on something new. They both wanted to write a love song. Fiona found inspiration from the novelist Virginia Woolf: 'She always looks at the minutiae and emotion of a situation. I'd been thinking about that a lot, and how the little things really represent the big things. I told Ed the idea and he loved it.'

They started putting old memories into words. In some ways, for Ed it was an extension of his song 'Wake Me Up'. Fiona recalled fondly how well they worked together: 'We were thinking of real people we loved, and the strange quirks and imperfections that made us love them. So everything in the song is real, which is a lovely thing to be able to say.'

Fiona was concerned that the song was sounding too happy and would be more effective if Ed stuck a few minor chords into the chorus. Eventually they were ready to run through the whole thing – Fiona on piano and Ed on guitar. This wasn't a session at Sticky Studios and Fiona didn't have any microphones or proper equipment in the tiny flat so they had to make a 'crappy' recording on Ed's phone. He promptly lost it – something he was prone to doing. Fiona didn't hear anything more and could only watch and admire as + soared to number one. A year or so later, she found the lyrics on a scrap of A4 paper and emailed them to him. Ed being Ed could still remember the tune.

Originally he went into the studio with a different song for the boys from One Direction. Instead, he decided to play 'Little Things'. They loved it. Their gentle stripped-back version was just as Fiona had imagined the finished track when she first heard Ed sing it. The old firm of Jake Gosling and Chris Leonard on guitar were involved in production, which probably accounts for the final version sounding so much like an Ed Sheeran song. Fiona could scarcely believe it when it went to number one at the end of the year: 'I cried because it was such a turning point in my life.' The song topped the charts in eight countries around the world and was Ed's first number one as a songwriter. He had co-written arguably the two best-loved songs of One Direction.

Ed was ready for his first getting-to-know adventure in the US. He was the opening act on Snow Patrol's American tour. As many British artists had to do, he needed to start off as a support act in order to become more widely known in the

States. At the same time, he was promoting the release of his debut album there later in the year.

'The A Team' was getting plenty of airplay but, as Ed knew from his experience in the UK, there was no substitute for building a fan base through live performances. When he started being interviewed in the US, he changed the description of his music. He was no longer acoustic hip hop. Now he was acoustic soul, which was much more radio-friendly for a mainstream audience.

Snow Patrol, the Irish–Scottish rock group, were a match made in heaven for Ed. He got on famously with them. It was during the tour that he formed a strong friendship with the keyboard player Johnny McDaid and together they would break the tedium of criss-crossing the US on tour by writing songs.

Johnny, like many of Ed's friends in music, is significantly older – in his case by some fifteen years. Ed seemed to thrive on their experience and wisdom, as if he was channelling the respect he had for his dad into new friendships. They already shared a mutual friend in Example. Johnny had co-written 'Say Nothing', which, in September, would be the lead single of the rapper's 2012 album *The Evolution of Man*. Born and brought up in Derry, Johnny had been the singer in London-based rock band Vega4 before signing to Snow Patrol's publishing company as a songwriter in 2009. He didn't join the group until a little later and had missed their golden years when 'Chasing Cars' was voted the most popular song of the noughties.

Ed and Johnny wrote two songs on the tour, 'Nina' and 'Photograph', both inspired by Nina Nesbitt – although the latter could be an observation about anyone who had only a photograph as a reminder of an absent lover. They finished the track in Denver when the tour played The Fillmore in the city.

Ed was becoming more obsessed with tattoos and was starting to fill his sleeve with important moments in his life. 'Photograph' contained a line about kissing under a lamppost on 6th Street. Many thought that must have been New York but it was in Denver. As a memento Ed had a tattoo '6 St' inked on his left arm. Embarrassingly, he later discovered he was actually on 6th *Avenue* but it was too late to correct it. He also had a drawing of a large snowflake representing his tour with Snow Patrol and the great time he'd had.

Unusually for a support act, Ed received almost as many reviews as Snow Patrol. His connection with One Direction, and the inclusion of 'Moments' on the deluxe edition of their album, seemed to attract an excited swathe of teenage girls. According to the *Orange County Register*, his fans 'shrieked their lungs out' through his entire half-hour performance at the Fox Theater in Pomona, California. The reviewer particularly noticed the 'vulnerable' opening song, 'Give Me Love', which was currently Ed's favourite track to perform and one in which he divided the crowd to encourage them to sing back at him. At the time, it was a low-profile song on the album, perhaps because it was one of the last to be written and had not featured in many of his concerts over the years. He was particularly proud of it, though. Ed was getting accustomed to the screaming now. He usually made a reference to it to get the crowd laughing: 'If there's more singing and less screaming, I think the world would be a better place.'

During Snow Patrol's set, Ed would come back onstage to perform a duet of 'New York', the band's elegiac ballad from their 2011 album *Fallen Empires*. The theme of the song – about missing somebody you have loved – was familiar to Ed. He and charismatic lead singer Gary Lightbody, would often have an arm around each other while they sang, just as two friends might on their way home from the pub.

After he finished the song, Ed, ever the professional, would leave the stage, walk briskly to the merchandising desk and make himself available to fans for pictures and autographs. He would sign CDs and T-shirts or just chat, making sure to remind them that he would be headlining his own tour in the US later in the year. There was always a long line. Ed's attention to the commercial detail was paying off. As one reviewer pointed out then, Snow Patrol had 100,000 Twitter followers; Ed had two million.

Ed did not perform the last few dates on the tour. He left after Phoenix, Arizona. Gary Lightbody was generous in his praise of Ed's contribution: 'He has lit up the tour and our lives and is a brother of ours for ever.' He wrote in his blog that Ed was not like other pop stars because there was 'no one pulling his strings in the shadows; no Svengali writing his songs and telling him what to wear. Everything he has done he has done on his own terms and all his songs are his own.' Gary predicted world domination for Ed by the end of the year: 'He's the complete pop star.'

Newspapers speculated wildly that he had left the tour to enter rehab. He issued an official denial, the first time he had needed to do that. In fact he had come home to attend his godparents' wedding and sing them 'Kiss Me' as promised.

The trip back coincided with the annual Ivor Novello Awards at the Grosvenor House Hotel in London. For a songwriter this is a more significant evening than the BRITS. Ed won Best Song Musically and Lyrically for 'The A Team'. Dressed in a suit and tie, he looked more like a school prefect than an idolised pop star when he collected his Ivor from singer David Gray. He was ecstatic: 'It's the highest kind of award you can get for songwriting – a big honour.' It was especially satisfying because he beat Adele's 'Rolling in the Deep', although she did pick up the premier title, Songwriter of the Year.

Nina Nesbitt wasn't there. She was appearing live at King Tut's Wah Wah Hut in Glasgow. While Ed was away, she had been working hard on her first EP, *The Apple Tree*, produced by Jake Gosling, and was also taking on more gigs. She was asked about Ed Sheeran in interviews and would be for years to come. She invariably denied any relationship. The situation was a difficult one – she wanted to be taken seriously for her own work and not just for her connection to Ed. But, then again, the *Guardian* reviewed *The Apple Tree* and referred to her as 'Ed Sheeran's other half'.

She would find it extremely difficult to ignore the subject if and when 'Nina' and 'Photograph' appeared on his next album. They were certainly running parallel lives and it's impossible to know whether 'Nina' is mostly autobiography or artistic licence. An insider observes somewhat harshly, 'It was a romance. It was very beneficial to her to be in that romance.'

While he had been away in the US, Ed had some sad news. A teenage girl called Abigail Fleming had died from bone cancer. In February, he had paid a secret visit to the

Bluebell Wood Children's Hospice in Sheffield where she was being cared for during her last days. Seeing Ed play live was on her bucket list of things to do but she was too ill for that to happen. So he took a guitar, caught the train up from London and played 'Lego House' and 'The A Team' at her bedside. Abigail gave Ed a card and a key-ring and he gave her one of Imogen's bracelets. Her mum Maria said afterwards, 'She loved it. He didn't just make her day. It made her life.'

Afterwards Ed told the hospice that he would auction his Lego collection to raise funds. The Sheeran family had long been supporters of their local East Anglia Children's Hospice (EACH) in Suffolk. A couple of years before, Ed had sung at a fundraiser organised by Woodbridge School that raised nearly £2,000 for the cause.

Imogen, meanwhile, supported the local EACH branch in Framlingham by giving them jewellery she had made, which they proudly displayed in the shop window. Her bracelets received national attention when the Duchess of Cambridge wore one when she made her first public speech. Kate had chosen a Smartie-inspired design of bright purple and orange beads. The bracelet was clearly visible when she wielded a spade to plant a commemorative tree in the grounds of the charity's Treehouse Hospice in Ipswich. Ed was thrilled and did not exactly adopt a restrained tone: 'Big up Kate Middleton who is wearing some of my mum's homemade jewellery,' he tweeted on the day. Imogen had already decided that all the proceeds from sales of that design would go to EACH, so this was a wonderful advertisement.

He continued the family's royal connection by appearing at one of the biggest events of the year in the UK – the Queen's

Diamond Jubilee concert. The celebration on a stage outside Buckingham Palace was seen by more than 15 million television viewers in the UK, as well as thousands of well-wishers crowding into the Mall and local parks. The participants included legends of music from throughout the Queen's reign – Shirley Bassey, Tom Jones, Cliff Richard, Elton John and Paul McCartney, who topped the bill as he does on these national occasions. Ed was the new boy. He gave a classy performance of the 'The A Team', which was still his best-known hit at the time. He performed before the Queen arrived, which was probably just as well as his song was about a teenage prostitute, Angel, who was addicted to crack cocaine. In a strange coincidence, Annie Lennox was on next and performed 'There Must Be an Angel'.

The event was quite cheesy and middle-of-the-road but Ed stood out. Neil McCormick of the *Daily Telegraph* noted his 'tender acoustic performance', which sounded oddly out of place: 'It was like an outbreak of authenticity at a camp cabaret.'

Afterwards, Ed was introduced formally to the Queen by Kylie Minogue. The best part of the day, though, was when Paul McCartney came over to speak to him. Ed was with his father, who had been a fan for many years. He was able to introduce them: 'Paul, meet Dad. Dad, meet Paul.' It was a lovely moment and Ed declared it to be the highlight of his year.

17

MOVING SWIFTLY ON

Before he left for two sold-out gigs in New York, Ed bought a house. He paid £895,000 for a six-bedroom mansion in a village a few miles from Framlingham. He had both feet on the property ladder at the age of twenty-one. He wasn't getting started with a basement flat in Ipswich. His new home was a hall, which suggested that this was a very desirable residence.

Ed had spent months looking for the right investment. One of the reasons he had waited so long to negotiate an advantageous publishing deal with Sony/ATV was that he wanted to maximise the amount of cash at his disposal: 'I wanted to buy a house. I thought, If everything fucks up, I've still got a house.' He had looked at several properties within a twenty-mile radius of where he was brought up, which caused great excitement in local villages when they thought Ed might be moving in. In the end, he chose the grand house, set in three and a half acres of land, just down the road from his mum and dad. Originally, he saw the hall as a party house where he could entertain old friends from school and his new ones in the music business – a crash pad in the country 'for me and my mates'. That ambition revealed there was nobody special in his life at the time – the relationship with Nina Nesbitt had fizzled out. He had big plans to turn the property into something that wouldn't have looked out of place in Beverly Hills. He wasted little time in buying the sixteenth-century Grade II-listed farmhouse next door for £450,000. Already, he was thinking in terms of an estate rather than a bolthole.

Ed's home had the precious advantage of privacy. Motorists speeding past on the school run couldn't really see the house because it was set back from the road down its own driveway – photographers with long lenses couldn't get a look either. The slight drawback of its location was that a car was essential. Ed couldn't drive yet so he needed to ask his dad or his friends to ferry him around when he was in Suffolk, although he could call on the services of a local driver whenever he wanted to. He needed to start some driving lessons but had no time. He could cycle if he was going to the pub, although he tended not to frequent the local, perhaps because it was too close and might attract unwelcome gawpers.

His desire to put his money into property followed some sound advice from Goldie. They had kept in touch since the drum and bass pioneer had seen a young Ed perform at the Access to Music concert. Ed explained, 'When my first single charted he rung me up and had this long proper in-depth chat with me. He was like "Never buy anything extravagant other than property."' Ed, who appreciated the value of money, was keen to follow this advice, especially as his friend Example had done the same thing when he initially found success. However, his first priority when he had a few noughts in his bank account was to pay off his parents' mortgage.

Now free from financial concerns, his mum and dad were able to pursue their own ambitions. When the children left home, John had embarked on a series of acclaimed art lectures. He gave more than eighty talks entitled 'Discover the Great Painters', which described the work of his favourite artists from the thirteenth century to the present day. He planned to expand the idea to describe the great masterpieces of a particular historical period, starting with the Italian Renaissance. The scale of his ambition reveals that the Sheeran family work ethic was by no means confined to the younger son. Imogen, according to Ed, was still happiest sitting with her cat at home and making her jewellery. Ed was fiercely proud of all his family – and they of him.

His brother Matthew, meanwhile, had been making giant strides in the competitive arena of classical music. His was not a world where fame would come calling suddenly, with a number-one hit record. Unlike Ed, he needed to progress academically. At the University of Sussex, he won the Thomas Beecham Scholarship – named after the great conductor – as an outstanding instrumentalist for his violin playing. His ambitions lay in composition. While still an undergraduate, he won the Presteigne Festival Competition for British Composers Under 35 for an original piece entitled 'Dreamtime'. He then claimed the Chairman of the Jury Award at the Shipley Arts Festival in West Sussex. In 2011, after taking a year out to work and study in Italy and Germany, he began a master's degree at King's College, London, and moved in temporarily with Ed, who finally had his own place in the capital.

In 2012, the year Ed set about breaking America, Matthew quietly graduated from King's with a MMus (Master of Music) degree in composition. The two brothers tried writing together but they didn't connect. They had different ways of looking at music. Matthew, as ever, was fascinated by theory and the challenge of composing in different styles and genres. He particularly enjoyed writing for film – the opposite of Ed's song videos, where the visuals were inspired by the music.

When Matthew moved out, Ed's long-term housemate was Briony Gaffer, an old friend from Thomas Mills. She had been in school musicals with him, including *Grease*, and had moved to London after graduating in English from the University of Sheffield, where she was publicity secretary for the Hip Hop Society. At first she worked as a fashion journalist, then moved into the world of styling. Eventually she took a job with Atlantic and was involved in TV promotions, including campaigns for Ed.

Briony was bubbly, vivacious and great company. Basically, she looked after the place, tidying and cleaning up after Ed. She cooked him chips and eggy bread while he unblocked the sink after she had washed her hair. They were like an old married couple, except there was no romance. He described her as 'a good lass'. She and Ed would enjoy funny Twitter conversations when he was away, which kept his fans amused, particularly when she sent him a picture of two cute kittens sitting on his bed.

She was left in charge when he flew to New York in June 2012. He was playing two gigs as part of the promotion for the release of + in the US. The first was at the Bowery Ballroom, followed by the Music Hall of Williamsburg in

Brooklyn the next night. During the day there was television, including NBC's *Today* show and VH1's *Big Morning Buzz Live*. Both concert venues, which had a capacity of about 550, sold out in ten minutes. Ed was clearly becoming better known in the States, thanks to a careful strategy by Atlantic. Like other artists trying to break America, he had to get used to the musical time delay: back in the UK, 'Small Bump' had just been released as the fifth single from the album. In America, however, + was fresh and new.

While he was in New York, Ed met up with Si Hulbert. His friend was also on a working trip to the US but got together with Ed to see some gigs. He also went along to both of Ed's performances to offer his support. They were vintage Ed from a man who knew how to make a connection with his audience. He stopped their hollering by his usual tactic of simply asking everyone to be quiet. Si recalls, 'The whole audience fell silent. And then he started playing "Small Bump" and all the phones went up in the air. It was just amazing.'

After the gig, Ed, Si and Stuart Camp were travelling in the back of a New York yellow taxi cab when they decided to check American iTunes to see how + was doing. The album was number one! 'He was stupidly excited,' recalls Si. 'He didn't get egotistical about it. There was no arrogance, like you might get with other artists. He was just like an excited kid.'

On the official Billboard 200, + went in at number five with sales of 41,000, which was still a great result. The album was number one in the folk-album chart. The majority of sales were digital downloads, which explained its success on iTunes.

While he was in the US, his first headlining tour was announced. The *VH1 You Oughta Know Tour with Ed Sheeran* would play twelve major cities, beginning with Boston in September and ending in Seattle in early October. This was big news for Ed because the tour was a trusted showcase for breakthrough acts and had helped promote Bruno Mars and Amy Winehouse in the past. Even more important to Ed in his ongoing efforts to break America was Stuart Camp's introduction to Taylor Swift. As has happened so often for Ed, it began as a songwriting initiative. The management teams for both artists had been in contact, realising that they could help one another in their own countries.

Taylor was aware of Ed's music, having heard and liked 'Lego House' when she was on tour in Australia in March 2012. The following month Ed performed in her home town of Nashville, which presented the opportunity for their respective 'people' to be in touch. Taylor Swift was little more than a year older than Ed but she was already a superstar. She had been brought up very comfortably in Reading, Pennsylvania, with idyllic summers spent at a holiday home near the beach in New Jersey. Her parents had a business background but they encouraged their highly intelligent daughter to express herself and explore the pursuits she most enjoyed – acting and music.

Throughout her life there are uncanny parallels with Ed's. She suffered bullying at school for being different. As Ed put it, neither of them was the most popular kid in school. Taylor's unhappiness with her peer group was one reason for her mum and dad's move to Nashville. Another was that their clearly talented fourteen-year-old daughter could pursue her musical ambitions. Her first album, *Taylor Swift*, won her recognition as a country artist and, more importantly, as a songwriter. Her second album, *Fearless*, enabled her to cross over from country to mainstream. She won the Grammy Award for Album of the Year in 2010. At the age of twenty, she was the youngest-ever recipient.

When she met Ed, she had just completed the *Speak Now World Tour* in support of her third album. She played 110 dates around the world before an estimated combined audience of 1.64 million. The figures were boggling, with tour receipts totalling more than $123 million. At the end of the tour, she needed to finish writing and recording her fourth album, which was scheduled for an autumn release. That was where Ed would come in. Her songs were particularly personal, which would often lead to speculation in the press on whom they were about.

Superficially, Ed's style of articulate and emotional lyrics would be a perfect match for Taylor. They wouldn't know until they tried whether they would gel or even like each other. They first met at his hotel in Phoenix and bonded over a burger. Ed was impressed that his very slim companion wasn't existing on a diet of fresh air. 'She's such a sweetheart,' he gushed, although there was no question of any spark between them. 'Too tall' was his rather blunt observation when pressed about the possibility. (She is five foot ten, and he is two inches shorter.) More significantly he appreciated her work ethic and thought her love of music shone through: 'She's not in it for anything else.'

Taylor was equally appreciative: 'You know when you really like someone and you meet them and it's a let-down? It definitely wasn't like that with Ed.' They wrote a song at her house in Beverly Hills, bouncing on a trampoline in the garden.

'Everything Had Changed' was very melodic with an anthemic chorus and probably sounded more like an Ed Sheeran song than one from Taylor Swift. Ed revealed that Taylor had written most of it before he became involved, although he did contribute a very important chord to the chorus.

In the small world of music, the backing vocals were provided by Gary Lightbody. He was in town when they were recording and popped into the studio in LA to talk to Taylor about a song he had written that he thought she would love. 'The Last Time' would feature on the new album, *Red*.

Ed and Taylor clicked in a genuine way. Her friends liked him and, importantly, so did her cats. By the time Ed flew home for a busy summer of concerts, he had been pencilled in for one of the biggest musical events of 2013 – Taylor Swift's *Red* tour. He added a tattoo of the name of the album to the growing set of images on his left arm. Ed was reassured to be told that if they fell out he could dispense with the R and it would just read 'Ed'.

Back in the UK, Ed took part in the second great occasion of the year – the closing ceremony of the London Olympics. The evening was entitled *A Symphony of British Music* and featured many of the nation's pop highlights during the past fifty years. Ed, with just one album to his name, performed on a bill that included The Who, Ray Davies, George Michael and, most memorably, the Spice Girls, who were perched on top of a fleet of black cabs.

Ed followed Annie Lennox to sing 'Wish You Were Here', one of the most iconic Pink Floyd songs. Once again it revealed Ed's bravery in performing such a well-loved song in front of a worldwide audience estimated at 750 million. In the

UK alone, the viewing figure as more than 26 million. Ed, naturally wearing a red hoodie, was backed by his first super group: the Floyd's drummer Nick Mason, guitarist Mike Rutherford from Genesis and Richard Jones of The Feeling on bass. Ed sang it simply, with no gimmicks, although his interpretation did not please all the Pink Floyd purists. His choice – and Nick's presence – however, neatly spanned the generations. For once, all eyes weren't on Ed: during the song, a man walked across a tightrope in the sky behind him.

Afterwards, Ed said that this appearance and his earlier one at the Queen's Diamond Jubilee were the two performances he would be telling his grandkids about. At both, he took his parents along for the day.

Ed was headlining his own UK tour that autumn and asked Foy Vance to be his support – another example of him leaving the ladder down. Ed had remained a big fan since he had first heard him and was thrilled when they finally met the previous year and shared some whiskey after the Arthur's Day Festival in Dublin. Foy recalled generously, 'We handed a guitar back and forth playing our songs. I knew instantly he was a special guy with a real heart.'

Ed couldn't understand why more people didn't appreciate Foy's talent. On tour, Ed enjoyed his company and the pair would stay up often into the small hours, drinking, writing songs and swapping stories. Sometimes Foy would be looking after his ten-year-old daughter Ella. She and Ed became firm friends when he discovered she liked Lego almost as much as he did. She was also the opposite of star-struck. Ed tells an amusing story of her turning down the opportunity to have her picture taken with Niall Horan from One Direction.

The + tour got under way with three nights at the HMV Hammersmith Apollo. His friends were pleased to see that his success hadn't changed Ed at all. Si Hulbert remarks, 'He literally gave everybody the time of day. He would socialise with people. When people nipped outside for a cigarette, he would be out there making a roll-up with the sound guy, with the guy who was making the coffee, with the guy who works behind the bar; and talking to everybody equally.' His cigarette breaks did slightly worry the powers that be, who were concerned that he wasn't doing his voice any favours, but Ed was a young man who knew his own mind and pretty much did what he wanted.

Not every gig went as well as the London ones. Ed became thoroughly disenchanted with the audience at the Empress Ballroom in Blackpool when they wouldn't shut up during Foy Vance's opening set. On that particular night, the venue was crowded with hen and stag parties up from Manchester and Liverpool. Ed coasted through his own set of familiar favourites but couldn't get them to pipe down. They ruined his duet with Foy on 'Kiss Me' and weren't any better for 'Guiding Light'. Then, during the encore, he sang 'Wonderwall', which he never played. He can't bear the Oasis song so everyone who knew him immediately realised something was wrong. At that point he should have been singing 'The Parting Glass' a cappella without a microphone.

One eyewitness explained, 'He was in a strop. People just weren't listening so "Wonderwall" was giving them a two-fingered salute without them realising. Then he smashed his guitar onstage – a £3,000 handmade guitar. The atmosphere was fucking horrible.'

Fortunately, that night was forgotten by the time he reached Barrowlands in Glasgow. 'Wonderwall' was not played. Instead, Paolo Nutini joined him onstage to sing his 2009 hit 'Candy'. As it was the last night of the tour, everyone was in a party mood and got very drunk.

The week had been a good one. Then Ed was a guest on *The X Factor* for the first time, singing 'Give Me Love', which had been released as the sixth and final single from +. He appeared on the Sunday semi-final show the day after One Direction had performed 'Little Things', so it was a good weekend for Ed songs.

Ed and Harry Styles were still good buddies, spending time together when their schedules coincided. In LA, for instance, Ed was there when Harry spent several thousand dollars on pizza and drove around the city handing it out to the many homeless people on the streets. Harry joined him when Ed was tattooed with a drawing of his favourite childhood TV character, Pingu the Penguin. Harry settled for just 'Pingu' inked on his left arm.

Ed remained completely silent when the media became excited by the brief relationship between Harry and Taylor Swift. One reason Ed and Taylor became so close was that they didn't gossip about each other. They might speak about writing songs and hanging out together but they never betrayed each other's confidence. Harry and Taylor were photographed for the first time when they dressed in woolly coats for an early December stroll around Central Park in New York. Ed was nowhere to be seen when Taylor flew into the UK for her birthday and joined Harry for a photo opportunity on his home patch in Cheshire. They went to the

George and Dragon in Great Budsworth and had a Chinese takeaway. A month later they broke up. Ed has never said a word about it.

In the future, Taylor would apparently write songs about Harry and vice versa. By not spelling things out, she could use the mystery as a marketing tool every time she had a new album to promote. When *Red* was released, much of the publicity centred on the huge-selling lead single, 'We Are Never Ever Getting Back Together', and the speculation about the subject's identity. The most common suggestion was the actor Jake Gyllenhaal from whom she had split earlier in the year, but she never confirmed it.

Ed has always been very straightforward about the inspiration for his songs. He hadn't played that sort of guessing game – yet.

18

THE UNIVERSAL SHUSH

Ed never stopped. Before the *Red* tour began, he had some headlining dates to fulfil in the US. When he and Foy Vance played Stage AE in Pittsburgh in January 2013, they took the afternoon off and decided to get tattoos as a permanent reminder of their friendship. They chose a line from 'Guiding Light' translated into Gaelic: 'When I need to get home, you're the light that guides me.' The lyrics in Old Irish are on the gravestone of Johnny McDaid's father, the respected Derry community leader John McDaid, who had died in 2011. Foy had sung it at the funeral. He wrote out the words for Ed's tattoo. Ed did the same for his friend, who laughed: 'It's become a bit of a bromance.'

For the moment Ed was not seeing much of his home. In fact, he was thinking of leaving the UK altogether for the foreseeable future. While the builders began the improvements he wanted on his Suffolk property, he decided he needed his own place in the US. He was, after all, going to be spending most of the coming year there so it made sense and would be a sound investment. He explained why he was going abroad:

'I think it's important to give the UK public a little bit of a break.' The States was the obvious choice because he intended to record much of his second album there. Although + had done very well in the US, his record company believed a move to America might improve the commercial prospects of the follow-up.

Ed was also drawn to Australia and New Zealand but it made more practical sense to settle across the Atlantic. Taylor lived in Nashville and she was keen for him to become a neighbour. He liked the attitude of the people he had met in the city. They were not impressed by celebrity. 'I don't think they'd care even if they knew who you were.' He liked the musical tradition, obviously, and the countryside, while the relaxed atmosphere reminded him of Framlingham. 'Nashville is full of very nice people,' he said.

His new home was an hour from the city, in an idyllic spot next to a lake. The house, which cost about $2 million, had four bedrooms and bathrooms as well as a swimming pool – although it didn't really need one when the lake was at the end of the garden. Ed found swimming slightly problematic and needed to wear ear plugs or run the risk of a burst eardrum. Taylor's house was an easy drive away. Her portfolio was handled by her astute father, Scott, who ran his own financial-advice company. He had encouraged her to build a property empire. Ed intended to follow a similar path. As well as their connection with music, Ed and Taylor shared a similar bond with their parents. Family came first for Taylor, and Ed fully appreciated that. When Taylor became successful, one of the first things she did was buy her parents a new $2.5-million home in Nashville.

Ed's move to the US was a further indication of his commitment to becoming a major star there. In 2012, despite his high profile in the UK, he had probably spent longer in America, and that presence would become even more pronounced when he began the *Red* tour. He reasoned that the new house would be the ideal retreat where he could write songs and work on the next album between gigs. He'd already invited Johnny McDaid to join him so that they could work together.

Before then, he attended the Grammys for the first time. 'The A Team' was nominated for Best Song but missed out to 'We Are Young' by Fun, featuring Janelle Monáe. Ed was in smart mode – clean-shaven, wearing a Burberry suit and admitting on the red carpet that he found it 'all a bit intense'. He correctly predicted that he wouldn't win and was more concerned with performing well during his first-ever duet with Elton John.

The organisers had been reluctant to let Ed perform solo, reasoning that he was not yet a big-enough name for the premier music-awards show. Elton stepped in to save the day, even though 'The A Team', which they sang on the night, did not exactly suit him. They ran through it just four times before their spot, and it was a tribute to Elton's professionalism that it went so well. When they had finished they shared a high five.

Amusingly, Ed rolled up to the after party a little late to discover that his mum and dad had already met everyone famous and were having a great time. He had his own celebration a week later when he turned twenty-two. He had to play a gig first at the Nokia Theater in Los Angeles. Randomly, he dressed up as a pirate for the occasion.

The *LA Times* went along and couldn't believe the way Ed controlled a crowd of 7,000 mainly teenage girls screaming at him as if he were Justin Bieber. He was like the 'most awesome counsellor at a summer camp'. Ed varies the song in which he employs the 'universal shush' – this time persuading the crowd to be silent for 'Wayfaring Stranger'.

Afterwards, Ed went backstage and chatted to Elton, Adele and the famous producer Rick Rubin, who had come to see the show. Rick was a character you couldn't miss in a crowd – his long flowing hair and beard made him stand out as a throwback to the great rock groups of the seventies. He was the founder of Def Jam Records, former chairman of Columbia Records, and is one of the most famous names in American music. He was the producer of, among others, Kanye West, Justin Timberlake and Shakira. He'd also won numerous Grammys, including one for Adele's *21*. He was just the person Ed wanted to work with on his next album.

Later, Ed started on the Jägerbombs – Jägermeister and Red Bull – helpfully provided by friends who had flown over from the UK especially to wish him a happy birthday. The night went downhill after the first seven or so drinks. Ed was merely enjoying himself like any other young man in his early twenties. He liked a drink or two and it was his birthday, after all. He ended up being thrown fully clothed into a swimming pool. His phone did not survive the dip.

Despite his success selling out venues like the Nokia Theater, which held 8,000 people, Ed was about to become a support act again. It made sense, as he would play sixty-six dates with Taylor on her *Red* tour in front of more than a million people.

His record company decided not rush out a second album when his profile was rising so well without it.

Ed still had further dates to fill for +. His old friend Passenger joined him for a short Australian tour. They had remained close since they'd shared cigarette breaks outside The Living Room in Cambridge. That was a long way removed from the Challenge Stadium in Perth, where the tour opened in late February 2013. Passenger had just enjoyed a breakthrough year when his multimillion-selling ballad 'Let Her Go' became one of the biggest songs of the previous twelve months. He had supported Ed at various gigs in the past and observed, 'It's really exciting for me and it's good for him because he has a mate on the road with him and not some stranger.'

The other act with Ed was Gabrielle Aplin, a twenty-year-old singer–songwriter from Wiltshire, who was just making a name for herself. She had followed the Ed path of self-releasing her first EP when she was seventeen and building up an online following on Myspace and YouTube. She had become more widely known when she recorded a version of 'The Power of Love' by Frankie Goes to Hollywood for the John Lewis Christmas commercial. When she joined Ed, she was gearing up for the release of her first album, *English Rain*, on Parlophone. Her voice has a purity that perfectly complemented Ed's when she took over the Foy Vance role on the tour for the duet of 'Kiss Me'.

Ed particularly enjoyed his trips to Australia and New Zealand because no one bothered him and he didn't have to worry about photographers. Nobody was too concerned, therefore, when Gabrielle's sultry tour manager, Athina

Andrelos, took his eye. Athina's parents are Greek, which accounts for her dark Mediterranean looks and dazzling smile. She had grown up in the Surrey commuter belt and gone to Surbiton High School but retained a strong sense of pride in her heritage. As a child, she attended Greek classes every Saturday morning and would dance in national costume for Greek Independence Day in March. After she left school, she worked unpaid as an intern at a management company before finding a job as a radio plugger. When she met Ed, she had been taken on by James Barnes Music in London, which represented Gabrielle and Newton Faulkner. She was an assistant music manager so, basically, she was Gabrielle's PA and buddy on tour.

She was also a singer on the London pub circuit with a guitar-led indie group called Joia, which means 'jewel' in Portuguese. The band had produced their first EP, *Match Light*, and received some radio attention. One critic noted Athina's impressive vocal range but felt Joia needed to work on their visual presentation: 'It's as if Eva Longoria was stepping out with the new collection from Topman.' An early interview gave an indication of Athina's fiery temperament. She was asked about her songwriting method and replied: 'If you piss me off, I'll write a song about you. Simple as that.'

Her musical progress had stalled, and the ambitious Athina was keeping her options open for a career behind the scenes. Nobody knew she had met Ed when he moved on to the *Red* tour. The media wrongly thought he only had eyes for Taylor.

Ed finished up at the Vector Arena in Auckland just four days before he opened for Taylor in front of nearly 30,000 people at the Century Link Center in Omaha, Nebraska, in

March 2013. He concentrated on tracks from + although, as a novelty, he included an acoustic version of the Britney Spears's classic '... Baby One More Time'. He came back onstage halfway through Taylor's set for a duet of 'Everything Has Changed', which had been number one on iTunes.

Right from the beginning of the tour, he had to deal with rumours that he was in a relationship with Taylor. He even had to contend with stories that she had ditched Harry Styles for him, gossip he condemned as 'lazy journalism'. He told Piers Morgan on *CNN Live*, 'I think you can be friends with someone without having to sleep with them. I've got morals.'

He enjoyed socialising with Taylor. He fondly recalled nights after the show where they would just play music. One memorable evening they were joined by Johnny McDaid, Foy Vance and Ellie Goulding. They sat in a circle and took turns to sing a song before passing the guitar to the next person. For her part, Taylor liked nothing better than Ed bursting into her hotel room to play her a new song. She loved being in at the beginning of something, then following it through. She observed, 'All those memories and a piece of art at the end connected with it.'

When the world realised there was nothing to the rumours of Ed with Taylor, they turned their attention first to the high-profile actress and singer Selina Gomez and then to Ellie. Selina had previously been the girlfriend of Justin Bieber and had just completed filming the action thriller *Getaway* when rumours surfaced that she was going out with Ed. In reality, she was a member of Taylor's girl squad, an entourage of close friends who would join her on tour occasionally. Ed was an honorary member of the squad.

Ellie, too, was a friend of Taylor's. Stories about her and Ed seemed to have more substance when they were seen holding hands at the MTV Video Music Awards (VMAs) at the Barclays Center in Brooklyn in August. At one point, Ed put his hand on her thigh. Newspapers immediately concluded that they were in a relationship. The situation was made more intriguing by the involvement of Niall Horan, whom she had apparently been kissing at the V Festival in Chelmsford the previous week. Ellie was very clear and constant that she was not in a relationship with Ed and never had been: 'I love that holding hands with my friends means that we are an item.' Ellie was next to Rita Ora while Emil Nava sat on Ed's other side. This was not exactly a cosy candlelit date in an out-of-the-way bistro.

Gossip was further fuelled by the song 'Don't', which appeared on Ed's next album. The track is about cheating, which everybody could relate to – according to Ed. More precisely it tells the story of a celebrity relationship he's having that dissolves when she disappears from their hotel room to have sex with another. He said it was therapeutic for him to write it, although it is a very untypical Ed song. For the first and only time he went along with the tabloid guessing game. Newspapers studied the evidence and concluded that Ellie had cheated on Ed with Niall. She's had to deny the story continually through the years – but has never wavered. Ed said it was about discovering another side to someone you thought was sweet. One of the obvious truths about songs is that they attract more publicity if they're negative.

Ed was happy to confirm that he'd had a fling or two on tour with some of Taylor's famous friends. He told *Rolling Stone* magazine that it was very easy: 'I would often find myself in situations just kind of waking up and looking over and being like, "How the fuck did that happen?"'

He undoubtedly had his moments, although this sort of boy bravado is not typical of a man who once said that he treated any girl he went to bed with as a potential girlfriend, which tended to put them off. He was in philosophical mood when a radio DJ asked him a trite question about what he looked for in a girl. He answered, 'The only thing you are left with at the end of your life is conversation – so someone who has good conversation.'

Despite the distractions, Ed was well on the way to completing the follow-up to +. He had composed many songs with Johnny and Foy but was finding Nashville less convenient than he'd thought it would be. He moved on to Los Angeles, where time had been set aside for him to record with Rick Rubin at his Shangri-La Studios in Malibu. Rubin's signature stripped-down sound was just right for Ed.

A less likely collaboration occurred after Pharrell Williams tweeted at the Grammys that 'This "Angels to Fly" song is great.' Ed, in his customary bold fashion, marched up to him later in the evening and introduced himself. They exchanged numbers and agreed they would get together soon. Everything Pharrell touched seemed to turn to gold (or, more probably, platinum). In 2013 he was the featured artist and co-writer on two of the biggest hits of the year, 'Blurred Lines' and 'Get Lucky'. He also wrote 'Happy' for the film *Despicable Me 2*, a song that would end up selling more than ten million copies.

Ed and his record company were understandably keen to associate with such phenomenal success. As an eleven-year-old, Ed had loved Justin Timberlake's first solo single 'Like I

Love You', which had incorporated hip hop into a strong melody. Pharrell and his partner in The Neptunes, Chad Hugo, had co-written and produced the track. Ed was hoping for some of that magic when he went in for a songwriting session at Pharrell's studios in LA. To his surprise, Pharrell seemed to be conducting three sessions in the building at the same time – flitting in and out to see how Ed was getting on with some beats he had laid down.

At first they didn't gel. Ed thought Pharrell's chords were too jazzy and wasn't enthusiastic even when Pharrell picked up on a riff he was playing. He persevered, however, and a song began to take shape, which he hoped sounded a little like Justin. They called it 'Sing' and it was nothing like his usual material. The lyric was inspired by one drunken night in Las Vegas with Psy, the man behind the hit 'Gangnam Style', and his Korean friends. Ed spent most of the evening trying to get off with a young woman while smoking a little weed and getting progressively drunk. Many of Ed's songs reference drink but a few talk about 'illegal weed', as he called it in 'Nina'. Elton John, a notorious hellraiser in his younger days, later said of Ed, 'He's not a big druggie but he likes a drink. He's a lot of fun.'

Ed was certainly in party mood when he flew to Ibiza for Jake Gosling's wedding. He tried MDMA mixed with a mojito cocktail. The effect was memorable: 'I fell in love with a bean-bag,' he recalled. 'I felt anxiety. I felt love. I felt warm. I felt a bit weird.' He wrote a song called 'Bloodstream' about the experience and told his mum and dad. He decided that once was enough. He told Spotify, 'I am not a big drug taker.' Alcohol remained his stimulant of choice.

Ed was enjoying his time based in Los Angeles. Ever since the early days when he had met Jamie Foxx, he'd had no trouble fitting in with the Hollywood A-list. He made new celebrity friends, including Courtney Cox and Jennifer Aniston, who both lived in Malibu. During one particularly lively party at Jennifer's home, he 'drank too much', eventually passing out on one of her poolside sofas. The next day he was round at Courtney Cox's beach house for yet another party. He had famously introduced Courtney to Johnny McDaid a few months before and the two had started dating, becoming officially engaged a year later.

His last big event in the US was to headline three nights at Madison Square Garden in New York. They weren't consecutive. Originally he was booked for one night – 1 November – but that sold out in three minutes so he added another date a week before and a third the week after. He had always dreamed of selling out the iconic venue. His dad had often spoken to him about it while Ed was growing up. When he had mentioned the prospect to his US management, they had thought he might manage it on his second or third album. But here he was, still playing +.

He announced it would be the last time he played the now familiar set. He had been touring the album for two and a half years. Snow Patrol joined him onstage for 'New York'. It was just like old times but what a difference a year makes: now they were the guests. Taylor came on during one show to sing 'Everything Has Changed' with him, and the crowd exploded with delight. This time the universal shush for the 20,000-strong audience was 'The Parting Glass'. The effect was slightly spoiled when a girl shouted, 'Have my babies', and the concert hall dissolved into a fit of giggles. Again the silence was broken when another girl shouted the same offer, but using the F-word. Ed stopped singing and said, 'I bet she came here with her dad.'

Madison Square Garden is, of course, the most famous venue in boxing as well as an important concert hall. Ed was so thrilled that he soon sported a new tattoo on his right arm of three boxing gloves, which also honoured a man who could truly appreciate its significance, his grandfather Bill Sheeran. Sadly, the following month Bill died, aged eighty-six, at home in Ireland. The family were devastated, even though he had suffered from Alzheimer's disease for many years.

Two weeks before Bill's death, Ed had begun writing the moving song 'Afire Love'. At the Grammys in January 2014, he wore a smart designer suit with his grandfather's British Boxing Board of Control tie and tweeted, 'Cheers Gucci for the suit and shoes. Gonna wear my grandad's tie, though.'

19
THINKING OUT LOUD

The throng of teenagers peering through the window of the Station Hotel in Framlingham could scarcely believe their eyes. It really was Taylor Swift having a drink with Ed Sheeran – in their sleepy town.

They were fairly used to Ed. The sight of him queuing for an Indian takeaway with a rapper or two did not send social media into meltdown, but this was different. Obviously a crowd gathered but, it being rural Suffolk, everyone was well behaved. The mood in the Sheeran household understandably was a little subdued following Bill's death so it was probably a relief that Taylor's visit didn't turn into media circus.

No journalists or photographers turned up to report a story that would have made the front page. Instead a local girl, Alice Dearlove, took a selfie of herself with two of the biggest stars in the world, posted it on her Twitter page, and that was it.

Ed had to contend with window watchers again when he slipped back to Thomas Mills High School for a workshop with some of Richard Hanley's pupils in the music room. Pride of place among newspaper cuttings about himself and other students on the wall was a gold disc he had received for +. He had wanted to go along and support his former teacher for some time but was never at home long enough to arrange something. Now that he had the chance, he emailed Richard to fix up an afternoon. They had to keep it top secret or the whole school would have been trying to crowd into the classroom. On the day, Richard even blacked out the glass in the classroom door so that no one could see in.

Ed listened to the young students from Year 11 and the Sixth Form perform some songs. Richard explains, 'It was mainly pupils who were like Ed – performing their own songs or singing in a similar style.' Ed offered some insight into how he worked. He suggested they always make notes of lyrics on their phone so that they could use them later. He told them that for 'I See Fire' he only had the first line about the 'misty eye of the mountain' and would sing it in the shower until he had thought of a second line, then a third. The lesson he had learned, he explained, was to prepare for songs and have 'oodles of lyrics' ready for the right moment. Ed also revealed that he no longer wrote songs every day as he had in the past.

Word that Ed Sheeran was in school soon leaked out, and when he left, he was waved off by a large and excited crowd. Richard recalls: 'There was a lot of interest – a lot of screaming.'

'I See Fire' had represented a new challenge for Ed. He had pitched songs in the past to the makers of both *The Twilight Saga* and *The Hunger Games* series but had no luck. Then, out of the blue, he received an email from the director Peter Jackson asking if he would like to compose something for his new film *The Hobbit: The Desolation of Smaug.* At first he didn't believe it was genuine but soon realised the Academy Award winner really had written to him. He discussed the project with Peter during a tour of New Zealand, where the film was being made, and over lunch agreed to his first movie commission.

Ed had always loved Tolkien's stories and looked back fondly to his dad reading the book to him before bed. He jumped at the opportunity and started thinking about the lyrics right away, the first time he had to compose to order. He set aside three days to complete the song and worked closely with Peter.

At the end of each day, Peter would meet him to check on his progress and give him advice. Ed observed, 'He knows what he wants but doesn't pretend to be musical in any way. He let me get on with it, but he also knows his movie, so he would tell me if something needed to be less energetic or more relaxed or whatever.'

The finished song played over the end credits. Ed had a secret ambition to be in one of Peter's epic fantasies but that never happened, although he did go out drinking with two of the stars, Luke Evans and Benedict Cumberbatch. They drank 'wicked' espresso martinis.

Having completed his first song for a film, Ed was promptly asked to write another – this time for an entirely different project. *The Fault in Our Stars* was a movie based on John Green's intensely moving book of the same title. Ed wrote 'All of the Stars' with Johnny McDaid and found it easier than composing for the fantasy blockbuster. He wanted his song to be 'sad, yet euphoric and lift people a little bit'. He thought it would be more relatable than dwarfs and dragons and added, 'I hope it doesn't depress people too much.' Neither 'I See Fire' nor 'All of the Stars' was written for the new album, although both found their way on to deluxe versions. Finally, × was complete and Ed could put his feet up and relax – the calm before the storm of promotion and touring that would inevitably follow its launch.

Many of the building works he wanted for his Suffolk home had been completed. As well as the obligatory indoor swimming pool, one of the first major improvements was a specially designed giant tree-house on a raised platform. The structure had decking so that he and his girlfriend Athina Andrelos could enjoy evening cocktails while enjoying stunning views of the local countryside.

He and Athina had reconnected when he returned to the UK and their relationship had become more serious. They could practically live in the tree-house complex, which had a TV room, a living room and study, all timber-clad and interconnected with separate conical roofs. The property also boasted an open-air hot tub that was ideal for parties, and a trendy eco-friendly pod which was his home studio.

Ed invited Amy Wadge to spend a couple of days with him. She had become more of a friend than a work partner and he was always pleased to see her and catch up. For a change, they weren't planning any songwriting. She was looking forward to 'some chilling-out time with my mate'. One evening they were going out for dinner with his mum and dad so Ed disappeared to take a shower and freshen up. Amy passed the time by grabbing the guitar that Harry Styles had given Ed and picking away at the strings: 'I played two lines. Ed came running downstairs and said, "What's that? We have to do something with that."'

Later that evening, when they returned to the house, they set about developing the song. They wrote 'Thinking Out Loud' that very night and Ed recorded it on his phone. The lyrics were from the heart and had a touching sincerity that was inspired by sad family issues. Ed was coming to terms with his grandad's death while Amy was facing up to the news that her mother-in-law was dying. They sat at the kitchen table and talked. 'We had conversations about everlasting love,' recalled Amy.

Ed was able to channel his romantic feelings towards Athina into this new song and imagine their life together. Whenever he talks about the song, Ed says he wrote it about her. The final lyrics had far more depth to them than a simple 'I Love You'.

He knew almost instantly that 'Thinking Out Loud' was special. The next day he texted Amy: 'This song's a banger you know.' The following morning he posted the briefest of clips, just ten seconds, but it was enough to create a buzz on social media.

Amy could only keep her fingers crossed that Ed was right. She had been troubled by some financial worries in the past couple of years and was in the process of turning her life around. She had given up alcohol after her last trip to Los Angeles two years before when she had partied too hard with Ed and his friends – she'd realised that Jack Daniel's was not a good songwriting partner.

Ed booked in with Jake Gosling, who had no writing credits on the new album but had produced several tracks, even though Ed had become more involved with leading American producers. Ed persuaded his manager and record label that they should shoehorn 'Thinking Out Loud' on to the album, even at this eleventh hour. He kept telling Amy, 'This is the one that will change everything for us.'

The first time Amy saw Ed perform the finished song was on *Later … with Jools Holland* in May. Jools offered some restrained light piano that gave the track a slightly jazzy feel, which was refreshingly different from the final album cut. Amy later admitted that she became emotional as she listened and started to cry. The song meant so much to her future.

After 'Thinking Out Loud' became track-number eleven, the album was finally finished. Ed admitted there had been times the previous year when he wondered if it was ever going to be ready. He had always intended it to be called ×, continuing his mathematical theme, but had to explain countless times that it stood for 'Multiply' and not for 'Mr X'. The idea was that he was building – multiplying – from the first album.

He chose green as the colour scheme for everything connected with × because he thought it important to have a particular concept for each album. This made perfect business sense from a merchandising point of view. The strategy is a bit like a football team's new strip – every fan has to have one, and after a couple of years you move on to the next in an entirely different colour.

Ironically, after the telephone directory of acknowledgements on +, all he had to say on the inlay for his second album was a succinct 'Thank you to everyone involved in the making of this album and to those who will be part of the journey.'

The most pressing decision was the choice of lead single. The front runner was 'One', the opening track and the last song he ever wrote about Alice. He had composed it in November 2011 while on tour in Australia not long after their break-up. Geographically the pair are a world apart but the song reveals his feelings are still strong and he is hopeful they will always be friends. For Ed, it represented closure.

Ed played the whole album to Taylor Swift and she was not keen on 'One' being the first release. She felt it didn't challenge people. Ed explained, 'She said, "If they listen to 'Sing' they can love it or hate it but they are gonna talk about it."' Elton John was even more outspoken in favour of 'Sing': 'That's your first single,' he declared.

The Pharrell Williams collaboration proved a wise choice. The track became Ed's first UK number-one single in June 2014. By the time of its release later in the month, it seemed as if × was the only album in town. The promotion of the launch was masterful. The high point came on the Sunday, three days afterwards, when Ed appeared on the Pyramid Stage at Glastonbury. He played for an hour at 7 p.m., immediately following Dolly Parton. Two acts performed after him, American rock band the Black Keys and the headliners, Kasabian. The *Guardian* described Ed's set as a 'whole lot of singalongs'.

The album swiftly reached number one in the UK, as well as in the US Billboard 200, and in thirteen other countries around the world. Mostly the reviews were good. Alexis Petridis in the *Guardian*, after the fuss surrounding his review of +, was more impressed this time around. He noted that Ed was an artist pulling off one of the 'harder tricks in rock – growing up in public – with ease'.

The *Daily Telegraph* felt it contained 'genuinely great songs', but the *Independent* found it 'authentically uninspiring'. Across the Atlantic, the *Washington Post* thought × was 'more accomplished, more assured and interesting than +'. A touch cynically, perhaps, the reviewer thought it felt like the work of a skilful careerist and that Ed was 'a well-connected striver, no offense intended'.

Ed was resigned to the fact that he wasn't going to get universal praise. He let the numbers do the talking. × went on to sell more than three million copies in the UK where it was the biggest-selling album of the year and would eventually become the twentieth-bestselling album of all time. The home-grown success was matched in the US, where sales reached four million. Reflecting Ed's supremacy in the modern world, Spotify announced that in 2014 × notched up 430 million streams.

Ed was in much better shape physically by the time the × tour opened in Japan in August. He had lost more than thirty-five pounds for the video of 'Thinking Out Loud'. When he performed the song on *Later ... with Jools Holland* he was clearly overweight, but he was fit and streamlined when he took to the floor for the now famous film of him dancing with Brittany Cherry. While on tour in the US, Ed had practised for up to five hours a day with Brittany. He had never concealed his lack of dancing ability so he had to put the hours in to make the idea work. In Emil Nava's film, dance is a metaphor for love, romance and sex – just as it always was in the great dances of Fred Astaire and Ginger Rogers.

Ed was never going to be a professional dancer but, dressed in a white shirt and black waistcoat, he carries it off with aplomb. Brittany, well-known in the US for *Dancing with the Stars*, found it rewarding to push Ed 'to do something he would never do in a million years'. As with the best professional dancers, Brittany, stunning in a white dress, made Ed look good. Ed did feel like packing it in when progress was slow, but he persevered and observed, 'When you get the hang of it, dancing is the most fun thing in the world.' His transformation from the teenager making a hash of his audition for *Britannia High* all those years ago is astonishing. Once again Ed revealed his steely determination, giving a two-fingered salute to anyone who thought he couldn't dance. The video was watched 2.7 million times on the first day of its release. Just four years later, it had been seen nearly two and a half *billion* times.

The film almost certainly helped. 'Thinking Out Loud' became the definitive Ed Sheeran song and a high spot of the tour. Athina was able to accompany him on many of the UK dates. She had given up the music business altogether and taken a job as a food-team project manager with celebrity chef Jamie Oliver's organisation. Ed seemed happy to be photographed with her, while she posted pictures of him eating chocolate dessert and referred to him as '2-Dessert Sheeran'. She joined him for a break in Ibiza with friends and they were in high spirits jumping into the sea from the deck of a luxury yacht. They were very much like any other boyfriend and girlfriend on holiday in the sun.

Athina was in the audience when he sang 'Thinking Out Loud' at the annual Victoria's Secret Fashion Show at Earl's Court in early December. Being surrounded by so many beautiful young women in their underwear almost proved too much for Ed. He had a goofy grin on his face and looked like a little boy trapped overnight in a sweet shop. Afterwards the *Daily Mail* said he had eyes only for Athina, which hadn't been strictly true.

Ironically, Ed was asked by a magazine to give some dating advice: 'For boys, don't focus on the people you see in magazines. I've never had a six-pack, like most guys. We want to eat burgers, we don't want to do sit-ups.' His message to girls was not to stress on the way they looked because 'There's someone out there who will find you beautiful for your thing.'

The first indication that his own relationship might not be as strong as some people thought came in December when Ed seemed to be putting his career first. He was asked by Yahoo! Entertainment whether he planned to settle down and start a family: 'I'm not getting to that point. I think had my star stopped going up then yeah maybe.'

His star certainly continued to rise in early 2015. Fittingly, he slipped into Dublin to play an intimate gig at Whelan's where, in so many ways, it had all begun for him at the Damien Rice concert. Only 400 people saw him in person but the concert was broadcast globally by VH1.

More glamorously, perhaps, he flew on to Los Angeles to take part in an all-star Grammy Salute to Stevie Wonder. Ed sang a storming duet with Beyoncé of 'Master Blaster', a hit in 1980. At the ceremony a year before, he had been asked with which artist he would most like to collaborate. 'Beyoncé,' he replied, without hesitation.

His parents and his brother Matthew made the trip. Amy Wadge joined them. She observed, 'It was like watching their son graduate. I was bursting with pride watching my mate singing with Beyoncé.'

Ed didn't win a Grammy that year – 'Thinking Out Loud' had missed the cut-off date for nominations – but he did have a triumphant night at the BRITs at the end of February. Eight days after his twenty-fourth birthday he secured the premier award, MasterCard British Album of the Year, for ×, and was named British Male Solo Artist. It seemed like the perfect night. Once again, his mum and dad, Matthew and Amy shared his table, alongside Stuart Camp and Ben Cook. Athina was next to Ed, beaming at his success.

Taylor Swift, in a spectacular scarlet-and-black gown, was on a different table but won her first BRIT award as International Female Artist. She was clearly delighted when she received it from Ellie Goulding, who was still very much one of her set, and made a point of thanking a special friend who had taken her to pubs and taught her to make a good cup of tea: 'I love you, Ed Sheeran,' she said graciously.

The man himself was not quite so eloquent as he stumbled through a point about what a great year it had been for British music. Afterwards there was a group photo with Ed clutching the BRIT and already appearing slightly the worse for wear. Athina looked happy as she posed next to Ed's dad.

By the end of the night she looked distinctly unhappy. They had broken up. Apparently she had moaned about him always bringing his family to such events. They had a blazing row and he told her he never wanted to see her again. A friend, who was there that evening, explains, 'You don't fuck with Ed's family. And that was it.'

Ed proceeded to get very drunk. He wasn't celebrating; he was very upset by what had happened. He had to regain his composure to continue his epic world tour, which would reach its zenith when he played three nights at the new Wembley Stadium in July, the first time an artist had performed there by himself. At every concert, he would sing 'Thinking Out Loud', a song that still meant everlasting love to his fans, if not to him.

Ed's tattooist, Kevin Paul, had much sympathy for Athina and Ed: 'They were a really good couple.' He acknowledged that being with Ed was going to change any girl's life. His advice to his famous client was to avoid a celebrity relationship: 'I think he'll meet another normal girl and settle down but until his career calms down it's not going to go anywhere. It's hard.'

Within a month, Ed was linked to a Victoria's Secret model, Barbara Palvin, who had been the girlfriend of Niall Horan. They had a burger when his tour reached Sydney, then headed off to a nightclub. The evening generated some publicity but nothing was going on between them. Ed had already made up his mind that he wasn't going to share a new relationship with the public until he was ready to do so. In any case, he had little time for that sort of thing as the epic × tour was scheduled to continue until December 2015. Love, however, was just around the corner.

20

HOME AND AWAY

Ed had some unfinished business with acting. He enjoyed it and had wanted to do more ever since those now distant days with the National Youth Music Theatre. He had not been able to secure a role in *The Hobbit* films but he was asked to appear in an episode of *Home and Away*. The Australian soap had become an institution since it had begun in 1988. Ed caught up with the storyline whenever he popped into the local chippie in Framlingham because the show always seemed to be on the television above the counter.

The popular soap is set in the fictional seaside town of Summer Bay in New South Wales, which, in reality, was idyllic Palm Bay in Sydney's Northern Beaches District. Ed found time between concerts for a sunny day's filming. The role wasn't too taxing as he was playing himself.

He was Teddy – his childhood nickname – who had been cared for by Marilyn Chambers, one of the show's best-known characters, when she worked as a nanny in the UK. In a scarcely believable plot line, Marilyn, played by actress Emily Symons, doesn't realise that Teddy has grown up to become

Ed Sheeran. When everyone in Summer Bay discovers Teddy's true identity, they persuade him to play a concert for the town's residents. He sings 'Thinking Out Loud'.

Ed relished the experience and decided to do more acting if he was asked. Being Ed Sheeran gave him the opportunity to indulge himself. He explained, 'I really don't care what people think, so I'm doing stuff because I enjoy it rather than because it might be cool.'

Ed had been in his best shape for years when he was practising his dance moves for the 'Thinking Out Loud' video but that new-found fitness hadn't lasted. 'I started drinking again,' he told reporters backstage after the Ivor Novello Awards at the Grosvenor House Hotel in May 2015. He was allowed a celebration that night, when he won the premier award, Songwriter of the Year, for the first time. Elton John made the presentation. He had continued to be at Ed's side for some key moments in his career and was on good form: 'This boy next to me will have a career – if he wants to – as long as mine. I hope he doesn't get into half the trouble I got into. He'd have to marry a man and a woman!'

Those comments were light-hearted and fitted the mood of the occasion, but Ed was single and in the middle of a gruelling tour schedule. A day spent filming *Home and Away* was a welcome diversion, but his love life was non-existent. Newspapers were trying to pair him off with Irish model Louise Johnston, but he had been too busy since his dramatic split with Athina. He confided during a radio interview, wistfully: 'I haven't really had time to sit back and re-evaluate my personal life because I don't really have a personal life.' He was spending so much time hopping on to planes and checking into hotels that he was in danger of burning himself out at the age of twenty-four. He was already thinking of taking a break: 'I'd like to live a bit. I feel like I've been in a bubble where normal happens outside. I'd like to get out for at least a year.'

By the time he reached the Hollywood Bowl the following month, his friends were getting worried about him. Johnny McDaid later told *Rolling Stone* magazine, 'I sat him down and said, "Look, man, please have all the fun in the world. But be careful because if that elastic snaps, it could take a long time to recover from it."'

Surprisingly, perhaps, Ed was not letting the standard of his performances fall.

On the × tour, he was clearly expanding his core audience. While his enthusiastic younger fans jumped into the air and sang along to every word, reviewers noticed a much wider age range in the bigger venues. One appreciative online critic described his Hollywood night as an 'all-you-can-listen music buffet'. She added, 'He was kind. He was funny. He carried himself the whole time humbly, but his music projected him as some sort of prodigy.'

America seemed to be completely in love with Ed. The *LA Music Blog* described the applause as 'thunderous'. While it was true that an Ed Sheeran concert was a one-man show, he brought sophisticated staging and special effects with him so it required five trucks to move the set between venues. Ed wouldn't have been human if he didn't make the odd mistake, though. At the Air Canada Centre (ACC) in Toronto a few days later, he flubbed a line from 'The A Team' of all things. He must have played the song thousands of times.

At the end of the summer leg of the × tour in Milwaukee, Ed had a week off before his three nights at Wembley Stadium. He flew to the east coast for Taylor Swift's Fourth of July party at her $17-million mansion overlooking the sea on Rhode Island and was able to catch up with Martha Baker-Woodside, one of his oldest friends from Framlingham and a welcome reminder of grand days at her parents' Dancing Goat Café. He was delighted to learn that another friendly face from school, Cherry Seaborn, was living and working in New York. She and Martha were part of the same set of high-flying ex-pats.

Ed and Cherry spoke on the phone while he was at the party and he asked Taylor if he could invite her to join him. He had seen her a few times since school, but this was the first time they had both been single and were free to explore the possibility of romance. She is a year younger than Ed so they were never classmates at Thomas Mills. It is ironic that, having grown up seeing each other most days, they finally made a proper connection 3,500 miles away from the teenage haunts they knew so well.

Cherry was brought up in a pretty village about twelve miles from Framlingham. Her father, Matthew, is an architect with a leading Cambridge firm, and among his many impressive projects is the Stephen Hawking Building at Gonville and Caius College. He specialises in the design of modern buildings that are sympathetic to the existing environment.

As well as being sporty at school, Cherry had followed an academic path by achieving her degree at Durham University in cellular and molecular biology. Her great love was still hockey. She was an exceptional young player, playing as a forward for the leading Suffolk team, the Harleston Magpies. Wearing her lucky number-19 shirt, she was a key member of the Durham side that were British University champions in 2012 and 2013. She was also selected for the England under-21 side three years in a row – it won a bronze medal at the 2012 European Championships in Den Bosch, Holland. They beat Germany 3–2 in the third-place play-off.

She wanted to continue her studies in the US where there was greater sporting opportunity for students. She secured a full hockey scholarship to take a master's degree in management studies at the renowned Duke University, which, coincidentally, was in Durham, North Carolina. When she graduated, she moved to New York and took a position with the accounting giants Deloitte, based in Manhattan.

She and Ed enjoyed a few days of private time in the city before he had to fly back to London for the biggest gig of his life to date – Wembley Stadium. They discovered that they had much in common besides missing home. Cherry was, like Ed, a mixture of enthusiastic and laid-back. She made friends easily and was relaxed in social situations. She also shared his literary tastes so they could chat merrily away about the Harry Potter books and Philip Pullman's His Dark Materials saga. Ed chose the fantasy trilogy as his *Desert Island Discs* book, declaring that he personally thought it was the greatest love story ever told.

He would be back in New York officially in late September for the final US gig of the year in Central Park, but he planned to see Cherry long before then. His work priority was playing Wembley. Three nights at the stadium in front of 87,000 fans each time was arguably the pinnacle of his career to date. Among his support acts were friends he admired who had been stops on his train journey to the iconic north London venue – Foy Vance, Passenger and Example. Elton John joined him for two numbers during the opening night. Ed sang the Kiki Dee part for a duet of the timeless 1976 number one 'Don't Go Breaking My Heart', then Elton provided gentle piano accompaniment for 'Afire Love'.

Ed told the audience that Wembley was not the fulfilment of a dream: 'It was always too big to dream about, so now we're here it's a bit mental.' None of the crowd realised that he wasn't too happy that the loop-pedal system failed each night, and that he had simply moved to the side of the stage and given an a cappella version of 'The Parting Glass', which everyone loved and thought was part of the show. The first night it happened he stormed offstage, demanding to know 'What the fuck was that?' Elton John went into his dressing room to calm him down. He succeeded by telling Ed that everyone loved the show and that 'The Parting Glass' was beautiful, then advised him to get over himself.

Whenever Ed had a moment between gigs, it seemed he filled it with something. He squeezed in another go at acting when he appeared in *The Bastard Executioner*, a Welsh-filmed medieval drama series that was being made for American television. He played the recurring role of Sir Cormac, the ambitious and sadistic prodigy of a high-ranking church elder. His lines would have challenged Laurence Olivier. He did his best with: 'I will ask but one more time, priest to priest, in service of your holy vow, where does the Seraphim hide?'

Perhaps it was trying too hard to cash in on the success of *Game of Thrones* but the whole thing sank without trace when it was axed after one series.

Ed, meanwhile, had to return to the day job and fulfil the rest of his × dates, but nothing could compare with Wembley. Inevitably there was a come-down. His new relationship, however, continued to blossom when he returned to the US at the beginning of September for the last fifteen shows in North America. He was seen strolling around New York with Cherry, then whisking her off to a baseball game. They sat in the front row, wearing matching home-team caps to watch the Mets lose to the Philadelphia Phillies at the Citi Field in Queens. They were now firmly on the radar of local photographers and were pictured getting money out of a cash point and popping into a liquor store. That kind of scrutiny is exactly what Ed hates.

A few days later a holiday weekend celebrated Labor Day, and they flew to Las Vegas with a group of friends that included Calvin Harris and Emil Nava. They were seen enjoying a party night at the Wet Republic club where Calvin was DJing. Ed was not keeping Cherry a secret; he just wasn't talking about her. While it was pretty obvious that she was his girlfriend, that didn't stop the media speculating wildly about him and *The X Factor* judge Nicole Scherzinger. Apparently, he had invited her to one of his Wembley concerts and subsequently taken her to Framlingham, where they had gone to the Station Hotel for a drink. The description in the press of an 'intimate evening' was slightly overstating things. The night out was easy publicity and everyone soon realised they were just friends and there was nothing in it. That didn't stop one newspaper hilariously suggesting that a heartbroken Nicole played Ed's songs on a loop.

Ed expected to have some new material soon for his next album. He had started writing again on tour, although the best song he produced during this time was destined for someone else. He originally had Rihanna in mind for a track called 'Love Yourself' but in the end decided it would suit Justin Bieber better. When he had come up with the lyric, which is basically a kiss-off to a lover, he called it 'Fuck Yourself' as in 'Baby, you should go and fuck yourself.' That would have made a memorable singalong at a concert. By the time it was released in November 2015, 'fuck' had become 'love'.

The single topped the charts in both the UK and the US, where Ed himself had yet to have a number one. 'Thinking Out Loud' had stalled at number two despite huge sales, kept off the top by 'Uptown Funk', the Mark Ronson blockbuster hit that featured Bruno Mars.

Justin Bieber had also been facing up to his demons, giving up drink and drugs at the beginning of the year after a period of bad behaviour that had led to several highly publicised arrests. Ed was not facing that sort of negative press so his fans hadn't realised the extent of his problems. His cousin Jethro was encouraging him to take a break at the end of the year and clean up a bit. Ed's problem hadn't reached rehab stage but Jethro observed, 'Ed likes a drink and he can't really hold his alcohol very well. He likes to party hard and he's still very young.'

Cherry was being supportive but she was in New York. They had begun to make plans for the following year. They talked about going travelling and Ed finally passed his driving test, which would help if they needed a car abroad. He had sailed through the theory element when he was in the UK for the Wembley concerts and backed it up with some lessons at a driving school in Ipswich. He had clearly needed the practice: while filming a guest spot for *Top Gear* earlier in the year, he had managed to drive the renowned 'reasonably priced car' off the racetrack at Dunsfold Aerodrome.

He kept his lessons a secret, but he was a familiar sight to locals as he edged cautiously along the A1120 back road from Framlingham to Yoxford. When he eventually passed, he announced it on Twitter: 'Passed my driving test. Zoom, zoom, zoom.' Ed had already bought a car, a Mini Cooper, although he joked that Harry Styles had told him not to be silly and to get an Aston Martin.

Before he passed, he needed to be driven to Ipswich to be given an honorary doctorate from the University Campus Suffolk (UCS). He loved his home county and had spent many happy times in the town, playing concerts or watching football. The degree was for his 'outstanding contribution to music'. Nobody seemed to mind that he had always been outspoken about not needing to go to university.

The × tour finally finished before Christmas at the Mount Smart Stadium in Auckland, New Zealand. The undertaking had been immense: 150 shows in twenty-eight months, grossing more than $150 million. Ed couldn't wait to take a break. Cherry left her job in New York and they started 2016 as a proper couple. Over the next year, they were apart for just three days.

Ed told his fans that he was temporarily signing off from social media. He had decided to give up his phone as well. He announced on Instagram: 'I find myself seeing the world through a screen, not my eyes, so I'm taking the opportunity of me not having to be anywhere or do anything to travel the world and see everything I missed.'

He had become a victim of the modern malaise of caring too much about what he was reading online. His day would be ruined if he saw a comment about him losing his hair – which he wasn't. He was progressively less relaxed in public, regretting that the days had gone of being able to stand in the crowd at a festival and watch a band. He admitted, 'I'm a very paranoid person in public spaces.' He had no intention of retiring, though, and promised that a new album would be on its way in the not too distant future. He added, 'If you love me, you will understand me buggering off for a bit.'

While he and Cherry planned their 'gap year', Ed still had some responsibilities to fulfil. The Grammy Awards had become something of an annual disappointment. For the past three years he had been nominated but hadn't won. Each time his mum and dad had joined him in Los Angeles, so it had become an occasion to put on a brave face and talk of success in the future. This time it happened. 'Thinking Out Loud' won the prestigious Song of the Year and Ed carried off Best Pop Solo Performance. He was presented with the first award by Stevie Wonder, who had told him he would win one day when they'd met up the year before. Taylor Swift embraced him, seemingly more excited than he was. As he went on stage, Ed put his arm around Amy Wadge, who, as co-writer, was accompanying him. He'd told her it was a 'banging song'.

For once he didn't stay up all night celebrating. Instead, he and Cherry took a plane out of LA and flew to the world-famous Blue Lagoon in Iceland. He rented the whole spa for the day so that when the clock struck midnight they could toast his twenty-fifth birthday. That was perfect, but the next day ended in a disaster that could have brought their trip to an abrupt end.

They were on a guided hike to watch what was promised to be the best view of the Northern Lights for twenty years when Ed ignored instructions to keep to the path and went to have a closer look at a bubbling geyser. The ground crumbled beneath him and both feet were plunged into scalding water. Cherry ran over to help as Ed screamed in agony. She pulled off one of his socks – which was a bad idea as his skin came away with it.

Poor Ed had to be airlifted to hospital for emergency treatment for a first-degree burn that included using fake skin to aid the healing process on the foot that had lost its skin. He could easily have called it a day and returned to Framlingham but he insisted on carrying on with their trip. When his foot had healed sufficiently, they flew to Japan where he wasn't that popular. He joked, 'There are maybe two people who like me in Japan. I deliberately picked places where I wasn't really liked.'

A ginger-haired man limping around rural Hokkaido stood out a little, but at least pictures of Ed and Cherry together didn't surface. They were left alone to 'eat weird food, soak in the hot springs and ski'. They moved on to Australia and New Zealand, where Ed indulged his inner daredevil by white-water rafting, bungee jumping and swimming with bull sharks without a cage. In New Zealand, he even allowed Peter Jackson to strap him to the front of his plane and fly him around as if he were a dancer in a 1930s Busby Berkeley musical.

On their way home they took in a trip to Ghana in West Africa, where they stayed near the capital of Accra with hip-hop singer Fuse ODG. They were still in activities mode, with jet-skiing and boat rides, although Ed dutifully followed Cherry around the local markets. Cherry's New York days seemed an age away: she had swapped her business suit for a sarong, her long hair in dreadlocks, as if she was on the trail to Kashmir rather than working in Manhattan. She looked happy and relaxed when she and Ed posed for pictures with Fuse and his crew.

Significantly, Ed was writing again. Fuse (Nana Richard Abiona) is half Ghanaian but was brought up in Mitcham, south London. He made writing fun and turned the process into one long party, which Ed loved. One of the songs they wrote together, 'Bibia Be Ye Ye', would end up on the deluxe version of the next album.

Ed arrived home wonderfully refreshed. He and Cherry were closer than ever. As he observed warmly to the radio DJ Zane Lowe, 'I have actually had the time to fall in love properly.'

21

PERFECT SYMPHONY

Ed was in the studio at his Suffolk home when he heard the news that his beloved grandmother Shirley Lock had died. She had been an inspiration to all the family, not just musically but also because, as Ed said, 'She was one of the nicest people you would ever meet.' He sat down and started to compose 'Supermarket Flowers', perhaps the saddest and most personal of all his songs.

Shirley had died peacefully, aged eighty-six, in August 2016 at the nearby Aldeburgh Community Hospital. Her two grandsons had been able to visit her regularly during her final days. One of her last wishes had been that Ed and Matthew would work together, and the two boys promised they would make it happen.

At first Ed thought 'Supermarket Flowers' was too private for his next album. The poignant and poetic lyric is written from the point of view of his mother, Imogen, sadly clearing out Shirley's hospital room after her death. She sweeps the supermarket flowers from the window sill while her husband John wipes a tear from her face.

Ed would later describe how 'intense' the moment had been when he played the song to his mum for the first time; it was his grandad Stephen, though, who persuaded him to include the song on his new record. Ed had sat next to him when he played it during the funeral, a small family affair at the town's parish church attended by the two of them, Imogen, John and Matthew. Ed recalled, 'My grandfather just turned to me. He was like, "You have to put that out. That has to go on the record. It's such a good memory." That's why it ended up on there.'

Shirley had insisted on colourful clothing at her funeral. She didn't want everyone moping around in black. When Ed gave a moving performance of this 'most special' song at the 2018 BRIT awards, he abandoned his usual dark suit and black tie in favour of a bright red jacket.

Ed was keen to finish the new album away from public scrutiny so kept a low profile, dividing his time between his growing Suffolk estate and his £9-million central London base, a former industrial space set over five floors that also included a studio. The album could be promoted as a comeback if he kept out of sight.

While he was away, Ed had let himself balloon again, and needed to get in better shape for the launch of his next album the following January. As usual, beer had been the enemy of his waistline and he was living in sweatpants until he had lost the pounds. Cherry wasn't his personal trainer but she was naturally athletic and encouraged him to start the day with a work-out in their home gym.

She began a new job at Deloitte's Holborn headquarters in London as a senior consultant in their risk-advisory department. She already had many friends in London, as well as her younger brother Charlie. He too had attended Thomas Mills and, coincidentally, was following a similar path in classical music to Matthew Sheeran – Charlie was making a name for himself as a promising young composer in the world of film and theatre.

Cherry also signed up to play for Wimbledon in the coming season's Investec Conference East division of the national hockey league. She would be playing against her old teammates from the Harleston Magpies. Ed made a point of supporting her whenever he could. The crowd at a hockey match were more interested in the sport than in gawping at Ed Sheeran. The big following for Wimbledon was due to the presence of Olympic gold medallist Crista Cullen in the team. Ed would arrive unannounced, watch the game, stay for some food and leave with Cherry. He enjoyed these afternoons, which gave him a break from music.

Ed had written far too many songs for the new album, using a mixture of old friends and new collaborations. Johnny McDaid was again his principal writing partner, although he composed many songs with Ryan Tedder, the lead singer of rock band OneRepublic, who had supported Ed on some of the × tour dates. Ryan was one of the most respected songwriters in Los Angeles and had written with Adele for her albums *21* and *25*, as well as working with Beyoncé on 'Halo'.

He and Ed wrote more than two dozen songs for the album but, in the end, only one – the sublime ballad 'Happier' – made the final cut. Ryan was very complimentary about Ed, describing him as 'laser-focused'. He added, 'Ed is super intelligent and savvier than just about anyone I have ever met.'

Ed was clinical in his approach to composing ÷, as the new record would be called. He originally chose that symbol to continue the mathematical theme with an album of collaborations, although it didn't work out exactly like that. He did a lot of solo writing. He told the BBC, 'I had in my mind what sound should be on what song, and which subject matter would be on which song – so I'd write ten songs on that idea.'

He employed that strategy with songs about Suffolk before choosing 'Castle on the Hill' as the best. Again, he wanted to write a wedding song and discovered that 'Perfect' was by far the most memorable. One song that did not fit this systematic approach is the underrated 'How Would You Feel (Paean)'. While romantics swooned over 'Perfect', this equally tender ballad was Ed's romantic gift to his girlfriend, a simple declaration of his love. Paean is Cherry's second name.

He had been inspired nearly two years before when Cherry had to leave him in the UK and fly back to New York, and wrote it as she travelled to the airport from the house in Suffolk. By the time she arrived, he had emailed her the song, which asked how she would feel if he told her he loved her. When they were chatting about the new album, he naturally wanted to know which her favourite track was. She told him, 'You've forgotten it existed and I have it in my email because I'm the only one you sent it to.' Ed dusted it off, recorded it properly and found a place for it on the album. He played the soaring guitar solo himself but thought he sounded like a poor man's John Mayer. So he emailed the acclaimed guitarist personally – because you can do that when you're Ed Sheeran – and it's John who plays on the final version.

Stuart Camp thought 'How Would You Feel (Paean)' would be bigger than 'Perfect', which would prove not to be the case. Ed considered it one of the best songs on the album. He produced the track himself, an indication that he was becoming more involved in that side of things.

The biggest outside influence on the overall sound of the album came from the fashionable American producer Benny Blanco, who also wrote songs under his real name, Benjamin Levin. Unusually among Ed's collaborators, he was just a couple of years older than Ed so in the same age bracket. His impressive credits included 'Moves like Jagger' by Maroon 5, and the Rihanna number one 'Diamonds'. He had worked with Ed on 'Don't' for the × album, as well as the Justin Bieber track 'Love Yourself', which had ended up as the world's biggest-selling single in 2016.

Ed had planned for Benny to come over to the UK to work on the album but faced a minor hiccup when he discovered that his friend refused to fly. Time was getting on so Ed decided that he would jet over to New York and they would sail back in luxury on *Queen Mary 2*. They put together a temporary studio in an old freezer room on board and worked on the new album together. One of the songs was 'Castle on the Hill', which was going to be the lead single for the album in January 2017.

Reintroducing Ed to the public after a quiet year proved relatively easy. He was still very newsworthy. The most bizarre story concerned a deep cut on his cheek, which had apparently occurred when he was fooling about at a party at the Natural History Museum in London with James Blunt and Princess Beatrice, the elder daughter of Prince Andrew.

Apparently she was pretending to knight James with a ceremonial sword when she accidentally whacked Ed with it. Ed had known Beatrice for five years: he had played at Holly Branson's wedding on the Caribbean island of Necker and she had been one of the guests.

Another account of what happened had James wielding the sword. A third version had Ed falling over drunk and managing to cut himself. The story was good fun, although Ed had a nasty gash on his cheek that required stitches. Ed was quite accident-prone, particularly if he was partying. The most hairy incident had been at a karaoke bar near Nashville in 2013, when he badly cut his hand drumming with beer bottles. They smashed, leaving a piece of glass embedded in his hand and blood all over the floor. His guitar-playing days almost ended then and there.

There was more publicity for 'Castle on the Hill' when Ed was pulled over for speeding in his Aston Martin DB9. He had clearly taken Harry Styles's advice and chosen the £140,000 sports car after all. On the track, Ed sings of doing ninety down the country roads near his home, singing to 'Tiny Dancer'. The local police force heard it and even suggested that he might like to slow down. The irony of him being caught doing seventy in a sixty-mile limit near Framlingham was therefore obvious. According to reports, he accepted a £100 fine and three points on his licence.

While the Aston Martin was an expensive purchase, classic sports cars like this – especially models no longer in production – are a good investment as they increase greatly in value. Ed soon tired of it, though, and said he'd given it to Stuart Camp's partner, Liberty Shaw. Generally, he was keen not to splash his money around in a way that would spoil his image of an ordinary bloke. He invested in property that his fans wouldn't see. He bought a villa, for instance, close to beautiful Lake Trasimeno in the Italian province of Perugia. The attraction for business-minded Ed was the vineyard that came with it. He also bought his parents a luxury flat opposite his place in London so that they, too, had a base in the capital. Ed was also quietly building his art collection – with the advice of his father. He favoured contemporary artists and was particularly proud of a work by Harland Miller, who is renowned for his giant canvasses of Penguin book covers. Ed's acquisition featured the c-word in very large letters.

Surprisingly, perhaps, 'Castle on the Hill', which was a ready-made stadium anthem, only reached number two when it was relesed, despite fantastic sales. The track that beat it to the top was the other lead single from ÷, 'Shape of You', which would prove to be Ed's most successful to date. 'Shape of You' almost didn't make it on to the album – it was yet another last-minute addition. Ed Howard at Atlantic had suggested Ed and Johnny McDaid try a writing session with Steve Mac at his studio in London. Steve was a hit-making machine and had huge commercial success with Westlife, Clean Bandit and Susan Boyle. He had initially thought Johnny was Ed's assistant, but when they'd got over that misunderstanding they had a great day. The first thing Steve came up with was the now famous hook for 'Shape of You'. He hadn't intended it to be anything more than a starting point for the song but Ed picked up on the pizzicato progression right away and started banging out a rhythm on his guitar while rap-singing along.

The three master songwriters took just two hours to build the framework of the song that would be the best-selling single worldwide of 2017. The one argument came over the line 'My bed sheets smell of you.' Johnny was in favour of 'my T-shirt', which he thought was more playful, but Ed was insistent and had his way. Johnny laughed about it afterwards: 'And what that did is take the guessing out of it. Ed is a fucking genius – I almost ruined it.' Ed has written many love songs. This was a sex song.

The boys took it to Atlantic, believing at this stage that it was better suited to an artist like Rihanna or perhaps Little Mix. As he was leaving the office, Ben Cook from Atlantic heard the demo, turned to Ed and said, 'This is a fucking smash.' On the spot, the decision was made not only to include it on the album but also to release it at the same time as 'Castle on the Hill'. Ed didn't think it was among the best tracks on ÷ but he acknowledged that it was a terrific lead single.

For the video set in a boxing gym, Ed famously took off his shirt to reveal all his tattoos – he wanted the world to see the extent of his body art. He often said that he would never have a tattoo that couldn't be hidden underneath his wedding suit so this was a rare opportunity to show them off. All his tattoos meant something to him. He had no design that was just pretty or ornate. He would be able to stand shirtless in front of the mirror when he was seventy and relive the memory of touring Australia when he looked at the picture of a koala bear climbing a tree. The kiwi bird was a reminder of New Zealand – a country he loved. Instead of three lions on his shirt, he chose just one magnificent big cat on his chest as a reminder of playing Wembley Stadium in 2015. He'd had

'Prince' inked when he was on tour in Philadelphia in 2012, with Rizzle Kicks, as a tribute to one of his favourite TV programmes, *The Fresh Prince of Bel-Air.* A picture of a tomato-ketchup bottle signifies the luxury he would take on his desert island.

He has more than sixty tattoos. They are his personal photo album and he's proud of them. Kevin Paul, his tattooist, once spent nine hours in a row working on Ed's sleeve. 'He's fucking hardcore,' he remarked.

The boxing element of the video for 'Shape of You' would have pleased his late grandfather. Ed showed off his best moves before it ended bizarrely with him in a fat suit taking on a sumo wrestler. The public loved it, and it took just ninety-seven days to rack up a billion views on YouTube. In late 2018, it was pushing up towards four billion and is one of the most watched of all time.

The atmospheric video for 'Castle on the Hill' was more straightforward, featuring Ed and a group of teenagers in scenes filmed around Suffolk, including, naturally, Framlingham Castle. There's a lot of drinking beer from cans and plastic glasses, suggesting that this was all there was to do if you were growing up in rural surroundings. Young Ed was played by Hugo Fairbanks Weston, a pupil at Thomas Mills, who bore a striking resemblance to him. They had a laugh making the film. Hugo recalled, 'I think in Fram, growing up, you do live the same sort of life that we filmed in the video, because we do a lot of those things too. It's pretty relatable for all our friends.'

'Shape of You' and 'Castle on the Hill' did their job well. The new album ÷ sold 672,000 units when it went to number one on its release in March 2017, the third-biggest opening ever, behind Adele's *25* and *Be Here Now* by Oasis. On the day of release, Spotify reported that it was streamed a record 57 million times.

As ever for Ed, the reviews were mixed, some hinting that the album was too safe. In particular, *Rolling Stone* singled out 'Perfect': 'Imagine a cross between Eric Clapton's "Wonderful Tonight" and Chris de Burgh's "Lady in Red" and you can decide for yourself whether to reach for a handkerchief or pass the sick bag.' The reviewer thought in the future it would be nice to see Ed 'take a few chances'.

Vulture magazine agreed: 'Sheeran doesn't break any new ground on ÷ but it has many admirable qualities. The ballads are gorgeous.' The *NME* noted, 'His latest album is as likeable as he seems in interviews: assured but unassuming and sometimes hard to fathom.' *Clash* magazine summed up its appeal: 'It's rare to hear a song for the first time and feel like it instantly lodges in your mind but on ÷ Sheeran somehow repeats the trick on sixteen separate occasions.'

Already plans had been made for an even more ambitious world tour than his × extravaganza: 210 shows spread over two years. The venues were going to be the biggest he could find and he was going to sell them out. He decided to start in Turin in March 2017 so that he could pop further south to inspect his vineyard and stay at his villa.

As the tour got under way, a civil case involving 'Photograph' was settled out of court. Two songwriters had sued, claiming Ed's hit was strikingly similar to their song 'Amazing', released by Matt Cardle in 2012. An agreement was reached with no admissions made public. Such cases can involve millions but no details of any financial settlement were revealed. Matt Cardle was quite clear that he was not involved in the lawsuit: 'I think Ed Sheeran is a genius and 100 per cent deserves all his success.' It would not be the last time Ed was involved in this sort of action.

The highlight of the tour in 2017 was playing Glastonbury as the headliner. Ed had taken six years to move up from being an also-ran in a tent to commanding the Pyramid Stage as the final act on the Sunday night. He played a consummate version of 'Photograph' and also included 'Galway Girl', which had been released as a single and had divided opinion. Some loved the song; others hated it. One reviewer described it as a 'huge, delightfully daft, pseudo-fiddle-dee-dee stomper'. It was perfect for a Glasto singalong.

Luke Concannon watched the set on television at his home in America. He loved 'Galway Girl': 'I think the British press don't like anything folky because they think it's naff. I think it's amazing. It's like a really cool hip-hop R&B song with this kind of country chorus, and then has a really good jig in it. The energy in it – I think it's great.' Luke remains a fan of the man he inspired so much when Ed was a sixteen-year-old boy. He sums up his Festival performance: 'To share that many gifts at one time is just so beautiful.'

While Glastonbury was undoubtedly the musical highlight of the year, Ed was seemingly just as excited to land a small role in *Game of Thrones*, his favourite television programme. He played one of a group of soldiers who just happens to be singing when leading character Arya rides through the wood where they're camped. When she asks him about the song, he replies, 'It's a new one.'

He sits beside her while she shares blackberry wine with them, which was a thrill for the actress Maisie Williams, who is a big fan of Ed. His five minutes on screen in the Season 7 premiere resulted in a huge amount of publicity for the show and a surprising backlash on Twitter. Many posts mocked him. The general feeling was that the cameo was too obviously Ed Sheeran. Ed deleted his Twitter account.

After Glastonbury, Ed flew to the US for three months of dates. In Boston in September, he was able to look up Luke Concannon. On the day of his first show at the TD Garden, he went round to lunch at his house. The lead singer of Nizlopi had fallen in love and settled happily in the Boston suburbs. The band had taken a break back in 2009 and Luke had hitchhiked to Palestine. He had written an album called *Give It All* about the 'incredible' experience. Ed turned up in a big black SUV driven by Kev, his head of security, who always travelled with him on tour. After lunch, he and Luke decided to write a song. Luke recalls, 'He grabbed my guitar case and the guitar flew out, smashed on to the floor breaking the head off it.' Ed was mortified and kept saying, 'I'll sort it.' He tapped a message into his iPad, and half an hour later Kev turned up carrying a small guitar case containing a beautiful Wee Lowden, as they're known, worth something like $5,000.

It was a replacement gift. Kev then went out to find the exact model Ed had broken, while the boys resumed writing the song. Luke had been talking about how he had hooked up with his fiancée Stephanie and had decided to settle where she lived rather than go back to England. They wrote 'The Streets of Boston', a song about falling in love in the city, although Ed's lines were about Cherry. Disappointingly, the song has yet to reach the public, although Ed may dust it off in the future. Realistically, there were already plans in progress for much higher-profile collaborations. As he was leaving Ed gave Luke a hug and said, 'I've got three heroes – Van Morrison, Damien Rice and you.'

After Nashville at the beginning of October, Ed was able to fly back to the UK for a three-week break before moving on to Asia. Things did not go to plan. He fell off his bicycle on a steep hill near his home in Suffolk and broke his right wrist, left elbow and a rib. He didn't realise at first how badly he was hurt and carried on to the pub. The next morning he woke up in agony and took himself to hospital in Ipswich where his right forearm was put in a cast and his left arm placed in a sling. He had to cancel a number of dates immediately when doctors warned him he would need to be careful or his guitar playing might be affected in the future. They recommended a minimum of four weeks' rest.

He was strapped up when he appeared on *The Jonathan Ross Show*. He talked about the accident but also about his 'gap year', admitting that one of the reasons he had dropped out of sight was to pull himself together. He said he'd found himself slipping into the pitfalls that always trouble the music industry. He called it substance abuse and didn't specify whether it was alcohol, drugs or both. He explained, 'I think you need to, when you get into the industry, adjust to it – and I didn't adjust because I was constantly working on tour.'

Ed hadn't given up alcohol; he cut back when he was away but was adamant he didn't have a drink problem and could go without if he had to. To protect himself from bad influences when he was touring, he surrounded himself with old school friends from Thomas Mills, hiring four to travel with him and keep him sane.

The first of two big collaborations for Christmas was a version of 'Perfect' with Beyoncé. They had to wait for the superstar to give birth to twins in the summer before they could finish the duet in time for its December release. Typically, Beyoncé recorded her part in one take.

The second was another version of the song, this time with the acclaimed Italian tenor Andrea Bocelli. Whereas Beyoncé's version was quite stripped back, this was altogether lusher, with exquisite strings orchestrated by Ed's brother Matthew, which gave them the chance to fulfil their grandmother Shirley's wish and finally work together. They called it 'Perfect Symphony'.

Ed had wanted a Christmas number one and 'Perfect' fulfilled that ambition in the UK and the US. In Britain, he kept George Michael's much-loved classic 'Last Christmas' off the top spot. George's iconic video for his song had been filled with melancholy and longing. Ed, too, chose a snowy gathering of friends, but his was full of happiness and love. There was even a kitten. 'Perfect' was now a wedding song *and* a Christmas standard.

In many ways it reflected his state of mind. At the end of January he made the official announcement of his engagement to Cherry on Instagram: 'Got myself a fiancé just before New Year. We are very happy and in love, and our cats are chuffed as well.' More revealingly, Ed explained, 'I always thought I'd end up dating like an actress or someone in the industry. But I don't think I'm that kind of person. I'm a hometown boy.'

He promptly took himself to Australia and New Zealand to continue his tour, returning in April via the Philippines and Japan, where he was fitting in concerts that had needed to be rescheduled due to his accident.

On his return he reportedly bought an eight-bedroom mansion in west London for an estimated £20 million. Fortunately he could afford it: the *Sunday Times Rich List* put his wealth at £80 million, the fastest-growing fortune of any musician in the UK and Ireland. He was now the second-richest artist under thirty behind Adele, but she was about to reach that age, leaving the way clear for Ed to claim top spot.

He also bought two more properties next to his houses in Suffolk and submitted a planning application for a chapel on the estate. This ran into problems when it was discovered that the land involved might be a breeding site for the great crested newt.

Ed enjoyed being able to stay at home – either in London or Suffolk – when he was playing his summer gigs in the UK. Cherry, with an eye to the future, had left her Wimbledon hockey club and rejoined the Harleston Magpies. They were both coming home, it seemed.

Ed topped his three gigs at Wembley Stadium in 2015 by playing four nights this time. The *Evening Standard* in London called it a 'joyful, communal celebration'. Just three days after he had played in front of 360,000 people at these concerts, Ed played for 400 guests at a fundraiser for the London Irish Centre in Camden Town. He had an affable chat with Dermot O'Leary, the evening's host and fellow patron, and played ten acoustic songs, including 'Thinking Out Loud', 'The Parting Glass' and 'Nancy Mulligan'. Some of the musicians who had helped make him what he is today joined him onstage: Gary Dunne, who organised the event, Andy Irvine, writer of 'The West Coast of Clare', Lisa Hannigan, whom he'd met at Whelan's in Dublin after the Damien Rice concert, and Luke Concannon, who had flown over from Boston.

Dermot had suggested asking Ed, so Gary had emailed him. 'Yeah, sure' was the instant response, even though he was in the middle of a world tour. 'It was that simple,' says Gary. 'Ed is a man of pure integrity – a gentleman.' The evening raised £250,000.

There's no one quite like Ed.

LAST THOUGHTS

The Castle on the Hill is looking impressive today in the mid-September sun. Looking up from the town side of the Framlingham College Mere, its towers loom menacingly through gaps in the trees. Small groups of teenagers stroll casually along the pathway by the water's edge, some listening to sounds blaring from a boombox.

It's easy to imagine Ed and his school friends finding a private spot on the grass or a tree stump on which to smoke cheap roll-ups and listen to the latest rap music. The best view of the castle is the stately picture-postcard one from the other side of Fram Mere, but it is not so discrete for after-school get-togethers – and you are liable to end up in the holiday snaps of tourists looking out from the top of its walls.

Since Ed wrote the song, the castle has become an even bigger attraction for visitors. His home-town anthem is not Framlingham's only recent exposure, though. The hit BBC comedy *Detectorists* is also set here, with the local scout hut doubling as the fictional metal-detecting club. Unsurprisingly, property prices here have soared since the town achieved such fame.

Ed's halfway through the US leg of his 2018 ÷ tour. For the past two nights he's played the Gillette Stadium in Foxborough, Massachusetts, this time with Snow Patrol and Anne-Marie as his support. The *Boston Globe* described it as 'one of the gutsiest shows ever performed in a football stadium'. A touch more insightful was the observation that Ed was 'affable' – quite a hard thing to be in front of an audience of more than 52,000 at the home of the New England Patriots American Football team.

Ed first played the stadium back in 2013 when he opened for Taylor Swift on the *Red* tour. Her $17.5-million Rhode Island estate is only an hour and a half or so from the stadium. He's been able to spend time with his good friend during breaks in the tour. She didn't take him to a pub, though, preferring a hiking trip to Percy Warner Park in Nashville and teasing him when he appeared to be out of breath.

It all seems a million miles away from the mere here in Framlingham, which is quite literally a backwater. Earlier in the book, I declared that my job was to discover how a scruffy, ginger-haired bloke climbed to the top of the music mountain. His look, of course, is part of the image that has helped him to get there. Tony Moore describes it as 'repetitively no image – so it becomes something'.

When *GQ* magazine named him worst-dressed man of 2012, he remarked, 'Glad they noticed.' He even used the 'accolade' in the lyric for 'Take It Back', a track on the × album. Typically, five years later he was back on the front cover of *GQ* wearing a Tom Ford tuxedo. He attributed his new-found sense of fashion to Cherry smartening him up by gifting him shirts for Christmas. Mostly, though, he still prefers jeans and hoodies, because when he goes to the pub everyone is dressed this way.

He is very striking, simply because there is no other major star who looks like him. He has always been self-deprecatingly funny about his ginger hair, but it has made him stand out from the crowd. *GQ* referred to him neatly as an 'everyman and a man apart'. He is clearly very smart and much more intelligent than he likes to let on. He says he doesn't believe in luck but in 'hard work and circumstance'.

Key events in his life would not have occurred if he had not put himself in a situation where something might happen. Perhaps the best example of that is flying to Los Angeles and being noticed by Jamie Foxx. Playing hundreds of gigs, entering talent competitions and never turning anything down all helped to create 'circumstance'.

One day when he was struggling around London, he caught the megabus to Manchester to play at the In the City Festival. On the way, he burned some CDs on his laptop to sell at the gig so that he could afford the coach fare home. He performed for an audience of just seven people.

One of them was Ian Johnson, of Access to Music, who recalls, 'He played as if it was Wembley Stadium.' Standing in the very thin audience was music lawyer Zubin Irani – a man who would be one of the most important players behind the scenes in the Ed Sheeran story – a happy circumstance.

Zubin became Ed's first lawyer and he is still with him. His philosophy on life is one that could equally apply to Ed: 'The harder I work, the luckier I get.' Five years ago Zubin discovered a new talent, Jorja Smith, and he has been quietly guiding her career ever since. She won the Critics' Choice Award at this year's BRITs. On the night, she sang 'Skin' with Rag 'n' Bone Man – Ed performed 'Supermarket Flowers'. She is following the Ed Sheeran blueprint by playing the Bedford and not signing to a major label immediately, although she does have a publishing deal with Sony/ATV.

Ed told the story of meeting Zubin when he played the Etihad Stadium, Manchester, in May 2018. In the retelling, the lawyer was the only member of the audience, which wasn't strictly true but made for a better anecdote in front of 50,000 people. Ed is prone to a little 'embellishment', as he calls it.

Of course, he has had some luck. He was fortunate to be born into such a talented family. In particular, his parents haven't just supported him, they have taken an active role in his life, which has been of huge benefit to him. Thanks to them, Ed has been astute from a very young age. Gary Dunne describes them as being 'promo savvy', something they passed on to their son. Just a small example of Ed picking up on that is how he always took – or arranged to have taken – a picture of the crowd from the stage or the floor of the pub. That would be posted online with the invitation to pass it on if you are in the picture.

The Sheerans don't just talk a good game, they do something about it. After Ed and his dad saw Gary perform for the first time with a loop pedal at the Shepherd's Bush Empire, John Sheeran didn't say, 'Oh that was good, let's go for a burger'; he got in touch with Gary and invited him to his son's sixteenth-birthday party. He forged a connection that was hugely significant for Ed and is still going strong today. The ability to make the most of every encounter is a priceless gift that Ed inherited from his parents. Everyone is a friend even if they have met him just the once.

His parents were among the rarer members of an older generation who understood the value of social media. Ed grew up at just the right time to exploit our growing obsession with online interaction. Tony Moore observes, 'Ed arrived when the world was ready for Ed.'

He also has no fear socially. He can be himself even when he is going round to dinner at Eric Clapton's house or other heroes that he has come to know, including Elton John, Van Morrison and Paul McCartney. Ironically, Damien Rice, the man who inspired him to become a singer–songwriter in Dublin all those years ago, is the one major influence who has never been in touch.

He's still close to Luke Concannon and the two meet up when they can. Luke sums him up in a way only a mate can: 'He's one of those kids who just comes along and can fucking do everything.'

The BRIT Award-winning grime star Stormzy says of Ed, 'He's a hard-working, business-minded, musical genius.' He wasn't always a genius. He has dedicated himself to improve and shown a consuming desire to be successful. From an early age, he responded to being told he couldn't achieve something with a robust, 'Fuck you, I can!'

He was the little boy who put his hand up in class to answer the teacher and nothing came out as he battled with his stammer. That was food and drink to school bullies who would ridicule his mannerisms. He overcame that by sheer determination. When he addressed the American Institute for

Stuttering's gala in New York he made the point that he wasn't the coolest child in school but revealed that the boy who was the coolest was now his plumber.

As well as a rallying cry, that remark could also be interpreted as a rare touch of arrogance. Good. Ed is not perfect. That would make him insufferable, even if his PR machine does overdo his ordinary 'everybloke' appeal. He loses his temper, he smashes his guitar, he gets upset and can be racked with uncertainty. He can sit outside a pub in Parsons Green and tell his friend Si Hulbert how unhappy he is that he is just not getting anywhere. He seems to love having his picture taken, always adopting a pose as if he is looking into a mirror. Taylor Swift once mischievously described him as 'peacocking' when he sat higher than her in a filmed backstage interview.

Genuinely, it wasn't all plain sailing for Ed. The music business is littered with senior figures who failed to spot his potential and passed when given the opportunity to sign him up. Fortunately for Ed, he was taken on by Stuart Camp, who has the precious gift of patience where his famous client is concerned. As one music critic observes, 'If Ed's happy, then Stuart's happy.' In February 2018, Stuart split from Rocket Music, taking Ed with him to his Grumpy Old Management company.

They have come a long way together. Of course, Ed's life has changed for ever. He has full-time security in the formidable shape of Kevin Myers – 'Security Kev' – who has become a big hit on Instagram in his own right with nearly a million followers. Like many megastars, Ed's world is diminishing rather than expanding.

One of my favourite stories about Ed is the time he had his crew in a panic back in 2011 when he was on tour in Newcastle with Rizzle Kicks. No one could find him and a search party was launched. He had just taken his guitar and gone for a stroll five minutes away in the notorious Bigg Market area of the city – quite a lively place on a Friday night. He had no idea where he was, but once found he was taken back to the venue at Northumbria University.

These days, he needn't leave his estate in Suffolk if he doesn't care to. He has everything he could ever want there. At least he was able to take himself off on his travels with Cherry a couple of years ago. He might not find that so easy to do in the future.

His private life seems to be in a great place at the moment. He has always favoured relationships over playing the field and is clearly in love and planning a family of his own with Cherry.

Professionally, though, how does he top or just match what he has already achieved? His original deal was for six albums. He will be exhausting the mathematical symbols. He could call his next album – (minus) and make it a stripped-back acoustic recording, although he will leave himself open to critics describing it as being less good than before. The greatest-hits album, when it comes, could be called = (equals).

He could continue with more acting. He has not set that world alight, which might not satisfy his ambitions. He has spoken of writing, perhaps a rom com, in the future.

My only concern is that Ed might become too corporate and safe – a record-company juggernaut. He is already a member of a very small superstar club, mixing, it seems, only with artists in his bracket – Taylor Swift, Beyoncé, Bocelli and the One Direction boys. Only in August 2018 he said he wanted to collaborate with Drake, another of the biggest stars on the planet. It's probably already set up.

Musically, he could grow by exploring more of the orchestra. Perhaps he could go from being the only man on stage to being in front of the biggest orchestra ever assembled, although that doesn't sound like a financially prudent venture.

He has no need to change, in my opinion, as long as he spaces out his albums and his touring – just as Adele as done. He has followed in the footsteps of the star from Tottenham in so many ways, not least in emulating her appeal. For her fans, Adele remains unaffected by wealth and fame, and that's a large part of Ed's appeal as well. He observed that, 'The real people that buy my records are Jenny in Stoke or Jasmine in Glasgow.'

Some critics like to whine about Ed's perceived blandness, but he writes about universal emotions that people of all ages, particularly women, can relate to – love, loss, heartache and the little things in life that make the days go by. His songs are as comfy as one of his battered old hoodies. He is a man to snuggle up to on the sofa to moan about the day at work, watch a box set and eat shepherd's pie.

It's time to leave the Castle on the Hill and wish Ed many years of enjoying the view. I'm off to the Co-op to buy the Sunday papers, which reminds me of one of the stories a local mother told me in the pub in Framlingham. She was doing her weekly shop when her seven-year-old daughter bounced over excitedly and said, 'Mum, it's Ed Sheeran!' Shyly, the little girl approached Ed for a selfie in the aisle. He did not disappoint and posed happy and smiling with her. The picture now has pride of place on her bedroom wall, a fan for life – as millions are.

ED'S STARS

This is a man who will place a high value upon personal freedom both for himself and others – the sort of freedom that honours individuality, change and awkward truths. Ed's Sun, indicator of life goals and aspirations, was placed in Aquarius at his birth – a sign associated with fairness, equality and a strong will. These qualities will be personally important for Ed, although the picture is complicated by the tense links the Sun makes to a planetary grouping that affects not just him but also a generation.

For a period (1988–96) two of the mega planetary bodies, Neptune and Uranus, both associated with irrevocable change, either through dissolution or unpredictable breakdown, were joined at the hip in the status-loving, change-resistant, patriarchal sign of Capricorn. This rare conjunction brings colliding, contrasting energies into play, which for Ed on a personal level will provide the thrust to reject or transform certain conventions. Out, for example, will be the flamboyance, glamour and window-dressing of stardom. In will be a more earthy, scaled-back performance. Out will be any desire to

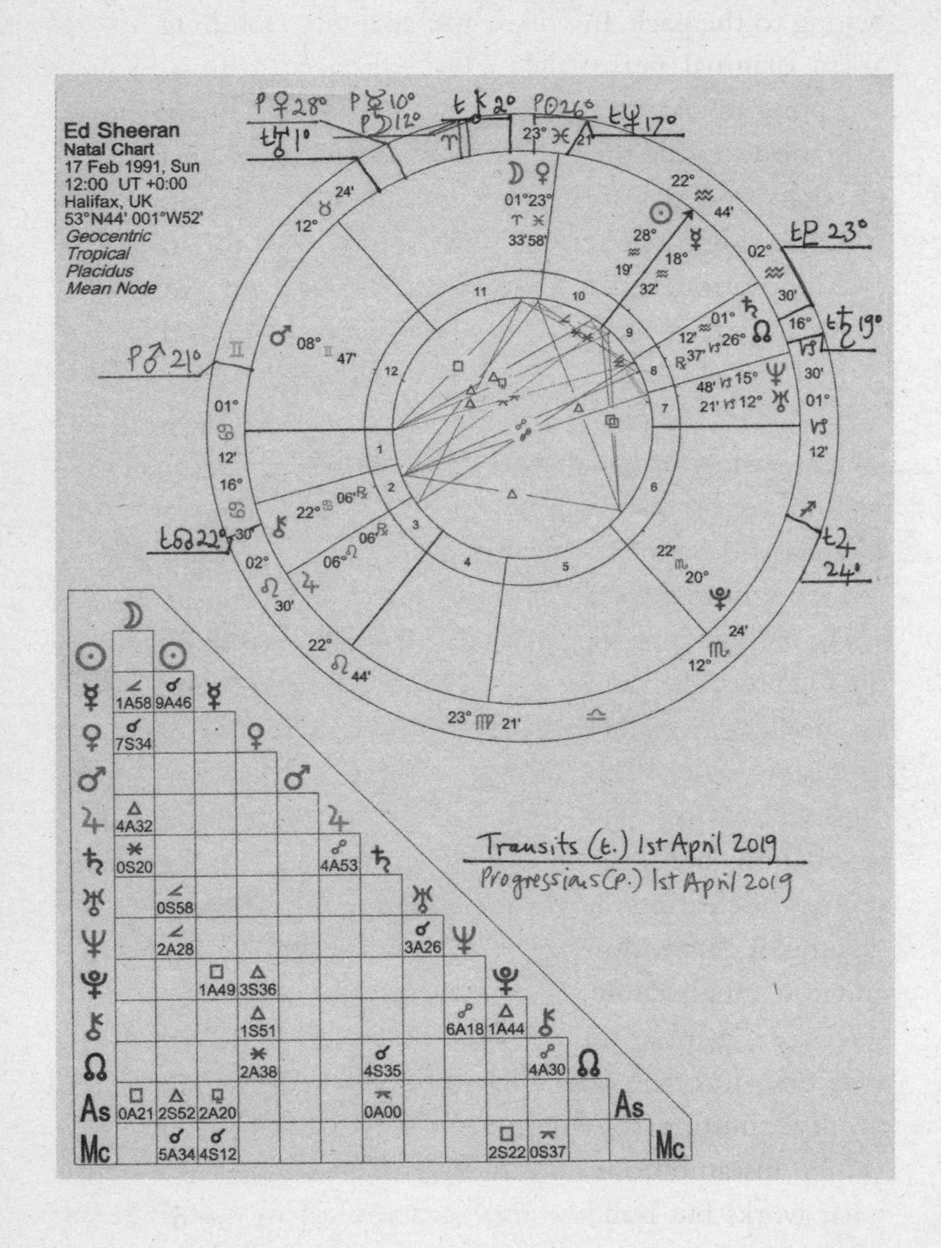
Ed Sheeran
Natal Chart
17 Feb 1991, Sun
12:00 UT +0:00
Halifax, UK
53°N44' 001°W52'
Geocentric
Tropical
Placidus
Mean Node
Transits (t.) 1st April 2019
Progressions (P.) 1st April 2019

belong to the pack. In will be the goal of establishing himself as an original personality. Out will be anything near to accepting mediocrity or the norm in any way. In will be the aspiration to scale the heights. With the huge, harsh, tortuous planetary energies of Neptune, Uranus and Saturn at play, the stakes are high. The tension, this pull between the status quo and innovation, reality and fantasy, security and excitement, needs a master – and thank goodness the master in this chart is the Lord of Creativity, the Sun.

Ed's chart has plenty of supportive and flowing planetary aspects – more of which later – but what stands out first is the uncomfortable element introduced through the Neptune, Uranus and Saturn combination. It is the bottom line, the tension within the man, the grit that creates the pearl.

He may wish to stand alone – that is part of him – but in the long term he cannot and will not be seen in such isolation because he so embodies the Zeitgeist of a very particular group. He is one of the millions of babies born in that decade who will navigate life in unpredictable circumstances, where foundations break down and boundaries are breached – the process of clearing out the old to make way for the new, the turning of conventions on their head. He will have too much, and too much choice can make every choice seem like a threat or a gamble: this partner or that, this sandwich or that, win one, lose the other. Decision-making, which always involves shutting down options, will be painful personally.

Like his ambitious cohort, he will be pragmatic, keeping what works but building new structures from the fragments of shattered institutions and traditions. For Ed and other millennials, distrust of authority will eventually lead to a new understanding of power. More responsible economic and material systems will evolve, kinder philosophies prevail, not least and most positively in developing the role of the male. He, along with others of the Neptune–Uranus contingent, will be fronting that huge progressive change. What lies ahead now, and over a few years more for this group, is mastery of the uncertainty – the willingness to live with the tension. This will be a catalyst for creativity, growth and strength. The group is growing forcefully into their time, and those who come through the cosmic tests, in whatever sphere – creative, legal, business – will be tough, have wisdom and be visionary future leaders.

Early success often depends upon good parenting. The planets influencing the patriarchal image are, again, those of powerful Saturn, planet of discipline, and non-conformist Uranus. Ed's father is likely to have valued success and have been able to achieve this through self-restraint, hard work and, when necessary, an innovative approach. An understanding of the past, combined with an instinct for dynamic change, would allow him to breathe new life into his workplace or family matters. Chiron, the planetoid known as the Wounded Healer, is opposite Saturn, suggesting an ancestral hurt, some issue that Ed's father needed to make a conscious effort to move on from. There may be a degree of melancholy and seriousness in his approach to things, a depth of thought and feeling. A desire to pursue a particular dream, with a fear of failure, would have driven him. He would have accepted his responsibilities square on, not least in acknowledging his bonds to others: a purposeful and compassionate man. The link between Ed's Sun and creative, boundless Neptune, with a Moon–Saturn link, suggests both parents acted strongly as a model for their offspring in seeking a life that was beyond the ordinary and showing how to make ideals a reality.

Ed's mother is likely to have been both aspirational and protective in his early life. The fast-moving Moon changes sign in the twenty-four hours of Ed's day of birth, making interpretation harder without an accurate birth time, but what is irrefutable are the positive links made either to regenerative Pluto or protective, expansionist Jupiter, the latter planet in particular associated with a desire to connect with something beyond the self. It brings an extrovert and optimistic energy to all it touches; it is kind and generous. Should the main positive aspect for the Moon be with Pluto, the matriarchal signature is of someone well able to create a safe place for exploring emotions and problems. Mother would have bolstered Ed's sense of self-worth, making it easier for him to form meaningful relationships with others. Ed would have known that she was unconditionally on his side, able to provide wisdom and help at moments when he questioned himself.

This is a chart of someone bouncing with cleverness, energy, an unrelenting determination to do things his own way, yet well able to use his sensitivities to delight and transform, to uplift and enrich the lives of those he comes into contact with. Ed has three planets forming flowing links in water signs – traditionally an element associated with emotional intelligence, based on the intuitive understanding of others. Harmonious Venus, the go-to planet for establishing how Ed will try to please, is in imaginative Pisces, linked to perceptive Pluto in Scorpio. The picture here is of someone who will use their creativity to find out about themselves and, with Chiron in the mix, will employ his own battle bruises to inform his creativity, generating a cyclonic swell of artistic force. How fortunate that, with his ability to access emotional truths and use them creatively, he has a sharp intelligence able to give pleasing form to them.

Partly this may have been down to a sibling relationship that incorporated a degree of helpful sparring. Aspects to Mercury suggest early years with someone who provided a supportive base from which to explore life but who may well have provided a different vision of the world – more rational, more grown-up and perhaps a little bleaker. A link between Ed's Uranus and his brother's Saturn suggests Ed will provide the impetus for growth and change while his brother models commitment and authority. Short and long term, Ed will be inspired by his brother's focused quest for meaning in life. Brother would have been able to have the last word but Ed would certainly have been able to escalate any disagreements. There would have been occasions when his brother's comments seemed very forceful and his position a powerful challenge: learning to stand up for himself would have entailed careful, stimulating thought and the development of his own skills, not least those of empathetic insight.

Healthy relationships thrive upon a sound degree of self-esteem. Those challenging aspects to Ed's rebellious Sun suggest early experiences may have contributed to a deficit here. Attempts to live up to standards set by authority figures will have been hard, leading to a lack of basic confidence. Mars, planet of action and initiative, placed in restless Gemini, suggests that at school happiness would have come from dabbling in multiple projects and completing none – it would be far more thrilling to start something new than face the boredom of settling to complete anything lengthy. An argumentative streak is never far from the surface with Ed, simply because he enjoys the world of ideas – contradicting the experts is fun because it is animating, daring, life-affirming and exactly what curious people with Sun Aquarius and Mars Gemini are programmed to do. It is fortunate that Ed's impatient Mars links well to optimistic Jupiter, providing optimism and the instinct to take lucky risks, which will make good use of the fidgety, nervy energy that can be combative, a little bit cavalier and needs generally to be on the move.

If the harder aspects connecting his Sun and the weighty outer planets, Saturn, Uranus and Neptune, provide the ballast in this chart, pointing to rational life goals, the flowing planetary combination of Venus, Pluto and Chiron speak of his creativity and also his inner world of relationships. Here is the clear evidence of the heart guiding the head because it is through his bonds with others that his life will yield the richness needed for his work and provide the development required for his role as a generational influence.

Ed has the capacity to love another in a way that acknowledges the person with all of their flaws. Venus influenced by Neptune can lead to unselfish, idealistic love, and there is the possibility that early on this energy and hope may be invested in someone not worthy enough. The regenerative Pluto influence will not allow naivety to prevail for long, though. Ed will want real engagement with a partner: nothing superficial will go anywhere near meeting his needs, but he will also understand the necessity for personal space. There will be close identification with the loved one, which may lead to the urge to fight their battles but this will not be in the traditional patriarchal manner of viewing a partner as weaker. Domestic peace will not always prevail – he has a deep instinctive Plutonic need to rock the boat and see just how the incumbents react when they tumble out – an absolute pain if you are on the end of this unpleasantness. More positively, Ed has a great sensitivity to fairness, commitment to equality. and an understanding of the vulnerability that loving someone fully entails. In short, he has emotional intelligence in spades and also the courage to articulate and be open about his feelings.

The Mars–Jupiter link in Ed's chart does suggest the potential for tricky amorous situations. On the other hand, the Jovian part of this irresponsible combination is held in check through an opposition to ethical, cool Saturn, suggesting he may steer clear of the obvious pitfalls on long-haul partnerships. Once again, there is a more generational message here. Many of this age group as children have experienced the trials of family breakdown. Perhaps Ed will have something to contribute, should a new ethical code emerge that acknowledges the often disparate needs of children and their parents.

During 2019, powerful Pluto in the sky will be moving in opposition to sensitive Chiron in Ed's chart. Chiron symbolises areas where we are fragile, and this transit is likely to bring the resurfacing of wounds going back to childhood. A natal midpoint link between the Sun and Chiron points to issues of self-esteem, some of which may be linked to physical imperfections, nurturing and a need to appear invulnerable. Any tendency Ed has to cover up painful issues (with Chiron in Moon-ruled Cancer, these may relate to his home, mother and emotional life) and weakness will be challenged: Pluto exposes and destroys so that healthy growth can emerge – the goal here would be an embracing and acceptance of the whole self.

In January 2020 an opposition to Chiron from Saturn, planet of material security and consolidation, follows. It may be that Ed will seek to heal, through attempts to establish secure roots, the creation of a place that is genuinely home. Ed may have to contend with frustrating demands and expectations from others that slow matters down. Patience is a virtue and he knows this because, while he has plenty of Martian impulsiveness, Ed has learned to live with and benefit from the forestalling energy of Saturn as co-ruler of his Sun. This is a time when he needs to draw fully upon his integrity because obligations must be met, codes of conduct considered, house rules established, standards laid down.

Ed has enormous resilience and strength and that will prove beneficial when, later in April 2020, Saturn returns to the exact position it occupied at the time of his birth. This is an astrological marker of the gateway to adulthood. It is something of a test, the effects of which are felt very much in the run-up, forcing questions as to whether one has been living too much for others instead of oneself. Things end now, and all change is loss, but the need to remove anything that will be inappropriate for the future will be paramount. Often this is a time when the responsibilities of parenthood are taken on – an obvious manifestation of a life transition. Should that be the case for Ed, it will be an easy rite of passage: the curious Saturn–Uranus mix of energies influencing his Sun support early fatherhood. At the same time there is a very beneficial link between transiting Mars to his natal Mars, which reinforces the initiation of new projects, not least those that endorse his confidence and the projection of a new facet of his individuality.

The period towards the end of November 2022 heralds a further period of dramatic change. This is when regenerative (although rarely without a struggle) Pluto meets the natal North Node, a point in Ed's chart associated with his life's purpose. Those he meets now and the circumstances in which he finds himself will ultimately move him further along towards those goals. Certainly he may feel there is a degree of Fate at play. These goals may well be associated with his creative output, indicated by links between imaginative, compassionate Neptune and Ed's Venus, but it should be remembered that life purpose is not the same as vocational objectives, although the latter can serve the former well.

Ed's North Node is in the solid and trustworthy sign of Capricorn, suggesting ultimately he must concern himself with developing reliability and authority. Once this is done, he can help others develop their nurturing capacity – again, one is reminded of the generational imperative for society to find greater acceptance of and triumph in a widening role/definition of masculinity.

Madeleine Moore
September 2018

LIFE AND TIMES

17 Feb 1991: Edward Christopher Sheeran is born in Halifax General Hospital, West Yorkshire. He has an elder brother, Matthew, who is two. His parents, John and Imogen, run an arts consultancy, Sheeran Lock.

Sept 1995: Ed starts school at Heathfield Junior, set in idyllic countryside ten miles from the family home in the market town of Hebden Bridge. At his first school, Ed is remembered as a 'gentle boy'.

Dec 1995: Just before Christmas, the family move south to a detached house in the quiet Suffolk town of Framlingham.

June 2002: Ed is inspired to learn the guitar when he watches Eric Clapton play 'Layla' during the televised broadcast of the Queen's Golden Jubilee concert in the gardens of Buckingham Palace.

July 2002: Goes with his dad to his first live concert – Green Day at Wembley Arena.

Sept 2002: Starts at Thomas Mills High School in Framlingham. On his first day, he tells the class all about his guitar. His teacher says he is 'very funny and endearing'.

April 2003: Travels to London with his dad to watch Paul McCartney in concert at Earl's Court. The former Beatle plays thirty-seven songs.

Nov 2003: Plays Officer Krupke in his school's production of *West Side Story*. Matthew is his boss, Lt. Schrank.

Sept 2004: Everything changes for Ed when he sees Damien Rice perform at an under-eighteens night at Whelan's bar in Dublin. Afterwards he meets Damien and decides he too is going to become a singer–songwriter.

Jan 2005: At thirteen, Ed completes his first album, *Spinning Man*, in his bedroom. It took him twenty-four days to complete fourteen original songs after his parents gave him a Boss Digital Recording Studio for Christmas.

March 2005: Records in a studio when his guitar teacher arranges a session near by at Summerhill School in Leiston. He records five tracks for a new EP named *The Orange Room*, in honour of his bedroom.

July 2005: Attends a five-day workshop held by virtuoso guitarist Preston Reed at his home in Ayrshire. Ed entertains everyone by making up rap lyrics.

Nov 2005: He plays Roger, the guitar-playing member of the T-Birds, in *Grease* at Thomas Mills, a part specially created for him by his drama teacher.

Jan 2006: Sees his heroes Nizlopi for the first time in concert at the Shepherd's Bush Empire, London. Tells his dad he will perform there one day. His father invites the support act Gary Dunne to play at Ed's fifteenth-birthday party so he could teach him how to use a loop pedal.

Feb 2006: A schoolfriend, Stuart Dines, is killed in a coach crash in Germany. As a tribute, Ed would write a song, 'We Are', which was played at Stuart's funeral. He later said it got him his record deal.

March 2007: Unveils *Want Some?*, a new CD he recorded over five months at a London studio. It features his tribute to Nizlopi, 'Two Blokes and a Double Bass', as well as his first cover, 'The West Coast of Clare', an Irish lament.

July 2007: Joins Nizlopi on work experience for a short summer tour. They agree that he can join their crew after he sends them 'Two Blokes and a Double Bass'. Sees singer–songwriter Foy Vance perform for the first time. Plays at Secret Garden Party near Huntingdon and hooks up with Alice Hibbert, a pupil at Thomas Mills, who becomes his first proper girlfriend.

Aug 2007: Appears in a musical adaptation of *Frankenstein* by the Youth Music Theatre UK at the Barbican Theatre, Plymouth. Ed has a minor role as a 'dude on a ship'.

Sept 2007: Gets selected to appear at Young Bands Night at the Norwich Playhouse, an opportunity for emerging talent in Norfolk and Suffolk. Impresses Ian Johnson from the city's Access to Music college, who recommends Ed to a London talent scout.

Oct 2007: Sings Foy Vance's 'Gabriel and the Vagabond' at a high-school concert in the Church of St Andrew, Marlesford, a village near his home.

Nov 2007: Makes his final appearance in a school production when he plays a German soldier in *The Sound of Music* at Thomas Mills.

April 2008: Opens for Nizlopi at the Norwich Arts Centre. More than one hundred people show up just to support Ed.

June 2008: Decides to leave school to try his luck gigging in London. His mum's concerns are eased when he secures a place on the Artist Development Programme at an Access to Music college in east London.

Nov 2008: Wins The Next Big Thing competition at UEA (University of East Anglia) in Norwich, despite having to improvise when four guitar strings break during his performance. Two weeks later he supports R&B singer Jay Sean at the university. Plays his first gig in London at Liberties Bar in Camden Town.

Sept 2009: Signs up for a degree course in songwriting at the Academy of Music in Guildford. Rents a student flat. He abandons his studies when he secures a support slot on Just Jack's UK tour.

Oct 2009: Meets Passenger at The Living Room, an acoustic night in Cambridge. The two become firm friends – many years later Ed will invite the singer–songwriter to support him on his × tour.

Nov 2009: Fulfils ambition of appearing at the Shepherd's Bush Empire, London, when he opens for Just Jack.

Dec 2009: Accepts an invitation to play a Christmas gig in the East End for the homeless charity Crisis and meets Angel, a crack-cocaine addict and street prostitute. Writes 'The A Team' about her.

Feb 2010: Films three songs with young video-maker Jamal Edwards, who posts them on his SBTV YouTube channel. After one week, 4,000 people have watched him performing 'You Need Me, I Don't Need You'.

April 2010: Goes to Los Angeles and impresses his American audience with gigs around the city. Jamie Foxx invites him to stay at his house in Hidden Valley and use his home studio. On his return, gets taken under the wing of Stuart Camp, a manager at Elton John's Rocket Music.

May 2010: Plays at a charity fashion show organised by sixth formers at Woodbridge School, Suffolk. The event at the school's Seckford Theatre raises nearly £2,000 for East Anglia's Children Hospice (EACH), which the Sheeran family has supported for many years. Opens for rapper Example at the Waterfront in Norwich. Ed is booked for one gig but stays on for the whole UK tour.

Oct 2010: Hires The Bedford in Balham to record a live CD and DVD. He is backed by a group of musicians called The Remedies. Tony Moore, who runs music nights there, charges him just £100 to cover the costs of an engineer. Ends set with 'Sunburn', a ballad from his latest EP, *You Need Me*.

Jan 2011: Releases final EP in his five-point plan. Called *No. 5 Collaborations Project*, it features Ed with several well-known rappers, including Wiley and Devlin. Celebrates the official announcement of his record deal with Asylum/Atlantic with a pint at the Station Hotel in Framlingham.

April 2011: More than 1,000 fans turn up to see Ed at the Barfly in Camden Town. He ends up playing three gigs there in one night and sings two songs on the pavement for those left disappointed outside. Appears on national television for the first time when he sings 'The A Team' and 'Wayfaring Stranger' on *Later … with Jools Holland*.

June 2011: His first single, 'The A Team' reaches number three in the charts. The atmospheric video had already chalked up a million views on YouTube. The song sells more than 800,000 copies and is the eighth-biggest single of the year. Plays the BBC Introducing Tent at Glastonbury. Breaks up with girlfriend Alice.

July 2011: Despite the pouring rain, gives a memorable performance at the Latitude Festival in Suffolk. Dedicates the encore, 'Make You Feel My Love', to his dad.

Aug 2011: Ed poses in jeans and hoodie – playing his paw-print guitar – on a bed at the Park Plaza Westminster Bridge hotel, London, for a photograph by Steve Schofield. The picture was acquired the following year by the National Portrait Gallery, London. 'Moments', originally a drum and bass number, is re-edited for One Direction – his first song for another artist. Meets Scottish singer Nina Nesbitt, who sings him one of her own compositions.

Sept 2011: His first album, +, sells more than 100,000 copies in its first week and goes straight to number one. Holds launch party at the World's End in Finsbury Park, London, where he had gigged many times. Gets tattooed with a + sign.

Oct 2011: Wins first-ever award when he is named Best Breakthrough Artist at the Q Awards at the Grosvenor House Hotel in London.

Nov 2011: Nina Nesbitt joins him on stage at the Shepherd's Bush Empire, London, to sing 'Hallelujah'. Actor Rupert Grint – Ron Weasley – stars in video for new single 'Lego House', directed by Emil Nava.

Jan 2012: Is photographed walking in Venice with Nina. She appears as the girl Ed is drinking to forget in the video for his next single, 'Drunk'.

Feb 2012: Wearing blue designer suit, white shirt and black tie, picks up two BRIT Awards as British Breakthrough Act and British Male Solo Artist. Visits a dying girl at a Sheffield hospice and sings 'Lego House' and 'The A Team' at her bedside – one of her last wishes.

March 2012: Begins first US tour as support act for Snow Patrol. Forms songwriting alliance with keyboard player Johnny McDaid and together they write 'Nina' and 'Photograph' while on the road.

May 2012: Receives his first Ivor Novello Award when 'The A Team' is named Best Song Musically and Lyrically.

June 2012: Ed is part of an all-star line-up at the Queen's Diamond Jubilee concert outside Buckingham Palace and sings 'The A Team'. Although she missed his performance, Her Majesty is introduced to Ed backstage after the show. Spends £895,000 on a mansion near Framlingham, and another £450,000 buying the farmhouse next door.

Aug 2012: Performs at the closing ceremony of the Olympic Games in London. Sings the Pink Floyd classic, 'Wish You Were Here', backed by the original drummer Nick Mason, guitarist Mike Rutherford from Genesis and, on bass, Richard Jones of The Feeling.

Nov 2012: Plays last gig of the + tour at The Barrowland Ballroom in Glasgow and is joined on stage by Paolo Nutini for a duet of the Scottish singer's hit 'Candy'. Makes first guest appearance on *The X Factor* singing 'Give Me Love', the sixth and final single from +.

Dec 2012: Achieves his first number-one single for another act when One Direction's 'Little Things' tops the charts. The track, co-written with Fiona Bevan, is produced by Jake Gosling, Ed's long-standing friend and collaborator.

Feb 2013: Buys a $2-million home in Nashville, not far from Taylor Swift. He says, 'I think it's important to give the UK public a little bit of a break.' Attends Grammy Awards for the first time and sings a duet of 'The A Team' with Elton John. Ends a drunken birthday celebration by being thrown fully clothed into a swimming pool. Meets Athina Andrelos, tour manager for Gabrielle Aplin, on a short tour of Australia and New Zealand.

March 2013: Opens for Taylor Swift in Omaha, Nebraska, the first concert on her *Red* tour. He joins her onstage for 'Everything Has Changed', a song they wrote together. Ed plays all sixty-six dates in North America.

July 2013: Drops into his old prep school, Brandeston Hall, near Framlingham, to watch the annual summer concert. Signs shirts and cards and poses for pictures with the excited children.

Oct 2013: Writes 'Bloodstream' about his experience of trying MDMA on a trip to Ibiza. Plays the first of three nights at Madison Square Garden, New York, and marks the fulfilment of another ambition by getting a tattoo of three boxing gloves on his right arm.

Dec 2013: Writes 'Afire Love' in memory of his grandfather, Bill Sheeran, who has died aged eighty-six after a long battle with Alzheimer's. Ed stuns locals in the Station Hotel, Framlingham, when he walks in with Taylor Swift.

Jan 2014: Honouring Bill's memory, he wears his grandad's British Boxing Board of Control tie at the Grammys.

Feb 2014: Holds a workshop for music students at Thomas Mills High School. His former head of music, Richard Hanley, blacks out the glass in the classroom doors so that his visit can proceed in secret.

May 2014: Performs 'Thinking Out Loud' for the first time in public on *Later ... with Jools Holland*. He had written the ballad with his long-time collaborator, Amy Wadge, after they had been out to dinner with his parents.

June 2014: 'Sing', written with Pharrell Williams, becomes his first UK number-one single. His second album, ×, also reaches number one on both sides of the Atlantic. In the UK, it would be the biggest-selling album of the year.

Oct 2014: Releases video of 'Thinking Out Loud', in which he dances with Brittany Cherry. Ed has lost more than thirty-five pounds to get in shape. The video receives more than 2.7 million views on YouTube during the first twenty-four hours.

Feb 2015: Performs duet of 'Master Blaster' with Beyoncé at all-star Grammy tribute to Stevie Wonder. Takes home two BRITS for the second time when he wins British Male Solo Artist and × is named MasterCard British Album of the Year – the night's most prestigious award. Splits with girlfriend Athina on the night.

March 2015: Films a guest spot for *Home and Away* at Palm Beach, Sydney. He plays himself and sings 'Thinking Out Loud' for the residents of fictional Summer Bay.

May 2015: Elton John presents Ed with Songwriter of the Year at the Ivor Novello Awards.

June 2015: 'Thinking Out Loud' becomes the first song to spend a whole year in the UK Top 40. Receives an award at a New York gala for the American Institute for Stuttering and tells the audience that kids should embrace their quirks because 'nobody can be a better you than you.'

July 2015: Ed is the first artist to play solo at Wembley Stadium, selling out three nights. Takes *X Factor* judge Nicole Scherzinger for a drink at the Station Hotel, prompting speculation that they are in a relationship. In fact, Ed has reconnected in the US with Cherry Seaborn, an old friend from Thomas Mills who is working in New York.

Aug 2015: Officially launches his own record label, Gingerbread Man Records, under the Warner Music umbrella. His first signing is singer–songwriter Jamie Lawson, an opening act on the × tour. Sits for Irish artist Colin Davidson at home in Suffolk. The oil painting now hangs in the National Portrait Gallery, London.

Oct 2015: Accepts an honorary doctorate for his 'outstanding contribution to music' at the University Campus Suffolk in Ipswich. Releases *Jumpers for Goalposts*, a documentary about his three nights at Wembley. Passes his driving test in Ipswich.

Nov 2015: Signs his friend Foy Vance to Gingerbread Man Records.

Dec 2015: Signs off from social media. Tells Instagram followers he is taking a break to travel the world and see everything he missed.

Jan 2016: Has an operation to repair burst eardrum, an injury he suffered jumping off a yacht in the Mediterranean.

Feb 2016: Finally wins a Grammy. 'Thinking Out Loud' is named Song of the Year while Ed carries off Best Pop Solo Performance. Flies to Iceland with Cherry where he badly burns foot in a scalding hot geyser, requiring a skin graft.

June 2016: On their way back to the UK from travels to Japan and New Zealand, he and Cherry visit rapper Fuse ODG at his home near Accra, in Ghana. Ed writes 'Bibia Be Ye Ye' with the London-born singer.

Aug 2016: While recording at home in Framlingham, he hears news that his grandmother Shirley Lock has died in hospital in nearby Aldeburgh. Writes 'Supermarket Flowers' about his mum clearing the hospital room, and sings it at the private family funeral.

Jan 2017: Releases two songs as lead singles for his next album. 'Shape of You' is number one for fourteen weeks in the UK and twelve on the US Billboard Hot 100. It becomes the bestselling single worldwide of 2017 and the most streamed song ever on Spotify, with 1.9 billion streams. 'Castle on the Hill', meanwhile, reaches number two in the UK.

March 2017: His third studio album, ÷, sells 672,000 units in its first week of release in the UK, the fastest-selling by a male artist. Travels to Liberia for Comic Relief to meet homeless and parentless children and produces a video for Red Nose Day. Opens his ÷ world tour in Turin so that he can inspect his new villa close to Lake Trasimeno, in Perugia. The property has its own vineyard.

June 2017: Headlines the Pyramid Stage at Glastonbury playing a set the *NME* describes as an 'absolute triumph'.

July 2017: Leaves Twitter after a backlash from *Game of Thrones* fans over his cameo appearance in the hit series. He plays a soldier who sings a song while camping in the forest.

Oct 2017: Falls off his bicycle on a steep hill near his Suffolk home and breaks right wrist, left elbow and a rib. Cancels dates in Asia while he recovers. Tells Jonathan Ross he had dropped out of sight in 2016 partly to pull himself together after slipping into substance abuse.

Dec 2017: Receives an MBE from Prince Charles at Buckingham Palace. Beats off competition from George Michael's 'Last Christmas' to claim the Christmas number one with 'Perfect'. Releases a version with Beyoncé and another called 'Perfect Symphony' with Andrea Bocelli, orchestrated by his brother Matthew. Working together was a promise they had made to their grandmother before she died.

Jan 2018: Announces to his 24 million followers on Instagram that he and Cherry are engaged. Says 'cats are chuffed'. Buys two more properties next door to his mansion in Suffolk, creating an estate that includes an underground pub complete with beers on tap and a urinal. Wins two Grammys – Best Pop Vocal Album for ÷ and Best Pop Solo Performance for 'Shape of You'.

Feb 2018: Attends the premiere of *Songwriter* at the Berlin Film Festival. Directed by his cousin, Murray Cummings, the documentary tells the story of how Ed and his collaborators created ÷.

May 2018: The *Sunday Times Rich List* estimates his fortune at £80 million, the second-wealthiest musician under thirty after Adele.

June 2018: Plans to build a Saxon-style chapel on his estate run into difficulties when it is revealed the land may be a breeding site for the great crested newt. Performs four sell-out concerts at Wembley Stadium in front of 360,000 people. Plays in front of 400 guests at a charity evening raising money for the London Irish Centre in Camden Town.

July 2018: Sets up an Instagram account for his two cats, Dorito and Calippo – @thewibbles. Within a day, they have more than 100,000 followers. Their proud owner has 25.8 million … and counting.

ACKNOWLEDGEMENTS

It's been a pleasure to discover that Ed Sheeran's immense likeability factor isn't an act. He is the proof that you can be nice and still pursue your ambitions rigorously in the cut-throat world of music today. Many thanks to all those who have helped me piece together Ed's journey to the top. They include, Jono Ball, Luke Concannon, Robert Dines, Gary Dunne, Richard Hanley, Si Hulbert, Ian Johnson, Katie Kalil, Keith Krykant, Tony Moore, Clare Nicholson, Neil Pascoe, Phil Pethybridge, Caroline Richardson, Georgie Ross, Nikki Sholl, Gillian Sunderland and Clare Wright. It's lovely that Ed stays in touch with people – popping in to see Luke in Boston for instance or helping Gary with his benefit night for the Irish Centre in Camden Town. By the way, Si's been working on the new Dido album so I can't wait to hear that. Thanks also to those who did not want to be named – your insights and memories were invaluable.

I loved visiting Hebden Bridge in Yorkshire and, of course, the Suffolk town of Framlingham. Many thanks to everyone who made me feel so welcome.

As always, I could not write these books without the expertise of the people around me. First, thanks to my long-standing agent Gordon Wise, who has guided me so well through another year. His assistant at Curtis Brown, Niall Harman, has once again been helpful and efficient.

Thank you to Emily-Jane Swanson and Jo Westaway for their brilliant research. My good friend Cliff Renfrew was as helpful as ever in Los Angeles. Astrologer Madeleine Moore has provided another fascinating birth chart. Reading her insight is always one of the highlights of any new book for me. I am grateful to Jen Westaway for transcribing my interviews expertly and coping so well when I am speaking to someone over lunch. Copy editors Hazel Orme and Helena Caldon have been outstanding.

At HarperCollins, many thanks to my editor Zoe Berville, who commissioned the book and offered such good advice throughout; Georgina Atsiaris for project editing; Claire Ward for her striking cover design; Dean Russell in production; Fiona Greenway for her sterling work researching pictures; and Laura Lees and Jasmine Gordon for looking after publicity and marketing.

You can read more about my books at seansmithceleb.com or follow me on Twitter and Facebook @seansmithceleb.

SELECT BIBLIOGRAPHY

Nolan, David, *Ed Sheeran: Divide and Conquer*, Music Press Books, 2017

Sheeran, Ed and Butah, Phillip, *Ed Sheeran: A Visual Journey*, Cassell, 2014

PICTURE CREDITS

Page 1: (top) Archives of Thomas Mills High School; (middle left) © Andi Sapey; (middle right) Photo by John Sheeran; (bottom) Archant, Suffolk

Page 2: (top) © Andi Sapey; (middle) © Andi Sapey; (bottom) Archant, Suffolk

Page 3: (top) Photo by Kevin Mazur/Fox/WireImage/Getty Images; (middle) Photo by Michael Kovac/Getty Images for EJAF; (bottom) Photo by Dave Hogan/MTV 2015/Getty Images for MTV

Page 4: (top) © Amanda Friedman; (middle left) Photo by Mike Windle/WireImage; (middle right) Photo by Dave J Hogan/Getty Images; (bottom) Photo by Gareth Cattermole/Getty Images

Page 5: (top) WENN.com; (middle) David Fisher/REX/Shutterstock; (bottom) © Avalon

Page 6: (top left) AP Photo/John Marshall JME; (top right) Photo by Yui Mok/PA Wire; (bottom left) Photo by Kevin Winter/Getty Images for iHeartMedia; (bottom right) Photo by Frazer Harrison/Getty Images

Page 7: (top left) Kate Wooldridge/WENN.com; (top right) Photo by Andy Sheppard/Redferns via Getty Images; (bottom left) Photo by Christian Augustin/Getty Images; (bottom right) Photo by John Phillips/Getty Images

Page 8: (top) Photo by Kevin Mazur/Getty Images for Global Citizen; (bottom right and left) © Avalon.red

INDEX

INDEX